D1571554

The Cost of the Kingdom

A Memoir by the Chief Estimator (Show and Ride) for EPCOT and Disneyland Paris

Carl L. Jablonski CPE

Theme Park Press
The Happiest Books on Earth
www.ThemeParkPress.com

© 2020 Carl L. Jablonski CPE

No part of this publication may be reproduced, distributed, or transmitted in any form or by any means, including photocopying, recording, or other electronic or mechanical methods, without the prior written permission of the publisher, except for brief quotations embodied in critical reviews and certain other non-commercial uses permitted by copyright law.

Although every precaution has been taken to verify the accuracy of the information contained herein, no responsibility is assumed for any errors or omissions, and no liability is assumed for damages that may result from the use of this information.

Theme Park Press is not associated with the Walt Disney Company.

The views expressed in this book are those of the author and do not necessarily reflect the views of Theme Park Press.

Theme Park Press publishes its books in a variety of print and electronic formats. Some content that appears in one format may not appear in another.

Editor: Bob McLain
Layout: Artisanal Text

ISBN 978-1-68390-287-4
Printed in the United States of America

Theme Park Press | www.ThemeParkPress.com
Address queries to bob@themeparkpress.com

For Alison
My Rock!

Contents

Introduction

This story is my personal memoir, of my education in show and ride estimating, and subsequently, the contributions made in that effort at Walt Disney Imagineering. In this story, I share my personal experiences about the many talented people I worked with over two of Disney's biggest theme park projects – EPCOT and Eurodisneyland (EDL or as known now as Disneyland, Paris).

I'll do my best to describe the incredibly creative environment I worked in on both projects. I'll share the trials and tribulations of my learning curve on developing cost estimates for shows, rides and attractions. A totally new profession that was my transition from the shop to an office environment. In both EPCOT and EDL there were similar learning curves. The first as a "rookie" and the other as "a seasoned" professional.

During my tenure at Imagineering with the EPCOT project, my new position became my vocation. Let me be clear; I would not have been offered the job as a show estimator without my education and experience in scenic design and technical theatre. I've placed these experiences in Chapter 12, called "Dues Paid." In the back of this book as more of a history of film and television. Dues Paid, speaks to my first several years of live road show experience, model making and a variety of hands-on experiences in theatre, film and television. Call it "my pre-show." It was the beginning of a lifetime of on-the-job theatrical experience and show biz industry friendships. Without these, my Imagineering career would not have happened. Lucky for me, my timing was perfect!

PART ONE

EPCOT

CHAPTER ONE

Zero to Sixty

When I have presented in the classroom or in a public setting, I like to start out with, "Hello! My name is Carl, and yes, I am a show cost estimator!" My introduction to Imagineering, known as WED (Walter Elias Disney) came about through a close friend of a colleague in 1979 where I was production manager in the Theatre Arts Department at California State University, Los Angeles. I was living my theatrical dream career, building three to four major shows a year and passing on my stagecraft skills to young theatre students! This possible new work schedule was a welcome change, when compared to my first few years out of Cal State Fullerton's master's program. No more last minute national and international gigs for Mark Wilson Productions. No more six-day weeks/14-hour days, and no more setting up six entirely new Operas for the City of Angels Opera Company. For theatre, this would be a 9 to 5 job with quarterly interruptions! That happenstance meeting with a friend in the theatre department at Cal State opened the door for me quite unexpectedly!

I was in the theatre shop working on some scenery construction for a new show, when I overheard a conversation between Byron Bauer and his friend Larry Weiss. Byron was our Technical Director (TD) and also operated a special effects company on the side called Cinesphere. This company contracted special effects services to a William Cruze for the Sean Connery version of the movie "Meteor." This movie became a second job to my regular full time Cal State duties. More about this in Chapter 12, Dues Paid! What was an easy schedule at Cal State, turned into two full-time gigs for about a year and a half! This schedule was further complicated when the theatre departments light opera, Candide, won the

Kennedy Center American College Theatre Festival region VIII competition. Candide, not set up as a road show, now had to be trucked and set up in Albuquerque, New Mexico. But I digress. Larry had dropped in to tell Byron about his new job for Walt Disney Imagineering. Larry was recently hired at Imagineering as a show set production designer. A job of transferring the EPCOT show model design into blue line construction drawings. (Blue line documents were created by using an ammonia fume bath. The sheets were fed into a roller tank with an ammonia tray. The fumes from the ammonia reacted to the ink creating a blue line drawing.) Of course, digital reproduction is used today, or simply read off the computer screen on AutoCAD or similar software. When I overheard "Disney's looking for model makers" this became my "career changing" moment! Very much like that first experience at Clokey, these five words set my career into an entirely new direction! I moved closer to the conversation, no longer eves dropping, but now a willing participant. Larry, what do you mean they're looking for "model makers?" Larry explained the new project called EPCOT, (Experimental Prototype Community of Tomorrow) would be a new theme park. EPCOT is fast becoming a massive model! Enough said! He had me at "model maker" which was a ready-made position based on my past television and film experiences. I thought, maybe I should just find out what this is all about?

Wasting no time, I did, and was called in for an interview with Maggie Elliott, then head of the model department at WED Imagineering. At that interview, I showed some photos of my past work wherein Maggie gave me a tour of the large EPCOT table model. If you didn't know, Disney Imagineering creates scale models of everything before designs are approved and sent to production. This is a costly effort, but its use succeeds in solving many design issues such as scale and sight-lines, among other critical design problems. They literally use a kind of tabletop "reverse" periscope to see the scaled models from the perspective of the guest. The model is also used to blend the color palette from one area to another. Sightlines if you didn't know, are what you "don't see" behind the scenes in Imagineering terminology! Next time you are at a Disney park, check out what you don't see! Things like the steel structure that holds up the rockwork or the building itself, beyond the façade! That is, "on stage!"

Maggie also explained that WED (originally called Walter Elias Disney) began in 1953 as a new company and was set up as a design group for "new" entertainment projects. That is, anything not related to film or animation. Imagineering, came later as a registered trademark in 1967, claiming its first use in 1962. You may not know that Alcoa actually "invented "the term in 1940! It appeared widely in numerous publications in several disciplines such as urban design, geography and politics, evolutionary economics, corporate culture and futures studies. Alcoa had, for a long time, sought a word to describe "what we all work hard for here at Alcoa... Imagineering is the word... Imagineering is letting your imagination soar, and then engineering it down to earth." Make Sense? Goes to show you (pun intended) that history does repeat itself!

WED, as the design group for Disney theme parks, had been approved for this new project (loosely) based on an original idea for EPCOT by Walt Disney himself. His idea included an urban city center, residential areas, and a series of mass transportation systems that would connect the community. However, after his passing, the company abandoned the concept, unsure about "operating a city". Much has been written on this subject so you might want to check it out.

Enough history, let's get back to my story. After my tour of the model with Maggie and a few other formalities, I was offered the position of model maker at Imagineering. I was very flattered (although this would have been the pinnacle of my experience in such work), and after much consideration, I turned down the position. Two reasons; 1) because of the salary and 2) the extra distance I would have to travel every day. The salary as offered, would have resulted in a lateral move financially compared to where I was at Cal State. While the salary was similar, human resources (HR) held the company line telling me that this is made up by the Mickey Mouse discount card and other perks such as the "silver pass." After all, who could pass up the same money and a 35% discount on purchasing Disney merchandise, with the privilege of working for the mouse? Well, I did! The Mickey credit card, which they promoted quite heavily, wasn't quite the "carrot" I was looking for. For Imagineering though, these perks confirmed you're one of the chosen few and had made it to the top tier of your craft. True enough, however it reminded me of that tune sixteen tons? Another day older and deeper in debt! It was a tough decision. The main reason being, Alison and I were starting to think about having a family and the potential for career growth was a strong consideration.

I remained at Cal State, continued on with my work, when another career changing telephone call came out of the blue just two weeks later. It was Disney Imagineering, a Joel Trinast from HR, and he asked me to come back and interview for a different position, this time in their estimating department. Estimating? I had no clue what he was talking about. Joel told me that a Dave Holtz, the Chief Estimator wanted an interview. To be honest, I was more curious than anything and scheduled an interview with Dave. At the interview, Dave told me that they were interested in hiring me for the position of Show and Ride Estimator. I said to Dave, I don't know what you are talking about and have never heard of a show estimator. As a production manager for the University theatre department, even for the various theatrical positions I had in my "Dues Paid" chapter, there was little, if any budgets for anything. Simply, there was nothing to estimate! I did not have to create budgets for MWP, Cinesphere or City of the Angels Opera Company! So why was Dave interested in me? What was his angle? Dave went on to tell me that this was a new position he created specifically to address cost concerns for the shows and the rides. Essentially "everything the guest sees" in Disney language. When you visit a Disney theme park you are considered a "guest." As a guest, everything you see in the parks is either "front of house or back of house!" This is also referred to as being "on-stage." The reverse of this is off-stage, and that separation from reality starts as you pass through the doors and gates into the operational areas. Or simply, "back of house." Dave explained that EPCOT was fully budgeted (at least as much as a self-funded, conceptual prototype community mega project can be funded) and in design.

The facility structures were at the design development (DD) level and (maybe) the shows at the schematic (SD) level from what I had seen.

Just a note, there are specific design levels for projects and Imagineering's version has become the standard. If memory serves, I believe the total project cost was budgeted somewhere around $1.4B. That budget was far beyond my comprehension and honestly overwhelming! Dave wanted someone with a theatrical/design/technical background to provide estimated cost information, based on the models and designs for the EPCOT shows, rides and attractions. He wanted to bolster his current professional team of construction estimators, with specialists, using entertainment cost professionals. Seemed like a good idea to me. Dave's vision was clear, he wanted my theatrical background. I would learn "on the job" under his mentoring. I knew design and production and had started with a "tool belt on" and knew the entertainment/production business. What Dave was offering, was an opportunity to learn something new! An office position that would take me out of the production shop and put me on a management track. Exactly what I needed; I wasn't getting any younger. I really didn't want to be hefting scenery in my 40s and 50s. At 32, my body was already breaking down from the 24/7 schedule and endless hours of bending, lifting, no sleep and working through the theatrical production lifestyle. All for the business of show, of course! It just seemed like it would be the right move and the right time, so I accepted. What did I have to lose? I was pretty excited! I recall going home and telling Alison, "They want me to sit at a desk, estimate scenery costs from drawings and models and pay me a lot more money!" By the way, I'd still get that card and the silver pass! Not too long after I received my letter of offer, I found out that Dave Holtz was "transitioning" out of Imagineering. He had decided to go out on his own as an Independent entertainment estimating consultant. Something he couldn't tell me at our interview. I didn't know at the time how much influence Dave would have on my career. Or that we would become friends and work on projects later. The business of show is really a small world!

My offer to become a show estimator still stood. However, my
new Chief Estimator's name was Craig Heller. Someone I had
not met yet. Craig would be an outstanding Chief Estimator
and I would learn much under his tenure. In fact, my favorite
line comes from Craig. It is "Buyer Beware!" This was a challenge that Craig repeated throughout our estimating review
meetings. A phrase I use to this day!

Officially, I started at Imagineering in the early summer
of 1980. When I first joined the estimating team, there was:
Loretta Hoffman, Carl Simmons, Mike White, Molly Rose and
Emil Kurylyand , the core team of facility estimators. Later, two
others joined, a fresh University graduate named Jeff Webb,
and a bit after that, a fellow named Gary Zinn. Gary became
the second show and ride estimator. His background came from
the Playboy Organization. I understood he was responsible for
"scenery" for the photo shoots. There was also one other show
estimator who had worked at the "fur and feather" shop (the
artists that applied the fur, feathers and costumes to audio-an-
imatronic figures) at the Tujunga show production facility.
His name was Cort Goudy, and his shop experience was very
valuable to a special cost-study analysis Lorretta began on AA
figures. Cort's mentoring also helped me in understanding the
different areas of work performed at the Tujunga shop.

These were the estimating professionals dedicated to the
EPCOT project (that I remember). This team was also responsible for the first overseas theme park called Tokyo Disneyland
(TDL). TDL was funded through an agreement with OLC
(Oriental Land Company). I only worked on a few attractions
towards the end for TDL, mostly to help out Peter Alexander,
who at the time was down the hall from estimating. He had a
management role in that project.

My first couple of weeks at Imagineering involved the
typical office orientation and "the getting to know you"
period that everyone experiences with a new job. However,
Disney Imagineering takes this a step beyond. We soon
received our official "Pixie Dust" tour. This orientation
consisted of three full days of "experiencing" each of the
main Disney operating groups in southern California. The
Walt Disney Studios, Disneyland and Imagineering. These

were well-organized introduction sessions designed to ori-
entate and immerse us newbies into the Disney spirit. The
indoctrination was intense, and the "cast" did their best
to make you feel "special and privileged" to work for the
mouse! Thus, the term "Pixie Dust." I'll give you an example
of what we experienced.

At Disneyland, our day began as one of the 'walk- around'
park characters. To experience what it felt like "from the
other side" of the (mask) costume. Because of my height I
was picked to play "Goofy." Some would say not too far out
of character. Participating in the "character walk" was mandatory for all Imagineering employees and that included (I
was told) Michael Eisner and Frank Wells. I always wondered what costumes they were put in. It is a very useful
experience. Seeing the expressions on the children's faces
from "inside the costume." I have to admit, was fun! I
loved it and got into character (a character "pro" from the
costume shop, provided us character tips and insights) for
the brief 20 minutes we were allowed to be "onstage" in the
park. Being in the park, in costume with kids all around you
is something you can never forget. The look in their eyes,
their smiles and exuberance really does change your perspective. The downside though, is it is very hot inside those
costumes, even on a cool day. Also, kids will be kids, which
is why they provide a "handler" to go out with you. You
know, to help prevent you "stepping" on any kids (the sight-
lines are limited from inside the mask) and to keep the kids
from kicking, gouging and doing whatever they think they
can get away with behind your back! And they do! The full
day tour also included many behind-the-scenes walk thru's
of some of the attractions. Seeing the Haunted Mansion, or
Pirates backstage was quite interesting, even though I had
constructed a lot of different theatrical scenery. We were
treated to lunch, met a few other management types and all
in all, the day was quite fun!

On the next day, we met at the studio for our tour behind the
scenes. Just being passed through the studio gate was a huge
thrill! Our tour included lunch at the commissary, the sound
stages, the back lot, the animation buildings and a very small

one room "museum" which collected and archived everything Disney. Dave Smith was the curator of this museum and it was his mission over the years to chronicle and archive all Disney merchandise and other memorabilia. I remember Dave. He had a twinkle in his eye, and you could tell he was smitten with the dust! RIP Dave! One of the most memorable parts of our studio tour was seeing (and touching) the "original multi-plane camera." The same camera that you see in the various archive photos with Walt and his animators crowded around! It is a very large machine in a very small space! It must have been very hot in that room when the animation cells were being photographed! Years later I saw the very same camera at the Walt Disney Family Museum in San Francisco where it had been moved. How many can say they had that experience? The studio tour finished with a visit to the employee gift store where we were "allowed" to buy studio logo merchandise. I purchased a "studio logo" 8 ½ X 11 tablet cover. Still have it! Here again, I am reminded of that old tune "Sixteen Tons?" The line "I owe my sole to the company store" seems relevant here?" The studio tour was the highlight of my orientation. It was very easy to get caught up in the privilege of it all. How many people get to tour the studio in depth? Not many people get past the security gates! Admittedly, I felt kind of special!

Our three-day orientation tour was completed at WED where we went through the MAPO shops, (Named after Mary Poppins) the special effects area, model shops, sculpting studio and other administration offices. All of these areas fully functioning in the production of various elements for EPCOT. The orientation highlight was touring the MAPO facility.

MAPO is where the animatronic figures, show action equipment and mechanical props are manufactured. I'd compare it to the special effects shop I managed at NBC Studios, Burbank later on, except MAPO technicians had full engineered drawings to work from. The NBC shop techs only had one concept drawing. Either way, each in their own right, excellent craftsmen! The tour also reminded me of the first time I had been in John Gaughn's illusion shop when I was with Mark Wilson Productions. John's shop was filled with master craftsman constructing the physical "illusions" you see on stage with master magicians such as the famous David Copperfield or Lance Burton. John's shop was truly "magical" and seeing MAPO for the first time reminded me of that experience.

With our tours completed and fully dusted with Pixie, I began to figure out what the heck I was going to do in the way of my new job as a show and ride estimator. But, before we get into that detail, I'd like to take a moment and review the EPCOT projects scope of work. Remember, this was the largest theme park ever built in the United States next to the Magic Kingdom at that time! Understanding the scale of the project, may give you some insight on why I was feeling totally overwhelmed from the get-go! As I say, it was "Zero to Sixty!"

You may not know that the EPCOT construction project was unparalleled in scale between 1980 and 1983. The U.S. economy experienced a deep recession, the primary cause of which was the disinflationary monetary policy adopted by the Federal Reserve. Think about it. Disney was pouring over $1B-plus in construction spending into the economy. Industries throughout the United States supplied materials, manufacturing, retail products, food and beverage supplies. I'd venture to guess it was the largest employer of construction staff in the United States at the time. The project was large; but there were many challenges. Many unanticipated due to its scale. At the peak of construction, there were thousands of construction laborers, contractors and subcontractors swarming like ants around this huge 600-acre site. The general contractor (under the management of Project Director Jim Nagy) selected for the project was Tishman Construction. Tishman, was a well-known general contractor and construction management firm and had been responsible for high-profile projects including the Twin Towers in New York City. (911! Never Forget!) Although Tishman had experience with big dollar projects, no firm on earth hired for this type of construction would have really known what they were getting into! Tishman managed hundreds of contractors and subcontractors on the EPCOT project site. And they did a fine job of bringing in the project on time. Whether it was "on budget," that's above my pay grade!

The local economy around the Disney World property flourished! I remember one place in particular that could not keep up with the demand of the construction crews coming in and out of the EPCOT site. It began as a small 7/11 type of store off of highway 4. As EPCOT's construction expanded, that little store became the place for "morning coffee" and a "days end" six-pack! It seemed like it happened all of a sudden. Suddenly, a massive exterior cold storage unit appeared adjacent to the main store in what seemed a matter of weeks! This is typical of what happens to the surrounding community wherever a Disney project appears. It's also why the potential Disney sites are selected "quietly."

There were also downsides to the EPCOT project. And that was related to the very scale of such an enormous endeavor! EPCOT became a target for some very clever fraud schemes. I'll tell you about one area taken advantage of by the site trades, as it was related to me. Apparently, there were trades people "clocking in" on different building projects within the overall job site. For example, a tradesperson might clock in at the Land pavilion for one contractor, leave that site and clock in at Spaceship Earth for another contractor. Same project, different job, two paychecks! I learned of this situation while I was on site later. To this day, I don't have a clue as to the extent of the problem. I do know that the on-site management team were doing everything possible to stop this practice. I heard that they did, eventually, but I can imagine it was an auditing nightmare. Integrated software reporting systems were not in common practice at the time. The technology was by "hand punching" timecards. Accurate tracking of day-to-day costs of a multi-billion-dollar project is difficult in any circumstance. I'm sure that there were many issues like this during the construction of EPCOT and I have a personal opinion about this. Disney was committed to the opening of EPCOT in October of 1982. It had the financial strength to fix problems as they happened. Not many companies can or will do this to see a project completed on time. Especially one of this scale! Any other project might be sold off in some manner, stopped and/or abandoned leaving investors in the lurch. I've seen it happen since. Not so for Disney! There was simply too much at stake! Disney was "all in."

The masterplan of EPCOT is divided into two themed areas: Future World and World Showcase. Future World is the main entrance with a monorail drop off, from service areas within Walt Disney World. You can ride the monorail from any other venue in Disney World to EPCOT. After you enter, Spaceship Earth is seen from the monorail station. There is a massive water feature separating the two. To reach World Showcase, you pass directly under the 18-story Spaceship Earth geodesic structure! Coming out of that passage, is Communicore with Future World pavilions surrounding both Spaceship Earth and Communicore.

Future World is a showcase of technology. The names chosen for the pavilions in this area are Energy, Horizons, Spaceship Earth, the Land, the Sea, Journey into Imagination and Communicore. Each pavilion explores technology and its contributions to the history of humanity. Where Future World is the entrance to EPCOT, Spaceship Earth is the guest's first impression! As guests arrive on the monorail, Spaceship Earth appears in the distance like a "golf ball" ready for its tee shot! It is a beautiful structure and catches the light of day from dawn to dusk on its Alcoa structural panel system. I first saw Spaceship Earth as a model in 1980 on my interview tour. At 18 stories tall, it is the largest geodesic sphere constructed at that time. Held up by massive footings, that cradle it like a loving mother, it has no windows and is "skinned" with an Alcoa aluminum product made especially for the building. The outer skin acts as a massive rain gutter, something you really need in Florida! Spaceship Earth reminds me that as I worked through the early design progress of Spaceship Earth, my daughter would refer to it as "Daddy's Golf Ball!" Doug Stapp, the project manager for the project, in fact had a golf ball on three golf tees in his office! Moving under and thru a tunnel, Future World is revealed, with Communicore the main attraction or core, and the various technological pavilions revealed on either side to form the Future World area. Each pavilion is "themed" to convey its intent and purpose. EPCOT would be Disney's largest park to date at 305 acres! Bring your walking shoes! As you exit Spaceship Earth, you see Communicore. This pavilion showcases the latest in personal technology. Initially, it was designed as a "super arcade" and was filled with all types of games and hands-on science exhibits. Directly around this "core" were pavilions that were very specific to the sciences. The Universe of Energy, for example, offered a one-of-a-kind ride vehicle that was "wire controlled." The vehicles hold over 97 guests on a journey through the formation of oil and natural gas. A massive recreation of the progression from dinosaur to oil is a journey that ended in a massive film experience! Then there is the Horizons pavilion, using an "over hanging rail vehicle" through the elements of transportation, energy, food and communications. Horizon's held a massive Omnimax film screen where the vehicle transports the guest into a full immersive film on the largest film screen to date produced for this format! Journey into Imaginations is described as "a symphony of volumes, forms, and tonal nuances." Its ride vehicle follows Figment and Dreamfinder (the main characters) as tour guides, "it takes the guest on a trip that mirrors the process of imagination," as noted in the book, past wonders like "Dreamfinder's Machine" and many exciting sequences brought to life by, of course, your Imagination! The Land pavilion is a vast complex, six acres in size, that includes a water ride called Symphony of the Seed! This is a passive journey through the process of agriculture-past and future! It a story "you can see, touch, and feel, and even eat at its revolving restaurant!" With food science on full display and used on the menu! The Living Seas pavilion is one of EPCOT's most ambitious projects. Built as an enormous seawater tank it immerses the guest into the watery deep! Feeding demonstrations, educational exhibits abound in a modern, stainless steel "under the sea" environment! Last but not least, the World of Motion, brings the story of transportation to life in animatronic realism! The ride vehicle tour starts with early man, with scenes filled with animatronics, exciting films and themed sets! Truly the first "wheel" and where we are today! At the ride's exit, GM, it's sponsor, presents the latest in automotive technology and the future of transportation!

The second and largest area of EPCOT is called World Showcase. This area is entered either by a central bridge from Future World, or from either side of the main Lagoon via the various pavilions surrounding it. The American Adventure is located just across the World Showcase Lagoon at the end of this bridge. It is the first major structure visible across the lagoon as you exit Future World. A unique bit of information concerning this "bridge" if I may. Between Future World and World Showcase, just under one part of the bridge, are "rising bubbles." I'm not sure if "the bubbles" have been resolved as of this writing, but you can see bubbles (if you know where to look) emitting from the water on the left side of the bridge. It has something to do with natural gas rising from below the lagoon. Check it out! World Showcase is an International show-case promoting the countries of, Mexico, China, Japan, Italy, Morocco, Norway, France, Germany, the United Kingdom, Canada and of course the United States. Each country pavilion is under contract by sponsorship of the host country to present the guest with a unique travel experience without having to leave the USA. World Showcase has become an opportunity to "brand" the tourism industry of each country. It has also come to be an opportunity for families to experience a piece of Europe without the expense and the passports! There are some that say that World Showcase was added and became necessary for EPCOT, because of the "sponsorship" funds derived from the various countries. Who knows and does it really matter at this point in time? No!

EPCOT's master plan, includes "Area Development" and is unique with the main manmade lagoon, water features, architectural icons and historically correct representations of each countries landscaping. EPCOT uses the same formula to "draw the guest to the back of the property." While Spaceship Earth is the focal point for the main entrance, the American Adventure anchors the back of the park much like Cinderella's castle. Both structures creating "a visual carrot" luring vis-itors deep into the property. Much like the reason "milk" is placed at the rear of the grocery store. Yes? There were seven Future World structures, and eleven World Showcase pavilions on opening day in 1982, although Horizons opened one-year later. That is a whole lot of estimating!

Over my tenure at WED, I provided estimates for every one of these pavilions, plus a few potential new "sponsorship" opportunities which never made it to funding. Each pavilion had a unique attraction, highly themed retail and of course five-star restaurants! Depending on the pavilion, there were shows and rides unique to each, all requiring an estimate. While I provided estimates for all, including sections of area development, my primary responsibilities were the Spaceship Earth and Horizons projects. Both, as I recall, exceeded estimated budgets of over $100 million each. I knew them intimately from their first footing, up to their last topping off flag!

Imagineering captured the look, feel and flavor of each country represented without question! However, back at Sonora, in early 1980 when everything was pretty much on paper, there were a few of us who had a bit more skeptical opinion of the potential success of World Showcase! Our feeling was that the general public would not spend "big bucks" to enter EPCOT, spend more "big bucks" to eat at four-star European restaurants and shops! I'm glad to say we were dead wrong! Even today, EPCOT restaurants are reservation only. Be sure to do this ahead of time, because it has been "reservations only" since 1982!

A little mentioned key to EPCOT's success, is the result of the original expat/educational programs for operating initiated by WED for each World Showcase venue. Each countries pavilion is staffed by world famous chefs, unique to each country. If you eat at the France pavilion, it's just like the cuisine you find in Paris! This is true throughout World Showcase. Also, each countries staff are "cast members" relocated from each country, adding to the authenticity. With all of World Showcase before you in exacting detail, each pavilion represented with its own unique iconic architecture, you are in Paris, or the United Kingdom, or one of the nine other pavilions experiencing the culture and ambiance of Europe!

I'll close this section and share a thought that many of my colleagues had during the EPCOT design phase. It is said, World Showcase is the alternative to visiting Europe. I've heard that from many people. Why go to Europe or Asia if you can do it at Disneyworld? No passport required!

CHAPTER TWO

Data

With the Pixie Dust quickly fading away, it was time to learn my new trade! Remember, I had no formal training, or for that matter had never estimated anything to do with shows and rides. I sat at my drafting table pondering the "learning" part, which was left to my own Imagination. (this turned out to be the real meaning of the word Imagineering) I had no knowledge or experience in this new specialty area. I was like a sponge that needed a very quick squeeze, ready to absorb all of the knowledge I could get! I was nervous, a bit frustrated but decided to follow that rule "if you don't know anything, start asking a lot of questions!" It was no time for pride. It was time to be humble and needy!

My first question was how do you do this? I was very much a rookie! I began by asking where I might find samples of the work product. Forthwith, (I just like that word!) I was directed to stacks of file drawers filled with old estimates. (Yes-This is 1980 and everything was in a file drawer!) This was a big challenge. However, in my master's program, I took a "research" class that established a methodology for discovering information. My theatrical education had taught me, how to research, organize and develop a plan of action! As I dug into the various project files and reviewed as many estimates as time allowed, I began to understand there were no detailed costs for shows and rides. And what nuggets of information did I find? In the nicely tabbed, legal sized file folders, the estimates for the show and ride systems were referenced in one words; "allowance." This was it? An attraction with twenty-six scenes had an "allowance" for the entire show? No detail? Not even a description of the definition of "allowance or what it was based on?" In contrast, the facility or construction estimates had line-item detail according to the standard CSI (Construction Science Institute, a national association of more than 8,000 construction industry professionals who are experts in building construction and the materials used therein) format. I would soon learn more about that! I also learned from my review process, that while the facility estimates were taken from structures well past the schematic design phase, it made sense that they were as detailed as they were. However, the show and ride estimates were often "conceptual" and depending on the attraction, had very little information available. Which is why there were allowances! I learned later that an "allowance" is really code for a WAG, a "Wild Ass Guess!" Could it really be that show estimating was this simple? Could I really follow the examples: Show, $100,000,000 - Allowance! Ride system $1,000,000, 000 - Allowance! The answer was no. There had to be a better way. This is where my right brain/left brain began to argue. What the heck does allowance mean? Is everything included? How would you know? Did anyone actually see a drawing? Was it based on a model? Did the estimator have a dialogue with the show designer? I needed answers! The answers to these questions became what is called the "Basis of Estimate."

As this was my first exposure to the profession of show and ride estimating, I began to quickly realize why Dave Holtz had brought me into the business of estimating. The experience of the staff simply wasn't there to take the show estimate ball and run with it! As alarm bells went off in my head, an action plan for figuring this all out began to develop! I didn't know anything about show and ride estimating, but I could certainly learn how to do it and devise a strategy to make it better. I decided that for my first step, I would "bug the hell" out of the pros in the estimating department. (Hint-this is a tip for you just starting out!) The two senior estimators I credit for getting me up to speed at Imagineering were Loretta Hoffman and Carl Simmons. They taught me the basics of construction estimating. How to approach the work. How to organize the work. How to get answers about the work! These two welcomed me looking over their shoulders, while I asked too many questions and generally disturbed their work! For their generous time to mentor me, I am forever grateful to them both!

Carl was an experienced "core and shell" estimator (again, that's the main building structural components) and Loretta, who originally started in the WED finance group, was doing a terrific job of detailing out the production/manufacturing process of the "animatronic" figures. We referred to these as "AA" figures for simplification. Lorretta had detailed the components of the AA figures, the first such attempt at detailing show estimates. Loretta was building the first "database" to understand how the pieces were put together and how the parts functioned. All on a "13 column ledger!" She led the way, as far as I am concerned in establishing show estimating! It was through Loretta's and Carl's examples, I learned how to detail out show and ride estimates! My faith was being restored on how and what I could achieve in my new profession!

Following Loretta's example, I set out to create the same level of detail, as much as possible anyway, for the entire show and ride systems. I would limit my use of the word "allowance." Allowance would become an excuse in my mind and not an acceptable show estimating term. I would create the details of a scene, sometimes designing far ahead of the show producers, using my abilities as a scenic designer and translate "that blank piece of paper" into a living document of show detail! To be clear, I was not designing the show or interfering with the design intent of the show. I was "filling in" the blanks in a generic form. This methodology was what I would later learn was referred to as "estimator's judgement." Sort of a license to fill in the blanks! All based on the estimator's experience.

My estimating process started with design packages. These were rolls of "blue-line" drawings. Once I reviewed the drawings, I could analyze the, model or a rendering that depicted the design intent. Often a fully developed design concept. Sometimes there was enough information, making it fairly simple to detail the show elements within. Sometimes, the design was a concept with lots of intent, but little factual information on the physical design. This is why I was called a "conceptual show estimator." That means "related to or based on mental concepts." Exactly what I was hired to do. My theatrical education and practical experience as a scenic designer and production manager, allowed me to understand the story or the script, and translate that into an interpretation of the intended visual form! In other words, in my head, I was creating the physical elements of the design intent! Essentially, estimating the "known and the unknown" materials in the designated physical space! I was creating the "basis" of the entire physical space to establish detail for my estimate! It was my experience from my live theatrical training, with over thirty-five productions designed and the same number actually constructed! I could estimate all costs associated with any concept provided, even though there might not be a set of construction drawing to base my conclusions. If you understand the story, it is not difficult to imagine the scenery required, or likely required, to bring the story to life. It all starts with a platform, exterior or interior walls, architectural detail, props and dressings or perhaps some artificial "greens" as they are called in the industry. Each of these elements confined to a space, alongside a ride track of some kind and as deep from the ride vehicle as the physical space allows. If you know the story that is being told, adding in the physical elements that tells the story was easy!

Creating a conceptual physical space is fairly straightforward. Estimators judgement is not! Let's think about the levels of platforming required for the scenes in Spaceship Earth. I use this example because when I first saw the show package, there was no distinction between the set platforming and the facility deck. Imagine, if you will, the ride vehicle "winding" its way up and through an 18-story geodesic dome in a continuous train of ride vehicles. The individual scenes are located alongside the track on odd level platforming, designed to maintain your POV on a level plane. Each scene staying at eye level as you reach the top of the dome. As the estimator, you have to ask yourself, are the show set platforms built to accommodate these levels? Or are the show sets going to be installed on platforms already in place when the scenery arrives? Either way, somebody has to provide them and pay for them! Is it a show cost or a facility cost? Make sense? Estimating the show platforms built at the same time in the shop as the rest of the scenery, would be in the WBS - show sets - category. However, if it is a cost for "non-themed facility platforms," one could argue that the cost belongs to the facility! This is not a trick question. If you are the show producer and have a tight budget, you will argue the latter! The same argument could come from the project manager of the facility! Can you blame them? Facilities logic becomes, "the building is delivered with a slab," anything above that related to the show or ride is a show cost! Show would say, "the steel framed platforms that our sets attach to are facility costs because they need to be structural according to code!" Guess who is caught in the middle. In this case, it was not an assumption on my part. I met with the engineers and asked the question. The steel framed platforms for the sets would be structural and require fire protection underneath. Next case! And on it went. It didn't matter to me who was paying for it, but only that the cost was in the estimate one way or the other! I would find many more examples of this as my show and ride estimates progressed. This is the theory I call "the grey area" of estimating show. Issues like the one above, kept me very busy between the facility PMs and the Show Producers. My theory suggests that you cannot put a show in a building without having some impact on its cost! My goal was to make sure that those costs were covered!

Then there is what is referred to as the "basis of the estimate." This could become an important document and should be included in all estimates. Whether you are estimating the facility, the show or ride, the basis for the estimate is derived from a variety of sources the estimator has used in their estimate. It usually begins with a dated set of drawings, including the date the documents were received. It could also include items such as meeting notes taken from project meeting, with the date, the verbal information received from project management, (or source) and a model review and discussion with show producer, (dated) among other sources. The point of the basis of estimate is to document where you received the information incorporated in the estimate. You didn't just make it up. Correct?

As mentioned above, there is what I call the grey area of show and ride. This came about as I dug deeper looking for those items between the facility, show and the ride that might "fall through the cracks!" in any estimate. I saw this happen between estimators that were estimating different elements of the same building! As I note in the above discussion, you could not "assume" that someone else was picking up the cost. You have to be "pro-active" and make certain! An "assumption" used in lieu of the facts, is easier to delete, than to miss the cost entirely! Assumptions create a dialogue with the project team and dialogue is good!

Another lesson learned from the facility estimators is called "estimators' judgement!" This is more than just an assumption and is based on the estimator's experience and knowledge in their field of practice. My estimator's judgement options came up often. Here's an example. Many scenes for the shows I received were incomplete with props, sets, murals, or maybe animated figures and show action equipment. It was not always a complete design. For example, show lighting, did not appear on most drawings. Either did audio. Then there were the special effects which could include special projectors, "Scent" cannons (an EPCOT first) and unusual effects like a volcano spewing lava! This left a huge gap in information and cost. Often, the information would appear in the scope documents and not on the drawing. This gap in information suggested that I needed to be "in the loop" to what every department was doing on their projects. Whatever the scope of work called for, especially the work it did not call for, I wanted to become an active participate in the planning, design and construction of these theatrical scenes. I could apply my "estimators' judgement." Because of this, I asked for and began receiving show and ride related reports from every department at Imagineering. There was a lot of paper coming into our department, but I justified it by telling everyone "I will be responsible for all of this!" I can quickly review the documents and "round file" (re-cycle) if it is not important. I simply did not want to miss anything that would make my estimates better.

This standard level of detail became the basis for my estimated show and ride costs of the attractions. The amount of detail opened up dialogue between the project team. (There were two sides of this coin - "Where the hell is that item called out in the scope of work" or "We hadn't thought about that!"). I learned, as the project developed, if "budget cuts" came up, and they always did, the amount of detail allowed for the team to "carve" rather than "slash" the scene. For example, it was easier to eliminate "four of ten AA figures" instead of taking a lump sum 40% out of an allowance. After all, what if six of those AA figures were estimated at $100K each and the other four at $20,000, $40,000, $50,000 and $60,000.? If you were the show producer, wouldn't you want a choice to maintain the integrity of your design? This then became my plan. I had learned this from the facility professionals, applied it to my own experience, and now all I had to do was work it! Fortunately for me, there was an existing roadmap at Imagineering called the Work Breakdown System or WBS. This was Imagineering's accounting tool created with show and ride categories, to organize "all the parts" into one nice neat package! It was designed for cost detail with the idea that costs could be tracked throughout the life of the project. Of course, one had to enter the information correctly to allow that to happen. You've heard of "garbage in?"

From my own learning curve on the terms and the methodology of preparing a show and ride estimate, I was now facing the bigger issue of Imagineering's unique process of creating the magic! By comparison, my previous theatrical background was simple. I would have one, maybe two drawings and a quick talk with the designer. And from that I built the show. No muss, no fuss, maybe a few more bits of dialogue with the director. Imagineering though, was complex and a much bigger challenge!

The quantity of documents, the meetings and the formal process of entering it all into a cohesive show and ride estimate was overwhelming! Besides learning the WBS system, there were scope writers, technical writers, show producers, special effects technicians, lighting designers, sculptors, model makers, audio/video specialists, MAPO manufacturing techs and the Tujunga production craftspeople! Then there was the management staff. Project managers show and ride engineers, production managers, project coordinators and project business administrators, isn't that enough?

The show and ride estimates were not being entered correctly into the WBS system. At least not to the extent it was designed. And the previous format of an "allowance" was easier to write at the top of the page then detailing all the various show elements. There was little detail on the show estimates because there were no show estimators with the educational background or theatrical experience with the elements in a show scene. Dave Holtz would have been the exception, because he was from a studio production background. Unfortunately, he had left as I noted above. That changed when I was hired. As I dug further into the methodology of estimating, I knew that I could work with the existing WBS system. Some revisions were in order, but why reinvent the wheel? This was the first part of the language of show. Theatre had taught me that there was only one important goal in the business of show. Deliver the production and open the show on time! With EPCOT on a fast track schedule, Imagineers had a huge learning curve ahead, no matter what department they worked. Meanwhile, the opening date remained at October 1982! Only two years away!

Of the departments I point out above, there were only two that interested me most. One was the project business administrators, (PBA's) the group responsible for accounting for every expense in the project budgets. The other the project scope writers. Their task was to organize the story for the show, including every piece of information that would make up the physical characteristics. Our estimates would eventually become their "budgets." I set out to make sure, my show and ride estimate line items "matched" the correct WBS category, and the information provided in the scope documents. The function of language, however, was open to interpretation in all three areas. What I knew to be an animated prop for example, might be included under animated figures and special effects between scope and the WBS. This I thought was due to the variety of industry backgrounds brought in for the specific tasks. I also learned quickly that the estimating department was not getting the WBS reports or the scope updates. And why would they? There was no one that needed the information. I saw this as critical information and requested both these reports delivered to estimating in a timely manner. At first, I received flack for asking for them! Why on earth would an estimator need to review these reports? Didn't they have enough to do with their estimating?

This was not a deterrent in my world. I am what would be labeled as a "pusher." That means that I don't let go once I have set my mind to something. I learned over time that being a "pusher" meant that sometimes I didn't get credit for something that changed and would benefit everyone. I like to say that even if the person I was pushing came up with the idea later on, I knew that I had planted the seed for the idea. My goal was for the benefit of the project, not a personal "atta-boy." Ego was not part of my make-up, then. My effort to integrate the three elements of estimating, finance and scope became my passion. It is what I now refer to as "the Language of Show."

This effort would become the foundation of a coordinated show and ride estimate package. It would represent the actual design intent with the goal to describe the design in a common language understood by any background in the entertainment industry. It would be a package that would include all elements of the show and ride, one scene, one system at a time. The detailed show and ride estimates, the scopes that described the work, would actually be coordinated within the WBS. This would allow each project to have a trackable "estimated/cost history." I was sure that talking to the PBA's would be easy. It didn't go as planned. "Territory" exists in every company and "change" always seems to be a four-letter word!

My first contacts in the PBA department were three individuals who helped me in understanding their functions as project administrators. Accounting is accounting, no matter what you call it. It is also not a "standard" language. The most troubling line item I saw was what was called "suspense." Suspend what? Was it "on hold?" Was it a slush fund? I don't think to this day I understood what it really meant, but at the time I went with "holding pattern!" Accountants, can't live with them, can't live without them! However, like every colleague I interacted with at Imagineering, everyone was very nice and easy to get along with. My biggest allies in my effort to understand PBA language were Bernard Freeth, Phil Jordan and Dick Riggert! Thank you, gentlemen, for all your guidance! However, it wasn't that easy to break the veil! They wanted to know, why do you need to know what we do? What is your motivation? This is information that is read by project management, not estimating! Fair enough. No one likes another department nosing around in their neck of the woods. Right? I told them that if I could understand the reports, actually see the reports submitted to the project managers, there was a good chance I could help them sort out any duplicate dollars in the shows or rides. At a minimum, I could "flag" funds that were not in the correct WBS category. I suggested that down the line, as the projects moved through the design phases, and into production, a proper detail and placement into the WBS, from the earliest estimate, could be monitored more closely. Things did fall through the cracks on a $1.4B project! I think I had them at "they really didn't need to do anything different." When I started to receive their reports in estimating though, there was quite an uproar and "some splain'n to do!" Nothing new here. I have a tendency to act and accept the fall out later! I should say at this point, that I would provide an example of the WBS language, but it is "proprietary" material, and this is one ledge I won't step off!

The second department I asked for help were the scope writers. Their job? To capture the story, in narrative form, to provide a detailed description of the story and maintain a timely update of the story for each attraction. There were hundreds of attractions! All moving targets and all needing a scope document. Imagineering as you may know, starts all design with a "story." The story being written by specialized writers working with show design. The scope writers' job was to transfer the information from the story into the various elements of the physical attraction. Show and Ride elements such as floor area, description of the scenery, ride track length, quantity of ride vehicles or lengths of films. It would also include the number of special effects, the number of AA figures and basics like the Theoretical Ride Capacity or THRC, the theoretical number of ride passengers on any ride (A formula for design purposes) Versus the OHRC - Operational Hourly ride Capacity (actual number of guests). And because Imagineering set the standards for a "gift shop" at the exit of each ride, the scope would also include retail environments, and food and beverage concessions, if any. The scope was the bible of the attractions.

As the program developed for EPCOT, many new attractions were added. The scope would also document backstage areas, new live stage theatricals, character parades and water spectaculars such as Luminaire in the EPCOT lagoon! It was the scope writers' job to capture the story, all its detail, and update it on a regular schedule. Estimators always had to check for the latest revisions. The scope document was an extremely useful "publication." Particularly to estimating. We did our best to match our estimates to the most current scope. Talented as they were though, there was a "learning curve" in this department too. When I first brought the issues of the WBS "language" to their attention, they understood the issue quickly. I would bring something to their attention, we'd have a dialogue and as a team resolved the issue. It didn't hurt though that one of the scope writers was in my daily ride carpooling from the San Gabriel Valley! I used that time to discuss and plan the seed for my idea. This relationship would continue when I went back to work on EDL (Euro Disneyland) in Paris. But that's the second half of this story.

EPCOT the project, was running like a freight train and every department had to keep up. If you were in finance, budget updates were the constant. In estimating, comparisons, a report (comparing the current estimate to the last published estimate) was mandatory. To "keep the train on the tracks" management needed information and they needed it yesterday!

For me, the day would begin with the delivery of "drawing packages" from the previous evening. The staff at "repro," created these documents (the rolls could be as thick as 12" in diameter and were very heavy) and we would joke that these "repro guys" were a bit "off" from all the ammonia fumes they had to deal with every single day! PC did not exist back then! There was plenty of good-natured fun and because we could all laugh together, it made for a fun atmosphere! I'm sure everyone is glad that the digital age has replaced that old system of reproduction though! My office looked more like document storage than an estimating space. Talk about being overwhelmed! Each day I'd review drawing packages, build new or update estimates and complete the process by summarizing the entire estimate onto an Excel spreadsheet. Estimating was my "crash course" into Excel spreadsheets. I go back far enough with excel that I remember management saying, "is this an Excel cost summary?" The answer was yes. Good, it must be correct if it came out of the computer! This actually prompted me to write in very small print at the bottom of each page; "Buyer beware! Just because this is excel doesn't mean it's correct!" Thanks again for that phrase, Craig! It was in a very tiny print and never noticed as far as I know! Excel was very problematic, not just at the outset, but I had headaches with it for most of my career! I was burned many times because of my own learning curve with the software. Not to mention the inherent flaws with the system. Funny thing though. Although I used this spreadsheet, I kept a desk top calculator throughout my WED tenure. At the end of the day, there were miles of calculator ribbon all over the floor of my office! I just couldn't trust the technology.

To be clear, the drawing packages we estimated from were not construction drawings. At best, they were schematic or maybe at the level of design development. Our estimates were not bids! Meaning, we couldn't provide estimates with labor and materials detail. Instead, we used a "square foot" method of estimating. Literally, we would create "unit pricing" for say, a show platform. Or a scenic wall, or a mural or a ceiling space. Our unit pricing would include a cost per square foot that included, labor, and material handling. Because of my shop construction experience, I had already built a variety of theatrical scenery. I could "picture in my mind" how the piece in question would likely be constructed. I knew the "quality" of material and workmanship required for the day-to-day operational requirements. How could I forget? "We don't use steel railing in the ride tracks for our water rides!" "We use stainless!" The tone was well taken. I had to learn an "operational" language to! I learned a lot from Wayne Jackson! Thanks Wayne! I had already been to enough project meetings to understand the "operational" requirements of a Disney attraction. All constructed to withstand the abuse of the guest and its own environment. All of this meant that it was not cheap! In other words, my "square foot" unit price was reasonable, an educated work up of what that particular item might cost in the field. Add ons such as crating, shipping moving into place, installation etc., were covered in other sub categories under each WBS show category. Our square foot estimates were as far as we went on the show estimates. A complete and final estimate of cost (for a bid package, for example) was not required. Due to the volume of work for EPCOT, all of the show sets, murals, AA figures etc., were built in-house. Perhaps not so much that other outside shops couldn't do it, but because of the high-quality standards required by operations. Our effort for management was to make sure the costs were realistic. If we noticed a "trend" of cost increases, we followed through with further investigation and fine tuning. The models did change, the shows and rides were often subject to being reduced with budget cuts. There was a constant blur of activity. The estimating process was not a relaxed, "take your good time" 9 to 5 task. We experienced, in our daily work, "fire drills", or work within work exercises. These were cost exercises needed by management "yesterday." Annoying, very much so! But like anything else, as you became more experienced and knowledgeable about the process, you develop somewhat of a numbness to the interruptions. You learn to let go, to shove the current job aside for later, and attack the new problem! They call this "multi-tasking now! Back then, we called it a "pain in the ass!" Not necessarily the best segues, but this memory reminds me that there was one, what I call the "granddaddy of interruptions." Occasionally management would come over to WED and "walk the EPCOT model." They would literally walk all over the model, asking questions, pointing out things they wanted to change or modify. Some might call this "Monday morning quarterbacking." You can argue this point if you want. I think the Disney shareholders though just might disagree with you! At least at that time in Disney history.

Come to think of it, how many people have seen top Disney executives walking around on an EPCOT show model with their socks on? You may ask, why was all this so important to me? The answer is clear now, but not so much at the beginning of my tenure at WED. Everything I did in my early estimating career. I did to learn the trade and make my job functional. I needed organization, planning and to understand what the heck I was doing and why. I have to be passionate about what I do. If not passionate about your work, why do it?

In 1980 there were no specific disciplines for show and ride estimating except what we created for the WBS system. There were no professional show and ride estimating organizations to provide guidance either. It made sense to me that something had to be done to elevate my new profession in show estimating. I also wanted to do something about my lack of education in the estimating profession. Through Carl Simmons, I discovered that he was a member of a National organization called the American Society of Professional Estimators (ASPE). An organization that promoted professionalism in the science, including a certification program. This certification was the same as having a CPA behind your name on your business card. In ASPE, if you qualified, you were a Certified Professional Estimator or CPE. One could get that exposure by participating in ASPE and successfully passing a certification exam in your discipline. Except, there was no discipline for show estimating! So, I wrote one! I found out that Imagineering would pay your dues, pay you to attend the meetings and provide time for your participation. Sounded like a deal to me! I began to attend the monthly meetings at the L.A. Chapter, No. 1. Through ASPE, I learned the discipline and techniques of facility, core and shell estimating. This knowledge came from dinner conversations and speakers skilled as professional estimators. Besides ASPE, I also enrolled into an evening class at USC (Paid by Imagineering too) in construction estimating. In this class I learned how to assemble a construction estimate for a small warehouse structure. Including the footings from the ground up! I also learned, that in the United States, particularly then, estimating was not an integral discipline in the construction industry. At least when compared to the United Kingdom. And there were no classes for show estimating in any school. This subject was not covered whatsoever in either my undergrad or graduate education. There was only one class that taught beginning construction estimating at USC. This class followed the CSI format (Construction Specifications

Institute) which was in contrast to the Quantity Survey (QS) system used in the United Kingdom and Europe. There were significant differences between the two. CSI estimating, the discipline in the U.S., was strictly a practice of providing cost information to the project management team. The estimator, typically, would begin early with the project, and upon a successful bid, turn the project over to the project team. Of course, they could be involved with change orders throughout construction, as required. The QS discipline, however, was a credentialed degree program with a University degree. The QS not only estimated the project but was responsible throughout construction for complete "cost control" of the project. I was surprised to learn later that their education included a specific procedure to "fold" the drawing packages. This instead of rolling or "hanging" the documents on racks! I'm not sure how more complete integration into the subject matter was possible! It would be on the Eurodisneyland (EDL) project later, where I would be "immersed" into the QS discipline.

My extracurricular activities with ASPE and the USC class would accelerate my knowledge of core and shell estimating. Understanding these construction fundamentals, helped me to be aware of the potential "cost impacts" (the effect on) the show and ride on the structure into which they were being placed. I started to ask questions. A lot of questions! Would the buildings frame need heavier structural steel? Would larger concrete footings be required because of the vibrations of ride tracks or as the ride vehicles passed thru them? What about show lighting? Would more HVAC (Heating, Ventilation & Air Conditioning) be required due to the heat generated by the lighting system? The Facility estimators did not discuss these topics. Why would they? Construction estimating was a time-tested science. Most construction estimators I know understand "what should be in a building." Would they think through the concept of what a roller coaster did or what the heat did from the lights in the building? Maybe they just relied on the engineers to factor these in? From my perspective, most of the building didn't have this information for the shows and rides in the early design packages. This "raised a flag for me." These structures were installing the latest show and ride technology. Maybe the engineering incorporated all of my concerns, maybe not. I did not want to leave this to chance! My goal was to be the show estimator that took care of this "grey" area between facility, show and ride for show estimating. With my theatrical background and experience to back me up, I was observing the entire package. My show estimating goals were expanding beyond my "scope." I didn't want to stop at the completion of the manufacturing process of an AA figure sitting in the box ready to ship! I wanted to know about the AA figure power requirements to operate it after delivery to the site. And by the way. What exactly was required in the facility utility package for this? Then there were requirements for compressed air or Liquid Nitrogen Gas (LNG). How much more power would be required in the electrical/mechanical packages? Would these show requirements be in the engineering packages? The utility packages. I was confident that if these packages were available, our professional construction and electrical estimators would pick up the costs. But I saw this as part of my responsibility too! I wondered, were these issues considered as part of that earlier "allowance?" These questions suggested I had to do more research. Sorting out the language of show wouldn't be enough. I also needed to be everywhere, see everything and meet the teams responsible. This meant that I would need to get invited to all project meetings that concerned show and ride. And this was not happening when I started at Imagineering. The first source I wanted to get to know, were the project coordinators. They were responsible for setting up all communications for the project teams. If you needed an answer, you went to the project coordinators!

There were a few roadblocks at the beginning. The culture in estimating was a discipline where the work was in your office, estimating from the drawing packages. Why would an estimator want to sit through a project meeting? What could you possibly learn that's not already on the drawing? Very much like my experiences in the theatrical world. The "cast" (i.e., what is called the "talent") were the people "on stage." Those of us that made the stage ready for the show were always "behind the scenes." More than once I felt this same attitude as I worked my way into the estimating process at Imagineering.

This was more of an educational problem than anything else. It was up to me to explain my need and how it would help the team! I like to think that many of our EPCOT alumni would tell you today, this was a project where most everyone got along. I think the truth is, everyone was so busy and so dependent on one another, that there just wasn't enough time to waste on petty issues!

It wasn't that I planned on going to the meetings and being a passive listener. If I were in an engineering meeting, for example, I asked questions about "electrical/mechanical systems" that supported the shows and rides. Everything was a prototype, so the information was not yet complete. If I was in a show production meeting (production for sets, props, AA figures, fur and feather, etc.,) I could ask questions on construction and manufacturing. These were my areas and sometimes my questions had not been thought of yet! Should the team see that I had the background and could ask relevant questions, I hoped they could see I was looking out for their interests. It might also demonstrate that I had their backs. The same objectives applied for show design. These sessions would help me understand the current design and provide a "heads up" on possible revisions to the show. If I found out that an AA figure was deleted, for example, or if its functions changed, I could revise my estimates. There was a downside to my interest in getting to know everything. Imagineering is known for its "meetings within meetings." And this is an understatement! For myself, I stayed in meetings only as long as I learned something new.

Perhaps the most important lesson from this chapter is "look beyond the scope of your job!" No matter what you do in your work, especially if you are just starting out, the task assigned to you will affect the project in more ways than just what appears on paper. Being aware of how your task fits into the project's goals, opens up communications with your team. The most important communication being, alerting the team of an issue that could affect the cost, the schedule or the scope! My suggestion. If you have to, get up on the table, stomp your feet and get the teams attention!

CHAPTER THREE

Implementation

My work was becoming easier and I had made in-roads into many departments that would assist me in getting to know everything I needed to produce a detailed show estimate. There was one area though, that eluded my efforts, and I wasn't sure why, until my introduction to a department that was called the "Tujunga Show Production" facility.

Remember those allowance's? Well, the one group that I could not gain access to had experience estimating to what they referred to as "project killers." The blame for these "project killers" were a direct result of those past allowances! There was a lot of distrust to say the least. That group was the Tujunga Shops. They were the core facility that produced the show production elements for EPCOT. The Tujunga facility was located "off campus" several miles away from WED off Tujunga Boulevard in the San Fernando Valley. What I had to dispel, I was told, was that projects were killed, and that translated to no budget approval and less production work for the Tujunga show production. I have no idea when this started to go south with estimating, I just know that there was not a lot of love from the Tujunga shops!

Fortunately for me, I went through my "Pixie Dust" orientation with a new friend, John Nelson. John and I had much in common having both started our theatrical careers with our tool belts on. In the shops! John was going to work at the Tujunga facility as a carpenter. That would become a huge advantage for me. However, our friendship benefited not only my relationship challenge at Tujunga but would later help me out at NBC studios in Burbank. I would hire John later on in the Scenic Operations Department where I was the Manager. But that's another story! John would quickly rise through the ranks at Tujunga. His accelerated through the management ranks and was extremely helpful in my eventual good relationships at the Tujunga show production facility.

This happened within the first six months of my tenure. But, there was only one person I had to convince that I wasn't a project killer! He was the manager of all show production and his name was Matthew Priddy. Matt was an imposing figure with his large moustache, his cowboy boots and a very gregarious personality. Not anything I hadn't run across in my live theatrical years. Most successful managers in the theatrical world were "pushers," a necessary trait to get the job done. But in my experience, most were also fiercely loyal to their crews and sort of "big teddy bears" off the floor! I would describe Matt in this way, knowing he operated a very close-knit family of technicians, carpenters and craftsmen at Tujunga. This I learned and used in my own theatrical experience. Particularly on the road. I too was protective of my team. It reminds me that I also used to tell my crews that "unless you're bleeding from the neck," I'll see you at tomorrow's 7 AM call! The not-so-nice part of being a successful manager! Matt was the key player and I had to convince him that I was not out to kill his future projects! But how to achieve this? At first, John set up a tour of the Tujunga facility for me. When I showed up, I remember a definite "glare" from Matt. This was Matt's territory and from that look I got his message! No estimators! However, intimidation is just a challenge for me. I was up for this one because I wanted to prove that I had paid my dues, had come up through the ranks with a hammer in my hand and win his trust. That turned out to be easier said than done. It would take time and an unexpected opportunity to turn it around. I was allowed to tour through the facility, with John as my escort. It was fascinating.

The Tujunga facility was divided up into sections to accommodate the various show elements. There was "fur and feather." Literally where the AA birds, props, small world figures, etc., would get their "outer dressing." There was the wood shop, metal shop, paint shop and final assembly areas where the sets were built for the various scenes. Like the model process, all sets were fully built-in place to the exact specifications of their final location on site so show design/management could "buy off" on the product before it shipped to Florida. This included the AA figures and show action equipment which would be pre-programmed and tested in place prior to shipment to Florida. I especially fell in love with the animated programming area. Sectioned off with large black velour drapes, the programmers, where legends like Wathel Rogers did their programming magic on the WED custom-designed computer. The number of hours that the programmers would take was intense. Like stop motion animation, I had watched so closely back in the day at Clokey Productions, the AA figures were "animated" move-by-move to the audio and sound tracks designed for the scene. A work of art and technology created by the masters of WED Imagineering. Often, these sessions took place with specific scenes fully set up and ready for shipment to Florida. For example, I recall watching "Ben Franklin" being programmed to "walk" up the stairs! Or "Guttenberg," readying letter plates on a fully animated printing press! These two, set up with only the immediate show set elements. (The Liberty Torch railing and the printing press) Many moments such as these are forever locked into my memory. How neat is that!

But not everything went as planned. There was a mostly complete and "dressed" Spaceship Earth scene, that did not meet the approval of Marty Sklar and John Hench. If I recall correctly, it was a "scale" issue. With a word from Marty, substantial revisions had to be made, all with "a wave of the hands." This level of design oversight was not a cost consideration. The change was all about excellence! However, last minute changes like this affected the schedule and the delivery to the site. Can you imagine the stress that the shops were under? I can. In my own way, later on I was responsible for a $12 million-dollar annual scenery operations expense at the NBC Scenic shops. Only there, we typically had a three-day turnaround from first presentation by the art director to delivering the set to the studio. Any delay could cost the production company $10,000 per hour of studio time! And yet, here at Imagineering, it was simply because Marty and John found it unacceptable. It was the only reason anyone needed.

Continuing with my Tujunga story, aside from the tours I was getting from John, a very unexpected opportunity came my way. To set the background for this, our estimating offices were located in what was called the Sonora building across Flower Street from WED's main campus. Although "off campus," we were tied into a public address system designed to remind us of companywide events. These were not annoying announcements like we had in our high school homerooms. The system was reserved for important events. It was within the first year at Imagineering that an "all call" announcement was made. The request was for "any staff available" to come to the Tujunga production facilities to help out for the coming weekend. Apparently, there was a scene from a show that needed to be completed by Monday for a load out to Orlando. The problem? There was a weekly shipping commitment between Tujunga and Orlando for the purpose of delivering sets, props, AA figures and all other show and ride elements to EPCOT for installation. The Tujunga shop was in jeopardy of missing this critical shipping deadline. As I heard this announcement I thought, maybe this was my chance to prove to the shops that I knew what I was doing. I figured it couldn't hurt! This could be my opportunity to convince them of my stagecraft abilities.

I showed up early at the Tujunga facility on Saturday morning and walked into Matt's office (they were still warming up for the day with coffee) and asked, "What do you need"? I recall Matt's face. He looked me up and down dressed in my jeans, T-shirt and tool belt as if I were an alien. With much skepticism Matt and John took me out to the shop to a piece of "suspended ceiling" that needed to be "dead hung" (rigged to hang from the ceiling) with aircraft cable for its eventual installation in the field. This was a plus because I had estimated this particular set and now could actually be part of its construction! Matt brought over the tool cart that had all the hardware required for the rigging set up and began to explain to me how to do the job. He was very skeptical (I cut him off short of his explanation) when I picked up the crimping tools and the "Crosby's" (these are U shaped clamps that you use on cables) and asked him to show me the drawing for the specifications. He did and I told him that I had "rigged" a couple of theatres in my day and that he could spend his time teaching some of the other volunteers! Reluctantly, Matt left me to do the work. I recall that look that said, sure, you can do this! It wasn't much of a problem to follow the directions on the drawings. Matt came back about an hour later to check and saw that I had completed the work to the specified requirements. I'm sure he was surprised. I said, what's next? And that's how the weekend went. I worked on many parts of the set and spent the entire weekend, late into the night making sure that I was there for the team! After this experience, I never had another problem with the shop and was invited to come back and work with them to shore up areas of my show estimates. With John's help, we came up with reasonable scenarios for production labor, which allowed me to develop better unit costs for the various show elements. I was eventually invited to some of their "beer party" get togethers at the local burger hang out which told me that I was ok in their book. Through this combined effort, we had achieved our goal of opening up communication between estimating and production. Now all I had to do was gain the trust of the show producers!

Like the issues at Tujunga, the show producers were tight lipped about anything they were doing when it came to estimators. This was another roadblock, but again I saw this as an opportunity. But how would I do it? I mentioned earlier, budgets were presented to Marty Sklar, John Hench and Orlando Ferrante as part of the sign off process to proceed. The results of these presentations were always the same. Craig would say, "This is the cost of the project!" Always the first thing management heard or saw in the presentations. This was typically followed by shock and awe by the creative management group. This reaction often translated to a "back to the drawing board" effort for cost cuts involving revisions to the show or ride. How could it not? Don't you get "sticker shock" when you hear the price of something before you know its value? This was the endless cycle between the creative/ cost approval process at WED during my initial tenure. After these presentations, Craig would hold an internal review to discuss our next steps. Next steps typically meant, going back to the show producer and helping "value engineer" the show. Value engineering is another way of saying "how can we do the same thing, maintain the same look and feel, but for a reduced cost?" This was a productive exercise because I could offer solutions based on my experience. But I had something else in mind, and it was at one of those meetings where I suggested to Craig, a different approach. An approach that goes back to the experiences my dad taught me selling cars! Yes, this is true! This would be the first time I hung my head out, exposed to the chopping block of criticism. I explained that we should attempt to sell the "value" of the design and delay showing the cost. With Craig's approval, I was assigned to lead the next presentation, which luckily for me, was a very small and manageable project. Small meaning about $4,500,000! The project was for the rehab of the existing Alice in Wonderland dark ride at Disneyland. Compared to the hundreds of millions we had prepared for most EPCOT projects, I thought it was the perfect "test" project for my new approach. So, what is the car sales approach?" It's really quite simple. "Don't tell the buyer the price until you have sold him on the value." This was my plan to reveal the cost of Alice-the rehab! Working with the show producer, Bob Kurzweil, I detailed out every element he wanted in the show and ride and made sure that the costs were in line with the work and his "design intent." This was the beginning of a trust relationship with the show producer. I wanted Bob to know that I was on his side and would do everything I could to help him achieve his design goals. Hopefully, this would get back to the other show producers and the word would get out that I was fair and, on their side, as much as I could be. Once the scope of his concept was completed, my estimate of the job could now follow that scope. We felt we were ready to present and try out our new plan. Of special interest for this particular presentation, we would be in the same conference room that Walt Disney used for his Wonderful World of Disney presentations on television for Disneyland in the 50s! This was a very special, if not sacred room at WED and there are those of us who swear we could "feel" Walt's presence during our meetings. No joke! The conference room itself had sliding presentation panels along one wall. Presentation materials could be placed in any order you chose. I made it a point to place the "final cost summary" (the number that represented "shock and awe") as the last slide to be revealed. Enter Marty Sklar, John

Hench, Orlando Ferrante and a few others (that I can't recall) and the meeting was set to begin. Craig introduced me, and it was now or never. I began the meeting with the introduction of the show producer wherein Bob proceeded to lead the group through his presentation boards and models. Not five minutes passed when John Hench asked, "How much does all this cost?" I stood up and asked John and the others for their patience, noting that we were going to answer that in just a few minutes. John backed off and the presentation continued. Just a few minutes later, the same question, how much does this cost? This time by Marty Sklar. I should point out that these guys already new the scope of the work from Bob and only attended this meeting to hear the costs, not another design review! For the second time I responded, may I please ask for your patience and all will be revealed. This pattern of questioning went on for about 15 minutes or so and every time I stood up, I could see Marty, John and Orlando glancing at each other, and slowly beginning to share a slight grin. I am sure they were catching on to my presentation methodology and the tension was growing as to the outcome of who had the most patience. Finally, after what seemed to be hours of presentation, it was time for the big cost reveal. I stood up and said with a slight grin myself, "I bet you want to know how much this wonderful rehab of Alice is going to cost?" There was one of those "pregnant pauses" and Marty and the team started to laugh. I slid back the panel and revealed the cost summary I had "blown up" in big numbers (We didn't use power point back then-in fact laptops were still not in use) and stated, "Here is the estimated final cost, $4.5 million!" You could have heard a pin drop. Everyone on our side of the table expected the typical Q and A on the various cost issues. To my surprise, Marty and the management team told us that it was a good presentation, and it was approved. With that they got up and left the room! I noticed that Marty and John both had a slight grin on their face as they walked out of that room. We were all a bit amazed at what had just happened. I had succeeded with the next step of my goal (To create trust with the show producers) and had begun to garner credibility with the creative team at Imagineering. My "connection" with

Marty (I'm not claiming any close relationship here) became "Here's the Bad News Guy," when he passed me in the hallways at Imagineering. I know it was said in a friendly way and I always saw a little grin as he said it, but the truth was, I did bring in budget news and it wasn't always good. Marty was kind enough to autograph my "The Art of Walt Disney" book later and it is part of my own personal Disney memorabilia collection. Marty Sklar is a "Disney Legend" and ambassador for WDI (that's Walt Disney Imagineering). I'd also like to share one story about the few times I got to work with Marty. It had to do with his "famous wall of sayings." Literally a wall behind Marty's conference table in his office. This "wall of sayings" was filled with post it notes and personal "Mickey" stationary (provided to all Imagineer's) and became a sort of catch all memorializing bloopers and poignant comments offered in his meetings. Often serious, mostly not, Marty kept his meetings relaxed and fun wherever possible. This was in direct contrast to the significant stress everyone felt at the time. I love humor and still like to use it in my meetings. If only Marty would have written a book picking the best of the best for everyone's enjoyment from his wall!

Another "Legend" I had the pleasure of meeting was John Hench. John (who goes back much earlier with Walt) had a close resemblance to Walt (he told stories of going to Disneyland and being mistaken for Walt Disney). John also did not disappoint autograph seekers, including me. He autographed my book too!

Here's something to consider. If we could step back and look at the "big picture" of EPCOT responsibilities, Marty and John were responsible for everything you see at EPCOT. It simply amazes me that EPCOT had such attention to detail, knowing that these two men were solely responsible. Being there throughout the planning stages and construction, I spent many hours in meetings with both Marty and John and I can vouch that they reviewed everything that you see as a guest at EPCOT. Just visit the park and you will understand the enormity of this responsibility. For example, there are no backstage "visual" intrusions! Looking between buildings, from near or far, everything was "on stage". The transition of color, from one area to the next, blended seamlessly throughout the park! An amazing artistic challenge executed perfectly!

Getting a bit more specific about my job at WED, I was the show estimator for two Future World projects. These were the Horizons Pavilion and Spaceship Earth. My main area of responsibility were the estimated costs for shows and rides. However, because of my interest in the facility core and shell, I worked very closely with the facility estimators. To accomplish this, I didn't just sit at a desk and read blueprints. I asked for and was given full and unlimited access to all design and production meetings related to these two pavilions. How could I estimate the projects without knowing what was going into them? For others though on the various teams, I was an outsider. This may have been the most important lesson learned in my show estimating career. Who, besides the project manager, is the one person on your design and construction team that knows and understands everything about your project! From scope to cost to schedule and budget, the show estimator has been there from the introduction of the concept, observed its transformation from "eye candy" (a reference to the typically beautiful and exciting artwork used to present the concept to the owners and investors) to its final drawing phase and on to its execution into a fully functioning building. That is, if they do their job correctly. May I add a note? The term "eye candy" is just what it says. While there is some resemblance to the creative first impression in an eye candy presentation, (typically a rendering) the project in its final physical form usually is not so "literal." It is meant to convey the concept in an upbeat setting, to create excitement and interest! WED is the only place I have worked that the term eye candy defines this excitement and energy into concept art. In that regard, I was very fortunate to meet and witness two Disney artists' responsible for creating what most agree are the best eye candy images at WED Enterprises.

The most memorable concept artist in my opinion was Herbie Ryman! Herbie began his career at Walt Disney Studios as an art director for the Pastoral Scenes for Fantasia, among many accomplishments! He also was a frequent visitor to the employee cafeteria where I had lunch most days. Herbie was often followed by John Hench. It was always a delight to see them both when they came in for lunch! I remember John was always accompanied by his longtime administrative aid Sandy Huskins. John is credited with background paintings for the Nutcracker Suite in Fantasia as part of his early Disney studio career. I remember clearly that when either came into the cafeteria, there was a "buzz" that seemed to animate the room! Both had a mischievous "twinkle" in their eyes and a friendly nod to everyone. Of course, they are both Disney Legends! I was very fortunate to meet both of these originals and have cartoons and autographs in my Art of Walt Disney book. Lucky me!

As part of my "all access" routine, I would also frequent the MAPO shops. This shop was created from the profits of the movie (Mary Poppins-hence the name). It was the manufacturing hub for AA figures, show action equipment, staff shops and other mechanical apparatus used in EPCOT and Tokyo Disneyland and eventually, all other parks. All of it managed by Orlando Ferrante. Orlando began his career in 1962 as an expediter for animatronics in the Tiki room at Disneyland. He too had a long career at Imagineering and is also a Disney Legend! I always felt welcome when touring through MAPO. I hoped that I could meet Orlando and share my production background much the same way that I did with Matthew at Tujunga. But that never materialized.

This never deterred my daily walks around the MAPO shops during the manufacturing process. It was like being a kid in a candy store! I watched the assembly of AA figures; show action equipment and other show hardware to be installed at EPCOT. Over the two or so years at WED, I walked through the vast spaces of MAPO's shops and witnessed many examples of Imagineering genius. There was Ben Franklin and Mark Twain, standing atop the flame of the Statue of Liberty! A key part of the American Adventure experience. Ben was also the first "walking" (up the stairs) AA figure and made his debut at EPCOT. There was Michelangelo, ready to paint "Adam" for the ceiling at the Sistine Chapel. There were the action figures for the Kitchen Kabaret destined for the Land pavilion. Of the many animated and show action figures, I think seeing the almost completed "Dream Machine" with "Dreamfinder" as the pilot, was one of the most exciting pieces and really, a piece of kinetic art! Meeting the very talented technicians and artists was icing on the cake! There was one such individual that helped me understand the MAPO manufacturing and production process. His name is Al Mirabella. Al took the time to give me a tour and explain to me the various functions of each department. Thanks, Al, for being so kind! For me, seeing the models and the renderings come to life, all I can say is, WOW!

While the MAPO shops created the engineering marvels, the actual full size "maquette" (a maquette being a small model or sculpture in 3-dimensional form) of the figure was created in the sculpt shop. Eventually created in full size, the maquette was used to "pull" tools or forms from which plaster, fiberglass or other materials became the finished piece. One of my very special memories was observing WED's number one sculptor Blaine Gibson. Blaine, also a Disney Legend, and his talented staff, sculpted many (if not most of the iconic) statues, AA figureheads and architectural features for the parks throughout his long Disney career. Reminiscent of my days at Clokey, walking into the sculpt studio was a transcendental experience. Outside the door, was chaos, hub bub and cacophony! Inside was quiet and peaceful with classical music playing quietly in the background! Watching Blaine, Adolpho and the others working, was like sitting in the library reading a good book! But how was this related to estimating? If you know anything about producing or manufacturing an object, it takes time and materials to make it happen. In the world of construction estimating, there is a variety of cost data for the construction components. Most construction estimators have field experience, so they know what they're looking at. In show and ride estimating, particularly in the conceptual and or/schematic phase of the design, there is not much more than an "image." As a "conceptual estimator," my costs for anything in the show elements, were "all in" or stated simply, complete with labor and materials. My visits to the various production areas of the manufacturing process like MAPO or the sculpt studio, provided a "sense" of labor used for the effort that it would take to produce any particular element. The observations became kind of a "database" in my brain if you will. And this routine happened almost every day as part of my daily tour throughout the various departments and divisions. Getting back to my visits to the sculpt studio, it was not a large space considering the amount of work involved. The studio seemed overpopulated with figures and architectural features ready for casting. The talented artists were working on individual pieces in whatever space they could find. I imagine it was a bit eerie at night with the figures all alone, coming to life, wandering the halls....! Excuse me for drifting off! Too many of those sci fi movies with the mannequins. More importantly, never once did Blaine say one word to me about my "standing around and observing." I know he saw me come in and stand there, but I suppose it wasn't that unusual. I found this out later from my EPCOT alumni newsletters. The place was a magnet for Imagineers! I always felt very welcome and enjoyed the solitude of space and the silent artistry of those working. Interestingly, twenty-five years later, through a mutual acquaintance in Santa Barbara, I was able to "close the loop" on my Blaine Gibson connection. Our 401k advisor (I met through my work at Bechtel on another theme park project much later) happened to know Blaine through a weekly dinner at their retirement community in Montecito, CA. Through this connection, Alison and I were invited to dinner to meet Blaine and reconnect. I could not believe I would be sitting down to dinner with Blaine Gibson! When we finally had the dinner, nervous as I was, Blaine made me feel very comfortable right away by telling me that he remembered me "standing around his studio" during our EPCOT days. I had no idea that he would remember me! We had a pleasant dinner conversation and talked about the good old days at Imagineering. After dinner Blaine invited us up for coffee to his personal apartment.

On display were some of the original sculpted heads that I had seen in the sculp shop! Blaine told us that a "limo" was coming to pick him up for a ceremony where he would receive legend status in the morning. I recall he was a bit embarrassed, because he said that if were able to drive, he wouldn't need that "limo" treatment! A very humble man! Having dinner with a

Disney legend of Blaine's caliber was a once in a lifetime experience! Closing the "loop" from my start at Imagineering to this night is a moment I will never forget! Speaking of closing the loop, later on (between EPCOT and Paris Disneyland) I commissioned Adolpho Procoprio, one of Blaine's sculptors. I asked Adolpho to produce a small bronze statue for me for a model called "The South Pointing Chariot". The maquette was to be approximately 3.5" tall and was a figure of the Yellow Emperor, (Circa 3rd millennium.) with one arm outstretched pointing the way. The South Pointing Chariot was a working model created by myself, Doug Beswick and Don Frantz! Once completed I had it cast in bronze using a lost wax process at a shop in El Monte, California. Interestingly, Adolpho would never take a dime for his effort! It was all about the art! The model was going to be an "executive desk toy" but we sold only one to a technical gauge manufacturer. Rest in Peace, Gentlemen!

Another special area I visited in my cost research, was the Special Effects Prototype studio. This area was "off limits," with "no access" to everyone except by special permission. This was the testing area for many of EPCOT's prototypical special effects! I received access because of my "need to know." I needed to see how these effects were being produced to create better estimates. Otherwise I'd have to use an allowance. And that was simply not the way I wanted to create my estimates. The special effects area was located in the main WED warehouse near the loading dock. Inside, it contained such "special effects" as the "lava flow" for the Energy pavilion. This was a very realistic flow of lava with steam and what "felt" like intense heat. There was the "leapfrog" fountain used in the area development water feature in front of Imagination. This was a very popular water feature and I recall seeing both kids and adults, attempting to "catch" the tubes of water as they appeared randomly in one flower bed and leapt over the sidewalk to another bed over their heads! The use of "laser" projection was also being tested. This effect would be seen in the Imagination Pavilion. EPCOT was the first theme park that used non-commercial lasers for the purpose of entertainment. The technology at that time was mostly for communications, the space industry and the military. WED would seek out these "secret" applications and find a way to use them to enhance a show. If you stop and think about this, many gaming and other entertainment technologies had their start in the defense industry! The lasers would be used to depict Figments smiling face and in other unique ways in the shows. Here's a little-known fact. A few of these special effect technicians went on to make their own future in the attractions business. Bill Novey, for example, created over 6,000 special effects for EPCOT and Tokyo, Disneyland. I remember seeing a measuring system "off campus" where Bill used lasers to measure 3D objects on a special platform. The lasers would scan the article on the platform and the computer would illustrate a 3D animated illustration on the screen that could be measured and transferred to a machine for exact tooling. If I remember correctly, Ford Motor company was there and interested in this technology. Then there's Mark Fuller. Besides inventing the "leapfrog" fountain and other water and fog effects for the parks, you might know his company called WET Enterprises. WET is responsible for major water features throughout the world with the Bellagio dancing waters fountain being his most recognizable water feature in the United States. There are many other effects companies that "spun-off" their specialties from the EPCOT project and too numerous to mention here.

These tours helped me to keep an emphasis on cost. It also created an awareness of the impact to future costs for EPCOT. That is the schedule difference between the time estimated and the finished piece installed in place. We carried an "escalation" line item in the total estimate to the end. This escalation factor would have to address this possibility. All we could do is publish what "todays" costs were for the show and ride estimates. Escalation factors came from government data to cover unknowns. Were they enough? We had no idea. For example, what would a "supply problem" have on these new special effect's materials? Let's take fiber optic cable as an example. Fiber optic cable (FOC) was first introduced commercially in 1977. How much FOC would you guess was available in 1980/81? Not much is the answer because it was for industrial use, not commercial use. The WED purchasing group had to literally search the entire United States to achieve the amount of FOC required for the EPCOT installation!

This we heard through a connection I had with the purchasing department. I don't know what that did to the estimates we had prepared and delivered before this news, but it surely impacted the cost when it was scheduled to be installed. Simply a matter of supply and demand! Hopefully our escalation factor covered the added cost. The special effects technicians must have been sweating bullets knowing that the FOC they needed might not be available for pre-opening day installation!

Another "all access" opportunity I had and probably the best, was my ability to go to the Disney Studio. And I did so every week! How cool is that? I was able to frequent the studio lot where many of EPCOT's prototypical effects machines and projectors were created. The studio sound stages were also used to produce the scenic murals for all of the shows. The sound stages were used due to the size of the murals, with most sized at 60'0 "tall x 100'0" long and larger. In the studio machine shop (the same place where many of Walt Disney's original film cameras were manufactured) the new EPCOT projection systems were being manufactured by Don Iwerks. Don was the son of Ub Iwerks, the creator of Mickey Mouse and Oswald the Rabbit for Walt Disney. (This machine shop was also where Walt machined parts for his "Carolwood Pacific Railroad." There is a really great book (*Walt Disney's Railroad Story* by Michael Broggie) on the history of Walt's fascination with trains and covers the entire history of this throughout Walt's life. This hit close to home for me because my grandfather on my father's side, was an engineer for the Rock Island Railroad in Calumet City, Illinois. My father also worked for Rock Island as a "stoker" or fireman for ten years before moving us out to sunny California! As busy as Don was, he was a friendly man accommodating in my quest to understand cost. I was allowed full access to his machine shop.

This turned out to be very important. Since each new projector, whether for film or for special effects, was a "prototype." All of it created from scratch by Don's talented staff. There was no "off the shelf" cost information. EPCOT was filled with many new special effect and film projectors. For example, Imagineering broke new ground for "35 mm film loop cabinets", the film support cabinets required for the new

EPCOT films. Understanding the mechanics of the machine, seeing it operate and tested, really helped me in assembling an estimated cost on this equipment. As a point of information, the film loop cabinets were stand-alone "boxes with glass doors" that allowed the films to "loop" (play over and over) throughout the days operating hours. For as much operational time required without stressing the film. The cabinets were temperature and humidity controlled and were all manufactured at the studio machine shop. Other special effect projectors being "one-offs" too, were also very pricey pieces of equipment. For example, what cost do you use for a "starfield" projector? How about a projector that "provides a streaming image of constant moving images past your ride vehicle? And there is always the projector that creates a disappearing shaft of light which "leads you" out of any number of transition tunnels between scenes! Remember, this is 1980. The many new theatrical effects lighting fixtures you see in the theatre and at concerts, were yet to be invented. If you want to know where these ideas came from, think about Don Iwerks and his crew and what they accomplished for EPCOT. Through my weekly routine of visiting the studio, I was able to observe the manufacturing and production of the various special effects and film projectors. Through this observation, I began to assign the number of man-hours required to create each type. Up to the time I started visiting the shop, all I knew was that the scope was calling out a particular effect or film equipment. I had a vague idea of what it did, but that was the extent of my information. Using the formula for labor (union labor) costs and material, I now had a good idea of what each unit cost. At the very least it was better than a WAG! Along with the actual projectors, the show estimator also added a cost for the software that went into or through these projectors. In the case of special effects, the "software" was custom designed media using anything from thin cut out plates of metal, to custom lenses that were "ground" specifically for the format desired to achieve the effect. On the film side, as cost was concerned, the only idea we had was to place a "cost on per minute of film." At the time, we used $1M / per minute/average. The issue with budgeting film, is you have to create a budget from the script and the actual "shot sheet" or storyboard. Otherwise, you really had to just guess on how the film would be produced. Better left to the professionals in the film industry who go through on the job training for this kind of estimating. In fact, the idea of this did cross my mind. I had access to the studio and thought about what it might be like to have a career change to the film industry. I did not follow this urge! But in finishing my thoughts on the studio machine shop, it reminds me that this is the same shop where Walt came in to build his own model railroad. Just standing there and observing the machinists, it wasn't hard to imagine that Walt probably used the same equipment. I thank Don for the privilege. It has to be one of the highlights of my estimating experience.

My ability to roam freely about the studio campus allowed for some other surprising perks! As I said, once through the main gate, I roamed without restriction. Well, almost. If the sound stage had a red-light blinking, I knew better to enter that door! I might go over to Walt's old office and look through the door to see his original workspace. One day I revisited the room where the original "multi-plane" camera was used for Snow White and other great Disney classics. Imagine being in the same room with that film history! Almost thirty years later, I would see this same multi-plane camera at the new "Disney Family Museum" at the Presidio in San Francisco. It sits in the retail store as a decorative prop. Visit this museum if you are in the area, you will not be disappointed. At the studio I also enjoyed lunch now and again observing costumed characters from films in production, and maybe a "Disney" celebrity or two thrown in for good measure. Not that I remember any names, I just don't do "trivia" very well! Sometimes, I'd walk into the sound stages and find a rehearsal going on for one of the Disney films or television shows. Again, fun to watch for a bit, but nothing jumps out as to what kind of production rehearsal was on stage. I would experience the same thing later at NBC studios where there were celebrities too. I had to take care of "standing shows" like Johnny Carson and Days of our Lives, for example!

There was one special perk that I did once a month though that I have to share. The studio barbershop was still in use in the 80s and I had my haircut done in the very same barbershop established in the early studio years. I was told that his was the very same barbershop where Walt had his haircut done. It still had its original decor from the early days of the studio. The barber told stories of Walt and other celebrities that came through the shop. The photos alone on the wall were worth the visits. It was cheap too! Such were my privileges at the Walt Disney Studio. I cherish every memory and am honored to have had the experience! Certainly, all access became a big advantage in understanding the EPCOT product!

CHAPTER FOUR

Semantics

As I suggest in the first three chapters, there was an immense learning curve in my introduction to show and ride estimating. I had pretty much exhausted what I needed to know with format issues, how to get information, had ironed out most of the relationships, and was finally ready to put finger to calculator! In this chapter, I'll highlight some of my "on the job" education on the two EPCOT projects assigned to me. Although I provided show and ride estimates for every single EPCOT project, my primary responsibilities were for Spaceship Earth and the Horizons Pavilions. Specifically, for the shows and rides. But my responsibility did not end there. I became very involved in the FF and E (Furniture, fixtures and equipment) for the common spaces, restaurants, retail stores and the area development. My interest and work in FF and E, usually assigned to a construction estimator, was necessary due to the nature of the décor, props and dressings that the Imagineer's created to fill up the space. Know what I'm talking about? If you don't, it's the "fun" stuff, that Disney creates for its themed interiors and exteriors. Inside might be a custom animated clock, themed windows or even an indoor water feature. Outside, there would be topiary figures or special monument statues, and did you think about "themed" trash receptacles? Not trash cans! No! Since they're custom and painted, they too would be considered part of the FF and E! As the project gained momentum, we could also count on "fire drills" to interrupt our flow of work. Just another day at Imagineering on a $1.4 billion-dollar project!

My mentor for the estimating skills learned on the Spaceship Earth project were greatly influenced by the project manager. His name was Doug Stapp. Doug was a seasoned Disney staffer and a dedicated professional. I would spend a lot of time working closely with him over the course of the project. Doug had an unwritten rule. "There is Doug's budget and the real budget." Doug asked me to be completely honest at all times in the show and ride estimating process. He would reciprocate by keeping me informed of changes, although the reciprocal part wasn't always forthcoming. The one thing I learned from Doug was what I now call the "semantics of estimating." This being a continuation of the "language of show." Our specific goal was to create line items in the estimate. Items in which only Doug and myself understood the "language." Specifically, we developed descriptions and titles for items that may, or may not be in the scope of work. Since my estimates were the basis of the show and ride details, my estimated line items were left to me to describe, I could write what I wanted. Of course, an AA figure is an AA figure. But what if the next line item became "accessories" to the line above? Since only Doug and I were scrutinizing the estimates for accuracy, the likely hood of line items such as these being discovered, was not too much of a concern. With the "published" estimates effectively becoming the Scope of Work, at least for the purpose of the project budget, it was Doug who maintained the control. The scope writing department kept up the best they could, but quite often the scope was far behind the estimate in many cases. It makes me wonder if the entire process was nothing more than an exercise. That crossed my mind a few times. As I worked through various budget phases of the design, I became very "creative" in our semantics game. Static props were the same as "prop," weren't they? A different line item for the same thing? Sometimes the "quantities" were not so accurate. Let's say that the "scope" called out for ten AA figures. I could easily change that to twelve or twenty or reduce the quantity for that matter. Only Doug and I knew the difference. Scope certainly couldn't keep up with the count of AA figures, nor did anyone dig deep into a review of the estimates. Doug certainly didn't volunteer this information to the project team. So "why worry?" The line items were real and self-explanatory. However, from any other perspective (design, engineering, management, etc.) their interpretation of these creative line items might be "That's a reasonable cost." Everyone had plenty to do without adding estimate reviews to their next to impossible workloads! I should mention one other way we utilized this technique. Our show cost items "may or may not" have existed. Sometimes show elements would be deleted. Interestingly, no one ever noticed. If a film was deleted for example, you could simply leave it in the estimate! Doug was certainly not going to acknowledge it. Even if it was found out, it was in the scope at one point, but everyone knew that the scope and the estimate were out of synch. This became its own art form, and I became quite good at it! I started this technique on Spaceship Earth under Doug's direction and would use it on Horizons as well. By now you should be thinking, what was the intended purpose of this semantics game? Bottom line, Doug wanted to create a contingency fund. A fund that only he had the key! A contingency fund is simply a "factor, such as adding 1%, 4% or whatever the estimator felt was their "confidence level" in producing the estimate. According to the CSI (a standard for organizing specifications and other written information for commercial and institutional building projects in the U.S. and Canada) format, there are specific "cost ranges or percentages" added to the total estimate, tpyically tied to design levels in progress. Make sense? However, estimates produced by Imagineering had no factored contingency added. Estimating would suggest a contingency factor in the estimate qualifications. But the fact of the matter is, no one really reads the "qualifications statement!" Not only at Imagineering, but I saw this throughout my estimating career!

We can argue whether our "semantics" technique was a legitimate project management strategy or not. Or that it was ethical or not. As long as I wasn't doing anything to compromise the project, I was ok with it. In over thirty years of estimating, it would be the first time I was party to this strategy! But not the last!

Considering the context of the total project, Doug's entire focus was on the construction of this unique geodesic structure. Show and ride was hardly on the map as the building construction began. Not only was the building a "prototype," but also the vehicle ride system. The shows had to fit within this unique structure as well. Looking back on it, I'd say Doug did the right thing in protecting the project budget! Spaceship Earth has become the "signature" building of EPCOT. Who can argue with that?

The ride itself was designed as a continuous train of passenger vehicles that would "wind" their way up, through and down the entire height of the 18-story structure. This unique layout required that the "show sets" were placed alongside the track. Meaning that each scene would have to align (level to the guest's perspective) sight lines throughout the length of the track. The track could be level for one scene, or 10, 20 or more degrees off level depending on the scene. I remember walking this layout and it was confusing enough to me and I knew the ride intimately! It took a while for me to figure out where each scene started and where the next began. Sound complicated? It was!

The Spaceship Earth story is told through "scenes" about the history of man and technology. As the guest, you were "loaded" (Ride term for getting on the ride vehicles) from a rotating turntable system onto the chain of ride vehicles (much like loading onto the moving walk belt on Haunted Mansion). You immediately traveled up (about a 20-degree angle) and into the main show after coming through what is called a "transition" tunnel. Disney is really good at creating these. They are added to the ride to create a "time transition," from reality to fantasy. Sometimes they're just simply a way to adjust your eyes from sunlight to the "dark" show. Thus, the term "dark rides," eh? Spaceship Earth's "transition" tunnel (a cacophony of electronic noise and visual communications) took you up into the start of the show. The ride then carried you through time, from the beginning of communication technology, starting with our ancestors, and on to the History of Man to the present time! At the finale, the vehicle was at the top of the dome where a "starfield" was projected and the ride vehicle would turn 180 degrees, allowing you to see this dome projection (Spaceship Earth) going backwards down to the area where you first loaded. That backwards travel was documented at 39 degrees! It was a severe change, that I remember! With design issues such as this, Doug knew that cost overruns were sure to happen on a prototypical project such as Spaceship Earth. Being the "rookie", all I could say was "yes sir!" This methodology would be used later during my role as Chief Show and Ride Estimator for Euro Disneyland (EDL).

Hindsight is 20-20 and in writing this down, I have to consider; was this technique a good practice? In Imagineering parlance was it "good show or a bad show? Maybe the real question is, would I do it again? It all depends on your perspective. Did it hurt anyone? No. In practice it helped save many shows and rides to meet their design intent. Did it disrupt the progression of the project? No. The project management reports on cost and design were never missed. If anything, this has brought up a topic I think about now and again. Especially since I have been involved with theme parks, that funded their project from a third party. Think of it this way. Since Disney was the "owner," no one could imagine the plug being pulled on the project. There was just too much riding on its delivery. So, what exactly did this tactic achieve? At the end of the day, nothing except "to keep the train on the tracks" and minimizing the need for conflict between management and design. I'd suggest that all we were doing was protecting the project budget. The so-called bottom line! Better to monitor the costs than to simply allow unlimited spending. There was no intent on our part to increase the project budget. In fact, the approved project budget was sacrosanct. Only the line items that equaled the total budget could be manipulated through revision, deletion or modification. The "bottom line" was just that! Unless corporate approved new funds, there was no more in the purse! Maybe we just weren't as "forthcoming" (still love that word) as we should have been? As we adjusted the project estimates for the various management exercises, if further design detail came out, we made the appropriate adjustments. But we always adjusted the "semantic" line items first, if at all possible, to maintain the integrity of the approved facility, show and ride budgets. I like to think of it as helping out the show producers. At least that's how I see it. If there is any criticism, I'd add that as a scenic designer at heart, I hated to see the shows diminished in any way. Guilty as charged! Even after 35 years, I would argue that what we did to keep the project within its approved budget, was worth it! I don't know how the other project managers operated, but I look back on what we did as doing our part for the success that is EPCOT!

My other project estimating responsibility was the Horizons Pavilion for our show producer George McGinnis. The Horizons Pavilion had a theme of technology and the future. George was the perfect choice as he was an incredibly talented "futurist." I recall that George was always available to answer my questions, or to show me the current status of the design. In fact, he would show me the models with enthusiasm! His talents and contributions include Space Mountain at Disneyland and Walt Disney World, as well as vehicle design for the Mark V and VI monorails and the people movers, among others. Horizons was another prototype ride. The ride was called the Omni mover system. The idea was to travel in a gondola like vehicle (much like the Haunted Mansion vehicle shell at Disneyland) except that the gondola would be "hanging from an overhead rail." As a prototype, a test track with vehicles was set up at the Tujunga facility parking area. This was a replica small ride track. A "working test model" to validate the engineering required for this unique new ride system. I watched the track go up and even took a test ride on it as the system came together. The ride was not simple. Each vehicle had its own motor system that "rode" the steel beam track much like a reverse monorail. Actually, seeing and riding the test track in person, gave me a good idea of the costs associated with this ride system. My estimate would be adjusted (up) accordingly. Similar to Spaceship Earth, it went up and around one massive area called the "Omnisphere." At eight stories tall and with the same in width, the "Omni-Max" screens dominated the space. The ride was set up to provide optimal viewing to the center of the screen as the vehicle traveled through and upward, "immersing" the guest into the action. Scenes such as; astronauts practicing construction techniques in space, the blast-off of the space shuttle or divers exploring our undersea frontier were larger than life. It was truly a film experience that no one had ever done, up to that time. Of course, systems like Omnimax and Imax are commonplace in today's world of entertainment. A note about Disney ride systems; the vehicles, propulsion systems, track and control systems, are "cycled" for testing purposes on a 24-hour, 7 day a week cycle. This is done because the rides and shows operate 16 to 18 hours per day, seven days a week. Most "off the shelf" ride systems cannot hold up to the operational requirements of a Disney park. Even so-called "off the shelf" systems purchased by Disney are re-engineered according to strict Disney safety and operational characteristics.

Seeking more information, I raised two questions specific to the cost of rides at management/engineering meetings. 1) Would there be "special ADA vehicles for the handicapped and 2) Were there going to be any "special ride vehicle" for the purpose of maintaining the show area around the vehicle? I brought this up because I knew that the ride systems were optimal for the guest, not operations. Show lighting for example, had some areas with no "catwalk system" for main-tenance of the equipment. As far as wheelchair access, this was not allowed for either at the time. At least I never read it anywhere in the scope documents. The answer was always no. At least the question was asked. No extra cost was allowed for these two items in my estimates. Eventually, after 1990, due to ADA (American Disability Act) requirements the ADA vehicles were added.

Are you familiar with "E" stops? When the ride stops, and you sit there wondering why? They are loading people into "ADA" specified vehicles and sometimes have to stop the load area platform to accommodate wheelchair's and other issues. As far as an operational maintenance vehicle, I have no idea if this ever happened.

Horizons, slated to open one-year after the official EPCOT opening in October 1982, became an easy target for a cost reduc-tion exercise. Sometimes being last is not the best situation. As EPCOT's total project costs were surely spiraling upward towards opening day, Horizons, opening in October of 1983 became the obvious target to go through a serious budget cut! I was fortunate because Doug Stapp, was the project manager for Horizons as well. This made it very easy for me having conti-nuity with the project manager. Not long after EPCOT opened, Doug called a project meeting to discuss the Horizon's pavilion budget. Behind him on the wall was a "footprint" (that's the plan view of the building from above) of the current Horizon's structure. In this meeting was the show producer, the PBA and of course, estimating. Doug started out with the bad news that Horizon's was "extremely" over budget and we all needed to cut 30% off the budget. This directive from the studio. To illustrate his request, Doug took a large straight edge and drew a line over the footprint taking one-third of the building and crossing it off. This is one way to do it, but at DD design, most of the pavilion was completed. The real problem being the show and ride systems were fully developed and already occupied 100% of the allotted space! This type of decision reinforced the practice of producing show estimates from an allowance to specific details. As I stated earlier, there were many "allowances" in the estimating files and no specific back up details. While the facility (core and shell) was well detailed in its scope (foundations, steel structure, walls, roofing, plumbing, electrical etc.) the rides and shows were not. This becomes a problem when the entire pavilion (facility, show and ride) budget is out of line with the approved budget. The facility estimates can be "pared" back with little difficulty. When you shrink the footprint of the building you can reduce the amount of concrete, steel and other materials that make up the building. However, how do you do that for shows and rides? As a scenic designer, I knew that the show and ride concepts were assembled in continuity from the story. Horizon's story was about mankind's future and how the planet's natural resources could be saved. This was well ahead of its time. The story was divided up into about 26 different scenes. Each one depicting an aspect of life as viewed in the future. One scene that comes to mind was a vast agricultural setting around a very futuristic home. The home, reminiscent of the original Disneyland "Home of the Future" (an attraction I remember going through as a child) had solar power, high technology with its agricultural crops surrounding the home in a rolling hill setting. This was a "green" project, 20 years ahead of its time. Understanding how developed everything was, imagine coming into a meeting with the Project Director and the rest of the team and watching him draw a line though a third of the building footprint. Again, easy to cut out concrete and steel, not so easy to cut 26 scenes with a ride track that snakes throughout the structure! Where do you start? What scene do you cut? It all seemed like a "lose, lose" situation!

How does this new line affect the ride track, or the ride engineering or the concept of the storyline? The answer is not simple and the approach, especially in this type of creative environment was devastating to the show and ride. All we needed to do now was to get our total budget down to under $100M (1980) dollars. I was fairly confident that this is where I could prove my show and ride estimating process. My revised status estimates detailed the ride costs in "lineal feet of ride track" instead of an allowance. My show costs itemized square feet of show platforms, individual AA figures and show action equipment, instead of the usual allowance used in previous estimates. The team could now "value engineer" the show and ride, just like they do with the facility construction. Value engineering by the way, is a well-known term in construction cost estimating. Simply stated, it is designed to provide the owner (in this case WED) with the same design intent, by placing the value where the guest can see it. An example in the facility is using concrete floors, unpainted walls and open ceilings behind the areas of the attraction that the "guest" cannot see. I've seen dirt floors used in backstage areas to trade facility dollars to show dollars! In show, it might be substituting a scenic mural in the background in lieu of dimensional scenery. Painted verses dimensional, that's what theatre is all about anyway. The problem is some of the production staff and the show producers were not theatre trained. The result of this "reduction" exercise was not a nice experience. It could have been worse! The team managed to keep all 26 original show scenes by shrinking the size of each to fit the new space. The ride track was affected too and reduced. Easy, because we estimated it by the lineal foot. Every scene was reviewed, and substitutions were made to maintain the integrity of the original design. The team simply used their talent and theatrical techniques to carefully look at the necessity of every item and its true value to the story. In the end, the Horizons Pavilion, although its footprint had been reduced, maintained its original show value! This scenario points out that every show and ride we estimated was a "moving target." We juggled these changes, constantly updating our estimates and quite often, provided a "cost comparison" to the project manager from one estimate to the previously published version. This is another piece of the "cost control" process I learned at Imagineering. Simply described, there were three columns. One column had the previous date of the most recently published estimate, and the other the newest published version. Going down the columns, each line item, show lighting, audio, show sets, etc., lined up exactly to its counterpart. To the right of these two columns, a third column would show the "delta." This is simply the difference between the two. The Delta could be a plus or a minus. For example, if I reduced AA figures from the previous version, I had to write a "justification" in my notes next to the line item. This became somewhat tricky as I noted before that the scope was necessarily correct in the first place. It's amazing though how creative one could get in their explanations. The important part of this was not to "trigger" an inquiry by the show producer. Not to say that didn't happen because it did! They were pretty sharp too! Sometimes you just had to bring the other side "in" to reduce the conflict!

One of the many experiences I looked forward to, were my frequent trips to Orlando, Florida. These trips didn't happen until later in year one. In fact, I had just missed flying on the *Mouse*, Disney's own corporate airplane. Mike White, our electrical/mechanical estimator had done it, but it was discontinued by the time I was ready to travel. From the start, I could not figure out why a trip to Florida, was not possible. I wanted to witness both pavilions construction from the ground up. However, it seemed likely that I would never experience this in the field. Management did not see, what I saw as an obvious correlation between what I saw on paper and what I witnessed in the field. The standard response being "the site is just dirt with a building going up!" There are no shows or rides yet! Eventually, once the "shells" of the structures were up and being readied for show and ride installation, I convinced our chief estimator how valuable it would be to my show estimating education. Helping in this was my argument that visiting the show production facilities, the Disney shops in Orlando, would help tighten up my estimates. Then there was my PICO argument. That's the Project Installation and Coordination group on site. PICO was a very important part of getting Walt Disney World built. Everyone understands that when you build or remodel something, a business, your home or any construction project, you need construction permits. Imagine a city or county inspector coming into your office or home, where you explained that you would be installing a roller coaster in the building? How about an animatronic show with special effects, fire and smoke? Can you see that a typical building inspector would not know what you were talking about? Getting permits approved in simple construction, let alone, a Disney building with a show and ride would be a challenge in any environment. PICO came into the picture as a "pro-active team to educate cities and counties for Walt Disney World. They assisted the inspectors by helping them understand the types of things they would be seeing on a Disney drawing and how it functioned on the construction site. And it worked! PICO with the collaboration of the cities and county planning departments, literally wrote the book on the type of specifications needed for a Disney Theme park. Having dealt with construction inspectors on post Disney projects, I can tell you that this was a great lesson learned!

Before I get into more detail on what I learned on site, I would like to tell my story of my first "flight" to Orlando from Los Angeles (LAX). With my travel arrangements approved, my flight on Delta airlines would leave on a Sunday morning. Delta being the sponsor for air travel at that time. Being the "rookie," I was advised by several of my colleagues that since it was a "first class" ticket (those were the days!) I should wear a coat and tie. Actually, this attire was appropriate at that time. I felt pretty good in my blue blazer and tie! I entered my flight and began to notice I was totally overdressed! I realized I had been hazed! My fellow Imagineers were dressed in jeans and T shirts! Everyone had a good laugh at my expense! Lesson learned. To this day, I fly in the most comfortable clothes I can, no matter what class I've booked. Included in my trips to Orlando were my studies of one of the more expensive construction items used in EPCOT area development. You've seen it at all the Disney parks. Its custom rockwork. Rockwork was a cost no one had paid much attention. It was always entered as a "square foot" unit cost. My question was "How do you get an accurate area of square footage on a multi-dimensional surface? Tinfoil! I attended field meetings, contributed to cost reports and participated in change order reviews. After all, when it came to the shows and rides, who knew better what was in the budget but me? I also observed the progress of the builds, facility, show and rides. It was also extremely helpful to see the work that I had estimated on paper, turned into its physical form on site. Typically, projects outside of Disney don't have travel budgets for this type of learning process, unless they are very close to the home office. However, management could see that there was benefit for me being there. I caught a few change orders that were "adds" and not the original scope as written. The changes went through, but the costs were adjusted. This was not a one-way street, however. The project benefitted by my "acknowledgement" of other items that I let slide, knowing that they would be covered under my semantics estimating practice! Each time I would visit the site, I had to "benchmark" (a point of the project frozen in time) costs from my previous visit and note the progress of work completed or in-progress from the previous trip. These trips, by the way, became quite frequent and I was spending about 50% of my time traveling back and forth between Glendale and Orlando. It was interesting to watch in-progress construction such as World Showcase Lagoon, before it was filled with water. The massive retaining walls and bed lining were built, and I watched as the lake began to fill. There were also the massive foundation "footings" being formed for Spaceship Earth. Each trip, an observation (and education) of the construction progress. Going from my reviews of the models, the drawing packages in detail and the countless meetings attended, I watched it all materialize right before my very eyes! How great is that?

Project safety was a primary goal and responsibility for the WED staff and Tishman Construction Management. This was especially important because construction on site was on a fast-track schedule. With every structure unique with the latest in electrical, mechanical and environmental systems, there was much to keep an eye on! American Adventure for

example, had an entire engineered stage changing mechanism in its basement, allowing for multiple scenes changes.
A huge advancement since my college days Drottningholm
Court Theatre model! There were so many moving parts, the
potential for an operational accident was high. The precision
of this system alone is worth an article, if not a book from an
engineering perspective. I hope someone tackles this topic one
day. Imagine going through OSHA's issuing of certification for
something this complex! Each pavilion had their own engineering issues. The Energy pavilion had a moveable audience seating
platform ride system (vehicles) that entered huge hanger doors
to reveal the show. The hanger doors doubled as film projection
screens when closed. These ride vehicles (holding upwards of
100 guests each) "followed" a thin wire embedded within the
concrete slab throughout the building. There were six of these
vehicles operating within this show space and it was very exciting to ride them during their test cycling at Imagineering in
Glendale. Spaceship Earth became one of the very early "free-
standing spheres" constructed in the United States. (An earlier
version of this type of geodesic dome was built in Canada for
EXPO 67) Spaceship Earth, however, was the first "freestand-
ing" dome. I was part of many of the job walks throughout
construction of this 18-story structure. I went on one of these
walks early in construction when the buildings "skin" (an Alcoa
aluminum product) was not attached, leaving the structure
completely open. I recall seeing the crews "resting" on their
breaks just inches from the edge of the concrete floor slab, 18
stories up with no barrier at the edge to prevent their rolling
off the structure. I saw one worker sleeping near the edge.
If it were me, I roll in my sleep and that would be the end of
that! There were mandatory OSHA barrier requirements in
place. But it was simply horizontal wire railing with no barrier
at the edge of the slab where they reclined. Sadly, there was
one accident during the construction of Spaceship Earth. Not
associated with the experience above. The accident took the
life of a contract welder working at mid-level on the side of the
structure. The site had specific designated main construction
roadways throughout. In the instance of this accident (told
me from staff onsite) the circumstances went something like

this. A contract welder had been assigned to complete a task on the outside of the Spaceship Earth structure. Working from the outside of the structure (his welders "torch" attached by hoses to a portable compressor at ground level) his focus was on the work. From what I was told, the problem was created by the placement of these hoses from his portable compressor. From his working position, some halfway up the outside of the sphere to his trailered compressor at ground level, the welder's compressor equipment was separated from the building. That is, between where the welder was working (somewhere up on the outside of the structure) and his compressor at ground level. The hose lines to his equipment were "draped" down from the structure and across the ground to his compressor trailer. On the roads near the structure, anyone traveling within and around the structure could choose their own path. Unfortunately, the truck that decided to cross the path between the welder's trailer and the building itself, allowed the wheels of his vehicle to "pick up" the hose and drag it forward and away from the building. This action "pulled" the welder off of the building where he fell to the ground. This truly was an unfortunate event, but a risk in high-rise construction. I don't know the final outcome of this but can imagine it was settled quietly. This story, sad as it was, was the story of the day during one of my trips.

There was one other accident that occurred a few months before opening. This time no one was injured. It occurred during the ride testing cycle at Spaceship Earth. Spaceship earth is a ride in a time capsule according to Wikipedia with the average angle of incline on the vehicle at 20 degrees. The steepest angle of the ride is at 39 degrees. The entry through the time tunnel area would be somewhere near the 20-degree angle and the end of the ride (coming down from the top of the 18-story structure) would be the latter at 39 degrees. The ride system is called an "Omni mover" system and is essentially a train of connected ride vehicles in a continuous loop pulled and pushed along the ride track. The ride vehicles are open and seat four people each and are entered from a moving circular pedestrian walkway, exactly like the Omni mover ride in the Haunted Mansion ride at Disneyland. The main difference is the moving belt is in a circle for loading to Spaceship Earth. The amount of stress on the "coupling" mechanism between each vehicle is enormous. Imagine this strain on the vehicles as they climb upwards at 20 degrees and downwards at 39 degrees in a continuous loop! You can feel this tension when you are on the ride, especially when you come down backwards at the end of the show and into the load / un-load area. Disney does not take these systems lightly as far as public safety is concerned. They go out of their way to separate themselves from the typical amusement park operator. Engineering performs "cycle tests" on the entire ride and show systems before opening day that are monitored not only by the ride manufacturer, but also by the WED Engineers. These 24/7 cycles are designed to ensure that everything is operating to plan and standing up to the rigorous demands of the 18-hour day-to-day park operations. WED engineers are known for their "over engineering" on ride systems and the public benefits from this practice. As an estimator, these costs to the budget are anticipated. It was during one of these cycles that the Spaceship Earth ride vehicles discovered a coupling design problem. Thankfully, it happened late in the evening and no one was on the ride or near the show area where it occurred. On one section of the track during the 24/7 cycling, the vehicle coupler mechanism found its weakest link! The coupling failed in the same manner as in a rubber band stretched beyond its capacity. When this happened the effects of the release of this energy was horrific! Ride engineering analysis discovered that the coupling hardware had "stretched" over time, creating a situation that allowed the coupling mechanism to eventually give way. The result was over a hundred feet of "whiplash" action around the area where the break occurred. The damage to the surrounding show areas and ride track was extensive. Fortunately, no one was hurt. What is more important, the resulting analysis of the ride vehicle connector indicated that this was a fixable mechanical issue. Yet, it was a devastating blow and put the ride in jeopardy, being so close to EPCOT's opening day. It turned out that it was a simple solution for a very complicated problem. The show areas were repaired, and the ride system began operating in record time. The 24/7 cycle of testing resumed with no further issues. I know because I saw the devastation and was able to ride the system just before opening day. With the ride system operating successfully for the past 25 years, they got it right!

There was one other new project following EPCOT's opening but before the Horizon Pavilion opened a year later. The design and estimating work began simultaneously and frankly, I couldn't decide where to place it in this timeline! I'll just finish this chapter telling you the story of New Fantasyland! New Fantasyland was a complete remodel, some say a rebuild of the original area at Disneyland. The scope included a total remodel of the interior castle courtyard, removing the Dumbo ride to where the Pirates Boat/Fast Food Restaurant was being removed altogether, re-locating the Carousel in what was Dumbo's space, and creating all new facades for the inner courtyard. Two new "features" were to be added. One being the "Sword in the Stone" live event. A live action recreation from the movie with a live "Merlin," located just next to the carousel, and a "transformation" effect of the Queen from Snow White changing into the wicked witch! This effect would appear behind curtains above the Snow-White Ride with appearances from one to the other, on a timed sequence. All existing "dark rides;" Snow White's Adventure, Peter Pan, Mr. Toad and Alice in Wonderland were to be given a complete interior face-lift! The remodel also addressed the food and beverage capacity, retail space and restroom facilities. All of which were outdated and inadequate for the park in 1982. One interesting construction surprise discovered during the complete demolition of the area asphalt, was the "maze" of underground utility pipes and conduit. This was the first time that Fantasyland had been remodeled, since its opening in the early 50's and there were no "as-built" drawings. These being a set of plans that the contractor typically updates as site issues change the original plan. Disneyland, having been built very quickly, did not have this done. Our on-site facility estimators had to deal with a ton of "change orders" associated with this issue! This was also the first project where I was assigned a particular ride (Alice in Wonderland) and where I would work closely with the show producer, Kurt Kurswell. A story I told you about earlier. This was also a Tony Baxter project. Tony was the executive producer and created some subtle but significant design influences on New Fantasyland. I think it's also where we started using the term "the Baxter Factor" in estimating. You see, if this were a typical construction project, the architecture, for example, would be illustrated and constructed in right angles. Not Fantasyland. Tony wanted all of the facades in the castle courtyard to have subtle angled deviations from this standard. If you look closely at the facades the next time you are at Disneyland, notice that the facades all lean a bit as they rise to the sky. It's a subtle design technique (very expensive by the way) that doesn't come right out and grab you. It does however, work on your subconscious. Everything is a "bit off" and perhaps you feel it, but just don't understand why you feel it. If you do, Tony achieved his goal!

Why "the Baxter Factor?" This was simply a "judgement factor," a cost multiplier, for any Tony Baxter design. In show estimating, we knew that his designs always had more than what was shown on the page. He had a reputation for detail and deservedly so! Visit Thunder Mountain or the New Fantasyland and you will see his work. Tony is also a Disney Legend! Since we never saw any reports on the final cost, nor participated in any "as built" cost analysis, we actually never knew the final cost of the project. There were rumors that it came in at twice over the original budget.

With this, here's a tip while we are on this subject. Any remodeling project is going to exceed the budget you have estimated. A good rule of thumb is to add 30% to any remodel project. Especially your own home! Fantasyland would have made budget if we added 100%. But that's above my pay grade!

On the Fantasyland site, I'd walk my show and ride projects: Snow White, Mr. Toad, Peter Pan and Alice in Wonderland dark rides. I'd also walk the site to absorb everything under construction. These walks included scrutiny of the "leaning" facades in the courtyard! One of the highlights for me was seeing the Carousel relocated. The rehab was a bit sad for me in that I had come to Disneyland as a child since the early 50s. But it was very exciting to see the changes and to be part of it all. One small treasure I have from the experience, is a little round gold (a plastic ball covered with genuine gold foil) ball that used to sit atop the carousel roof structure. It is a decorative piece that goes back to the original carousel and a family treasure! One of the facility estimators brought it back for me as an unexpected surprise. Disney uses genuine gold foil for the castle turrets and other architectural facades that would need special high reach access equipment. While more expensive at first, it saved cost because the areas where it was applied, did not need painting, if any! This "tradition" started by Walt during the initial construction. It is said that his brother Roy, did not want to spend the extra cost. Not a problem, Walt just waited until Roy went back east on a business trip and that is the story of how the genuine gold foil came to be used!

New Fantasyland was also the project that got me in hot water with Carl Bongirno, President of Imagineering and Ron Dominguez, Vice President of Disneyland. Along with my responsibilities at EPCOT, I was asked to go to Disneyland to help the SQS (Show Quality Control) team from Imagineering. I attended the on-site review process with a design team from Imagineering. All for the purpose of creating an estimate on the show and ride elements. This is where I observed the different rides at off-hours. Rides like Haunted Mansion, Pirates or the Jungle Cruise during non-operational hours. Usually at 7 am in the morning. I'll give you an example. We would ride the river cruise boat and our SQS Imagineer (I believe it was Wathel Rogers) would point out things like; that elephant needs new paint, that lion, the male, its fur needs a re-fluff! I'd make a note of it and confer with the Disneyland estimating department and the shops, to arrive at an estimate.

And this is how I came to work at Disneyland and the estimating department. The Disneyland estimators job required more "hands-on" estimating. Meaning they estimated from construction and engineering documents. They interacted with the various Disneyland shops to assemble their estimates. There was very little, if any, conceptual estimating. However, like Imagineering, they did not have anyone with a show production background. It wasn't long before the chief estimator asked me if I was interested in coming over to work at the park. This got my attention for two reasons. 1) it was only 30 minutes commute from my home and 2) the job would have been permanent, unlike project assigned as for EPCOT. I decided I wanted to do it, but it was not to be. Weeks later at Imagineering, I was called into a meeting where I was asked "why are you participating with Disneyland about an estimator's job?" I was a bit surprised, because I hadn't accepted the job formally. I was aware I had to go through the proper channels at Imagineering to let them know I wanted the job! Unfortunately, Disneyland had not "asked." I heard it was more of a "transfer Carl now" approach! A story behind this revealed something I didn't know. A very real "family feud" was going on between Disneyland and Imagineering at that time! I never once felt it when at Disneyland, except for jabs I took about my moustache and the mickey "golf" shirts I used to wear to the park. Both not acceptable at Disneyland. I also never heard about this at WED! Yet here I was being told flat out "you cannot go to Disneyland!" "You are needed here!" Not exactly how I thought it would turn out. Resigned to my fate, I accepted the fact that I had a job, a project and a career at Imagineering! I continued working on the New Fantasyland project, EPCOT opened and every once in a while, I would visit my estimating friends at the park!

CHAPTER FIVE

Mouse Perks

I'm going to take my publisher's advice and include the fun side of my Imagineering experience. Why not? Many of the "perks" I received were not available at most entertainment companies in 1980, let alone any corporate or private business. Because my previous career in live theatrical was a 24/7 job, there wasn't much of a chance to indulge in some of the more fun things one might do for recreation. I went into this job thinking that the physical aspects of live theatrical I left behind, would be less stressful to the almost sedentary work of sitting at a drafting table for 10 hours. But "stress is stress," and the mental/emotional can take a toll on the body too! The long hours and physical lifting of my stagecraft did take its toll on my knees and back. I was looking forward to my new "desk job," leaving this behind. It was great for a while, until I learned that "mental stress" could actually be worse.

Don't misunderstand me, working for the mouse was a good move for myself and my new family. It truly was a once in a lifetime experience! There is nothing like working for one of the most famous brands in the world! In fact, the main reason this story is told, is directly related to encounters with the public. On frequent business travels for the mouse, total strangers would ask me what it was like to work for Imagineering. Of course, the first five minutes was an explanation that I didn't work for the theme park! Often, I'd just forget and have my "mickey" badge on, prompting the question. It has been said that the Disney brand is the most recognized in the world. You can "not go a day anywhere in the world" without hearing or seeing something about the Disney brand. There is truth to this statement. With that said, I'll begin with the "mouse perks" I enjoyed at Imagineering.

The "silver pass" was the single best employee "perk" as an Imagineer. This pass was provided to employees only at a certain level, luckily for me, I had one. This pass allowed the entire family to go to Disneyland every day of the week with up to three other guests. And if you ask, I don't have a clue as to what Imagineers are offered today! We used it often, sometimes just inviting friends along for a night out. And why not? We lived thirty minutes away from Disneyland, so it was easy to pop over to the park for a lunch or dinner and perhaps a ride or two. Often, Alison would take the kids while I worked, just to window shop for an afternoon outing. This was both a good thing and a bad thing. These early Disney visits stayed with them and to this day they have annual passes and use them frequently. My grandson is fast becoming another generation of supporting the mouse! The other side of this though, is that they have to pay for it now and the annual passes have more than kept up with inflation. Not to mention the new black out days depending on how much you love the mouse and the annual pass you purchase. Not so much for me. It's like going to work and standing in a long line. I'd rather watch it on TV. I guess the magic has left the building!

The silver pass allowed access to many other park events, and the holidays were especially memorable. Christmas is a special time of the year to go to Disneyland. Every year we attended the Candlelight Parade held at the Main Street train station. This event, which I understand is once again open to the public, is an evening parade of local choirs, caroling up main street with lighted candles to special stage platforms set up against the train depot stairways. Once assembled, the choir represents a human Christmas tree! The event featured a reading with a live orchestra with choir music from the "First Christmas." Told through song and scripture, the readings were by celebrity guests. During the three years we went, our hosts were; Michael Landon from Bonanza, Ed Asner and Jason Robards and Pat and Shirley Boone. This event was always a special treat for the family. However, there was no special seating for anyone but special invited guests. We had to hold a place near the stage podium hours earlier just like everyone else. There was one time though, where seats opened up just in front of the rope barrier we had staked out. This was just a bit of good luck. The usher came up to us and just like that we were treated like VIP's! Not only was my silver pass good at Disneyland, but also at Walt Disney World. We did take the family there for vacation, even though our daughter was a toddler at the time. Because I had traveled there on business so often, I knew where we could stay and how to get around. The best place I found is at Camp Wilderness. There are single wide trailers set up with bunk beds, a full kitchen and a queen size bed. It was a quiet place to stay and great if you have kids. You could also eat breakfast and dinner at the camp, and it was very easy to get to Walt Disney World. Either using water taxis that picked you up at Fort Wilderness, and dropped you off near the monorail station, or riding one of the many buses for free on the Disney property.

A very special perk (only after hearing that it was a possibility) was getting access to Club 33 at Disneyland. I don't remember exactly how, but someone told me that it was a possibility to get permission. Again, I think it had to do with one's management level. Somehow, I figured out who had the "key," and I did manage to get approved. We went there whenever we had the chance. Club 33 is an exclusive, members only club, established for corporate sponsors and high-end guests. It is a five-star restaurant and the only place that serves wine and liquor in the park. The original entrance to Club 33 was in-between the Blue Bayou restaurant and the retail shop in New Orleans Square next to it. To get into the club at that time, it was coat and tie only. Maybe in one of your visits near the door to the Blue Bayou restaurant, someone came up to you and asked you to please move? They needed to access the speaker at the door. WTF? It happened to us several times and to be honest, we were a bit annoyed at this "intrusion" into our space. It was not only the fact that someone asked you to create a space so they could enter, it was also a bit embarrassing because those entering were dressed in formal attire! While we were typically dressed comfortably for the park. We did not know much about this then, but after this happened once, that is what prompted me to find out about club 33. Just an update. I 've heard that the club's private entrance has been moved and guests are no longer interrupted while they wait in line.

I remember making that first reservation. It was for one of our anniversaries. We went to the park, feeling a bit awkward being "dressed formally," and once at the door, politely asked the people waiting in line if we could reach the speaker at the door. I remember that look. It was a combination of "WTF" and "What door?" This time we were the intruders! To be honest, it felt kind of special! This could maybe go to one's head. After excusing ourselves and "parting the line," I rang the door buzzer. A voice from the speaker asked, may I please have your name? Honestly, it wasn't much better than a drive thru order box! This done, the electronic door release buzzed, and we went in. It was a relief to get this part of it out of the way into the safety of the foyer! We had a choice of a small ornate lift or a beautiful staircase to take us to the dining room. The furnishings were very ornate throughout and the atmosphere transformed from a theme park to a five-star restaurant. We checked our coats and confirmed our reservation to the hostess. The hostess seated us at a window table, complete with white tablecloth and exquisite china place settings. Our table overlooked New Orleans Square and the Rivers of America. It was every bit a first-class experience. Club 33 shared the kitchen with the Blue Bayou restaurant. But the cuisine could be found at any five-star dinner house, prepared by chefs dedicated to club 33. There also was a fully stocked bar and an excellent wine list. We had to stop and realize that we were not really in Disneyland anymore! It was that special.

Our family also went to club 33 during my EPCOT tenure. Every year we would take the family for Sunday brunch, especially at Easter. Alison's mother would entertain everyone in the lobby playing classical music on the harpsichord while we waited for our table. Easter brunch events offered a special buffet with both black and pink caviar, among other entrees like eggs benedict, fresh salmon and shrimp. It was not your typical buffet! We became rather fond of those Easter Sunday brunches.

Club 33 also offered a very relaxing atmosphere. This of course, was the opposite of what was going on outside in the park. At any one visit, there might be a string quartet. Sometimes a soloist accompanied by the harpsichord. There was always something going on. Visiting the club at night was even more special with the lights of the park twinkling outside the window. This atmosphere made for a very romantic anniversary or special birthday celebration. We miss our Club 33 experiences but are appreciative to have the memories. As far as my other colleagues, I do not have any memories of their asking me about my club 33 experiences!

One thing that hasn't changed over the years, is the cost of visiting club 33. It has changed and is now a very exclusive and private club. Whether or not Imagineer's can attend, I do not know. We did have an opportunity to go back as "civilians." That was through a friend of my daughter Andrea about ten years ago. There was a fixed price per person of over $100 each. But you get what you pay for. It was just nice to reminisce about the many events we celebrated there as a family.

All Imagineer's in Glendale had access to the free video library. Every single Disney film was available and that included the now controversial "Song of the South." This title cannot be found anywhere today. Seems silly to me, it's such a sweet story! We'd have Disney film nights frequently in our house, thus beginning the "next generation total Disney immersion" process! Oh, remember that "Mickey Mouse credit card" I downplayed at the beginning? I actually came to love it and used it quite frequently. It offered a 35% discount at any Disney owned store. There were many at the Disneyland Hotel. In fact, I purchased my first two suits at the men's store. Not for work, but for special occasions. Then there was the Pendleton shop located in Adventure land! That was the best store ever! Alison purchased several very nice dress suits for work and of course, everyone knows the Pendleton long sleeves shirts for men!

I have to also credit Imagineering for my entry into the world of personal computers! Within the second year they offered a discounted purchase program from Apple computers. These weren't the highly sophisticated versions we have today, but the Apple II. Basically, a typewriter with a screen! I've always been a soft touch for electronics and to this day, I buy the latest tech out there. However, in 1982, the Apple II was as high tech as it got! I purchased one and if I remember correctly, it was about $2,000 for the set up. That's a lot of dough at that time and remember it was discounted from retail! I think I mostly played "pong" on it. My kids though had a very early start with computer technology.

Speaking of computer technology this reminds me. In the early 80s, computer technology was quickly coming into business and the home. In our estimating work, we used excel spreadsheets, something "I learned by doing." I do not remember the hardware, but it took up one quarter of the space on my drafting table! Do you remember how big the monitors were? My daily use was strictly for entering the quantities of the show items into a spreadsheet. I did not trust the excel formulas and used my table top ribbon calculator to double check everything. I think I said earlier my office had calculator ribbon all over it! I was just an "old dog" who had not accepted the new technology. Worse than that, all my notes, or memos or whatever I had to write, I still did on a yellow pad. Only after I had edited that hand written piece, did I type the finished piece into the computer! I think it took five years to get out of that habit. Emails were just coming into use and I only remember my attempts at "retrieving" an email I had sent, because I had sent it to the wrong person or worse said the wrong thing!

Besides all the fun stuff at the parks, the activities at our Glendale Campus were unlike any I have experienced at any employer since! The holidays were always a highlight with special family events held at WED. These events were designed for the children (or the child in all of us – ok, from Walt's plaque at Disneyland) and the costumed characters were always present. The food was always amazing, the decorations straight out of the Disney event warehouses and it was truly a memorable experience. I brought the family to many holiday events.

One year, we were invited to the studio for a very special event. The Disney film Tron was released in 1982 and we attended an employee preview at the studio theatre. This is the same theatre where I saw music being "dubbed" into a Disney film during my "all access" visits. I would just sit in the back and observe how they added music tracks to the film. Seeing a new release Disney film at the studio was a very special family event.

Then there were the sports activities for those that wanted to go all the way to Disneyland at four AM in the morning. Four AM because all employee sporting events had to be completed by opening which I think was ten AM. Each year I participated in two different events. There were the 5K and 10K runs around the park, and the Canoe races in Rivers of America at Adventureland. I was a daily jogger back then (when I had my real knees) and was in decent shape. I jogged three to four miles a day and wanted to give a 5K a try. As I said, it's a very early start, but fortunately I lived only 30 minutes from the park-verses over an hour's drive to the Glendale campus. The 5K run is very popular and I'd guess it attracted over 100 runners of various ages. Because of the start time and I'm quite sure the distance, I don't recall meeting too many participants from WED. The really neat part of this experience is actually running through Disneyland! The course is set up throughout the park and the early shift operating employees stood along the way to cheer us on. It really was an interesting perspective of the various lands in the park. There were no guests, nothing was operating, and at 6 AM eerily quiet. I ran in this event for two years and am happy to have it in my memory.

The canoe races were a different challenge! There were a few of us at WED estimating and from the Project Business Administrators that wanted to form a team for the canoe races. I didn't know anything about them but was told that the "Indians" (there really were Indians operating the canoes) always won! Sure, they would! They were in the water every day, mostly young guys that "owned" the Rivers of America. I don't believe they were ever beaten, especially by a WED entry. So, we were the first to try. I can only remember two of the WED employees that made up our team. There was Craig Heller, our Chief estimator and Phil Jordan, one of our PBA's. Forgive me guys for the rest of you! My old memory fails me at this moment! The total crew was somewhere around six of us and this detail escapes me too! What I do remember, is that we had to show up at 6 AM in the morning for canoe practice on three separate days. By our third practice, we felt like we were quite a powerhouse and had a real chance to beat those Indian crews. Exhilarating because you could actually "feel" the canoe moving forward in the water. The canoe would actually lift and move forward when we were synchronized in our strokes. As I think back, I believe we had the speed, but were outclassed by the Indians because of their knowledge of where to "aim" the canoe around the course. In any event, we succeeded in getting a third place which I understand was a first for any WED team. We did it one more year and it was really a blast and a great way to get to know my fellow Imagineers.

I would be remiss in the last part of this story if I didn't mention many buttons, souvenirs, plaques and other "thotchke's" I accumulated at Imagineering. We all had to wear Mickey badges (I have four of them). To this day I look for a name badge on people to know their name! And each project or project milestone represented an opportunity to receive a memento of that event. Openings day for major projects were Tokyo Disneyland, EPCOT, New Fantasyland, and later Horizons. These warranted more than a button. Special commemorative keys were given and "presented" in custom folders describing the project. Special commemorative coins were also given for other milestones such as a new attraction or a special Disney anniversary.

Of course, what Imagineer could pass up the purchase of an Imagineering jacket or an EPCOT book, or the many logo items on clothing. My entire wardrobe had a Mickey on it! As you probably know, it didn't stop there. There was character household décor, special license plate frames for your car and other Mickey temptations! In fact, my cars license plate was "Mouseki," polish for mouse. I still have my Imagineering jacket (it still fits). It's not "special" anymore because anybody can purchase one.

Writing this and sharing these stories with you, reminds me that it was not all work and no play during my EPCOT Imagineering experience. I am also reminded by the many new projects that have been delivered since my tenure. We have what we call our "story" display cabinets at home. In this cabinet is a display of many of the mementoes I have just mentioned. My most treasured though is my "The Art of Walt Disney" book which has many autographs and personal cartoon drawings. With all of this, I am reminded, that but for that call to interview in the model shop, I wouldn't have any Imagineering memories to share. I've been very fortunate!

CHAPTER SIX

Pixie Dust; Fade to Black

Even before EPCOT post opening activities began to wind down, there were rumors that funding by corporate for the next big project was not going to be approved. Having just completed two of the largest projects in company history, EPCOT and Tokyo Disneyland combined, had been a $2B investment. Many of the staff (including estimating) were also worn out, had many vacation days available, mostly because we just never had the time to use them. Each week the atmosphere at WED was heavier with the anticipation of layoffs. And still there was only silence out of corporate Disney. There was one day I remember quite well. In estimating we gathered and were told that we would be hearing about upcoming layoffs. However, for us, the company's investment in our development of the estimating systems for facility, show and ride, would be useful in the future. So, according to our chief estimator, WED was going to keep us around. We asked about the kinds of activities that we might be doing and were told that we'd get into post opening cost analysis and assist the financial group to develop a standard of EPCOT's costs history for future parks. If that wasn't enough work, we were told to "bring a good book." Some might like to pass their workday like this, but it was not what I wanted to do.

Soon however, just after EPCOT's opening day, a "hail Mary" pass came from corporate Disney! Fantasyland, the original land in Anaheim was going to get a complete make-over! The project was to be called Fantasyland 83' (New Disneyland). This would be a $25M investment with a schedule of about one year to pull it off. But I've already told you this part of the story. I bring this up again because for me, it was a transitional period. I had to make a decision to stay and work on

Fantasyland, instead of leaving after EPCOT. In fact, I was being "courted" by NBC studios at that juncture. I decided to delay that decision and see if there would be further projects for us after New Fantasyland. There wasn't!

There is one more story about EPCOT that sums up "a general attitude" we as Imagineers experienced. It happened during a "memorial photo shoot" after EPCOT opened. Some would say it might have risen to a "revolt!" Imagineering was assembled in the Glendale parking lot for a "team" picture. The area had been marked out as an outline on the pavement, spelling "We Did It!" Similar to what CSI does to memorialize a chalk outline of a dead body! As instructed, we randomly filled in this statement. The controversary wasn't the photo shoot. It was the appearance of two characters who had nothing to do with EPCOT! And all of us were not happy at their appearance! EPCOT was designed to be a new experience and there was no mention or any reference about Mickey and Minnie Mouse in the EPCOT story. There was no Mickey Mouse merchandise, branding or any retailing connected to EPCOT on opening day. Most of my colleagues, myself included, thought that this was as it should be. Wasn't EPCOT the Prototypical Community of Tomorrow and not Disneyland?

There was no doubt in my mind that we were "blind-sided" by the presence of both Mickey and Minnie. I don't think that this poster was ever made public, but if you happen to see this poster (on EBAY or other memorabilia source) you'll notice in the photo that Mickey and Minnie appear waving in the foreground. If there was a video of the photo shoot that day upon Mickey's entrance, it would tell a different story! There was plenty of booing, hissing and much disappointment. If the poster photo was in better focus, you would notice a few one-finger salutes! I'm just saying! Poor Mickey, poor Minnie, at best, these poor costumed characters were very uncomfortable. Sadly, we lost our battle for a mouse-less EPCOT. The poster is forever "tainted" as far as we are concerned. Sorry Walt!

And what's a grand opening without a healthy termination of staff? On what is known as Black Friday, over 2,000 WED staff were released from their duties. It was a very depressing time for everyone and for me quite awkward because I knew I had a safety net! There was even a rumor of one individual who managed to keep ahead of the "cuts" for several weeks. The story was it took several weeks to hunt him down because he had two different offices, and somehow managed to never be in either of them! I heard this story in my carpool. One passenger worked in the Human Resources department. The stories I heard on those long commutes, Oh My! However, I was getting a bit restless, even with the layoffs and the slack time up until New Fantasyland was eventually approved and opened.

Getting this part of the story out of my system has both fun and cathartic. Funny how when you are doing the thing you love; time just seems to stand still-until one day you find yourself looking back 40 years! I have to ask myself, what had I accomplished? Imagineering had invested three years training me in a new position called show and ride estimating. There was no job description, no formal training available, nor was there any way educationally to have prepared for it in my bachelors or masters' programs. What I had accomplished between EPCOT, Tokyo Disneyland and New Fantasyland, was estimating over $500M of value of shows sets, rides and attractions. I had also educated myself in construction estimating, learning the basics of "core and shell," and a specialty area known as Furniture, Fixtures and Equipment (FF&E). My approach to this new career was unique in understanding the special requirements of shows and rides in construction. What I came to call the "grey area," between facility, the shows and rides and their place in the building structure! Because of Imagineering, I became (still am) the first certified Show Construction Estimator (CPE) in the American Society of Professional Estimators (ASPE). This through a certification program I wrote for the CSI area known as 13.10, Show Construction. Sadly, it no longer exists because there are no other show construction estimators who have taken advantage of the certification, or ASPE for that matter. As I look back, if this were a university, I had just completed a master's degree in show and ride estimating! Three years of on the job training, providing estimates for a $1.4B prototype theme park and a New area of Fantasyland budgeted at $25M! What University teaches that?

Even with all I had accomplished, the idea of loyalty was on my mind. On the one hand, no one was telling me I had to go. On the other hand, I knew I was at a crossroads in my career. But for that hail Mary pass of New Fantasyland, I would have been doing what they call "forensic estimating." Historical analysis of the estimates to the actual cost of the project. Would the system allow for that level of detail? I doubt it. Not exactly the kind of work I was interested in. I love to be challenged and have always had a "restlessness" since I was a child. Without the hint of another work project, it was time for me to feed that restless spirit! NBC studios had been courting me for about a year for a position that would challenge my theatrical background and my new estimating skills. It would be a great career opportunity. Who could pass up working on the Tonight Show and the rest of the NBC lineup just down the street in Burbank? But that's another story!

PART TWO

EURO DISNEYLAND

CHAPTER SEVEN

Back to the Mouse

For four years, after EPCOT, I was adding to my portfolio in cost control and estimating at NBC studios, Burbank, California. As the Manager of Scenic Operations, it was a very stressful and difficult position. I tell people that "TV is where I turned my hair grey!" Even with the stress, I really enjoyed being part of the studio operations and would not trade the experience for anything. During my NBC tenure, I really expanded my participation in ASPE. Kind of a crazy juxtaposition, since my job was entirely all show related and except for a new studio 11, I did not have anything to do with construction. However, with my CPE (show construction certification), I participated in monthly meetings and the once-a-year convention. I have to say though; it was fun to be the only entertainment estimator in the organization. I was invited to speak at many functions provided by ASPE. I must have been crazy, because my work was pretty much 24/7! Even with that schedule, I volunteered in various board positions at the ASPE LA chapter number 01 and eventually became the chapter president, two years in a row! At NBC I was managing $12M annually in new scenery construction with a staff of 60+ union carpenters, artists, stock scenery handlers and transportation drivers. My work was actually part of television history, with building the most expensive game show in television! And as I said before, this is an entirely different story!

With everything going on, I heard that WED, which was now called Walt Disney Imagineering (WDI), was preparing to approve a new project in Paris, France. This was of definite interest to me and I made some inquiries. However, Craig, our chief estimator had departed his position there. I did not know the new chief whose name was Steve Sock. I had put this idea out of my head for the most part, you know, "What and give up showbiz?" and received a call from WDI human resources.

Would I be interested in a senior show estimator position? To be clear, they said it was not for Paris, but specifically show estimating. Always looking ahead and recognizing another possible once in a lifetime opportunity, I said sure! I interviewed with the new chief, the offer was made, I accepted, and it was "Goodnight Johnny!" My crew and the fine staff I worked with at NBC gave me a really wonderful sendoff party. I miss going down to the studios and watching the Tonight show being taped at 5 pm. I miss dropping into KNXT and watching Fritz do the weather. As much trouble as I had with that damn wheel, I missed the taping of Wheel of Fortune! With my graduate school minor in television production, I had been living the dream!

My new office was in the main WDI campus instead of across the street at Sonora! It was very strange walking into the front door every day, having to show my Mickey badge to the front desk. At Sonora, we just walked in! There was just a different sense of the place. Maybe I should have taken some time off from the end of my tenure at NBC before starting at WDI? Television was a lot of fun and I really put myself into it. Maybe I was just older and wiser? Not sure if that's what it was either. For sure I was older, but wiser, I doubt it. These were all possibilities. But in the rear view, I can tell you what it was. Imagineering had grown up and there was the definite "smell" of a corporate culture emanating from the halls! I should have picked up on it starting at Human Resources. The new staff was definitely more professional and the questions much more in depth. There was just more processing! I suppose with EPCOT, we all lucked out because we all were so young, focused and passionate about the work. If you asked me today, my response would probably be "you can't ever go back!" No matter what you think or "want to feel" that everything will be the same, it is just not possible. People change. Businesses' change. We change! I find it's just better to keep moving forward!

The return to WDI was not without its perks! There was the time I participated in a World Showcase Day costume contest held outside in the patio outside of our Glendale campus cafeteria. This was very unusual for me. Being a backstage kind of guy, I thought I had a great costume idea and my estimating colleagues "egged" me on to do it! My idea was sort of a takeoff on Lady and the Tramp. I created a flat plate contraption that had "meatballs" on it for my head. Under that "hat" I wore a "mop". To tie it all up, I draped a red checkered tablecloth around me complete with attached dinnerware! I definitely felt very foolish, but my effort earned me a second place! I received a Mickey telephone" which had a push button dial! You don't see those anymore, but I still have it.

Another great event held just prior to going to my Euro-Disneyland work was the 35th Anniversary of Imagineering in 1987. The park held a special employee only event that started after eight pm. The park was shut down to guests and all rides and attractions were available. Everyone received a special commemorative key. There were white tablecloth buffet tables positioned along Rivers of America with character ice sculpture as centerpieces. We talked about the food of that evening for weeks! There was a special "Imagineering" edition of Pirates of the Caribbean. Many of the scenes had Imagineering management and show design staff as "new" live characters! Some of the recordings had been changed too, just for that event. We had only heard a rumor about this beforehand. To actually see this ride with the changes and the new characters, was very special! It was an evening of appreciation for all those who made New Fantasyland a success! That is how Imagineering treated its employees!

Of the staff from my WED days, only Mike, Jeff and Cort, were still there. The work assigned to me was a brand-new attraction scheduled to open at Disneyland, and then Walt Disney World. My early expectations hoped it would be the Paris project. However, corporate had not officially approved the Paris project when I first arrived. But that's fine, the attraction, you may have heard of it, was "Star Tours." A prototypical dream attraction in the testing stages that began in early 1986 and changed the theme park industry!

I also had no idea that Star Wars would play a different role in my career later on. I ended up working for Industrial Light and Magic (now Lucasfilm) in San Rafael, California, a few years later. How cool is that? And that's (you know what's coming) another story!

When I first saw the Star Tours drawing package, I recall thinking that this attraction was going to knock the ball out of the park and change theme park entertainment! Was I wrong? As I studied and flipped through the pages, it was clear to me that this was going to be a very challenging show and ride estimate. After all, it was entirely a prototype and every single element in this attraction was new. Aside from the massive "simulator" used to hold the audience, I realized that the "loading ramps," used for guest access to the simulator would be an engineering marvel! By the way, do you remember the attraction that was originally in this building in Tomorrowland? (It was "Adventure through inner space" sponsored by Monsanto! Remember the eye in the microscope?) Allow me to go through this as I remember how I estimated the attraction.

Let's start with the simulators. If you didn't know, Star Tours began its life as an attraction through a licensing deal with Lucasfilm. Disney had tried for years to get the IP (Intellectual Property) from George. As you may know, they eventually purchased the IP for $4B in 2012. Star Tours was actually the second IP with Captain EO being the first. That's public information. But here in front of me, in 1987, was the actual use of the first IP as a ride from a Lucasfilm brand! It was like the holy grail of theme park attractions! A coup of the highest order in theme park licensing! It was, well, BIG! Was I a bit excited? DUH!

Opening a new show/ride attraction like this can be daunting. Show estimating is much like being a detective. The project as a whole can be overwhelming, you need to break it down into its components. Many of the parts are either a prototype, or a use of some existing technology with a twist of the Imagineering magic. Where on earth would I get the purchase price of the simulators, for example. There would be four in the attraction. During EPCOT, I had my friend in purchasing, so I started there. A dead end. With a few telephone calls though after I figured out the manufacturer, I ended up using an estimated cost for each simulator purchase at $1M each.

That included packing, crating, shipping, delivery, installation, tax and a factory representative for starting up the test unit. I should note here that we did not have Google or anything like it's used today. My "sleuthing" for information came from the yellow pages and lots of telephone inquiries. I see that according to Wikipedia today, there were four military simulators purchased for $500,000 each. But that was just the cost of the simulators. The simulator had to be set up, tested, tweaked with the ride engineering group and tested some more! Only then could the TV screen, the AA figures and the seating be installed and then, tested some more. Where do you think all of that happened? It was in the main campus parking lot out to the side of the building! And for this particular attraction, it was a good thing that I was able to see it being tested. As my estimates were frequently being revised higher than my original first pass on those drawings!

With the simulator in an enclosed test building, I was able to walk around and under the simulator set up. It sits on "legs" which are actually "pneumatic actuators" that provide the motion for the cabin. It reminds you of a giant spider! On my frequent tours of the test set up, I recognized that the one big cost item was going to be for the loading ramps. These ramps, if you have never been on the ride, slide out from directly beneath your feet as you stand near the loading door! And why is that? It's because the simulator has to operate completely free and unattached to any structure-except the floor. In other words, if you "loaded" the ride, without this sliding ramp, you would be walking into thin air! If that isn't complicated enough, as the ramps slide out from the facility structure underneath you, safety rails, meeting OSHA specifications, fold up from the sliding ramp. Do you think these were "off the shelf" purchases? No, they were not. This is where the Imagineering ride engineers did their magic. These one-of-a-kind slide-out ramps were designed from scratch! It was the most difficult ride element I ever estimated up to that time. After much discussion, many hours of reviewing all of the parts, I did come up with an estimate. I'm not too sure if I remember correctly here, but I think that estimate was $750,000 each! Almost as much as the simulator. This created quite a moment of "shock and awe!" with both engineering and management. However, I stuck to my guns and used my favorite tactic which is; Never say no. Simply ask the person that is adamant about changing the estimate, the work or service order; I'll be happy to do that. However, it will cost more and probably affect the original schedule! Just sign your name here! Sort of a FU, strong letter to follow if you know what I mean!

Now, let's look into the simulator cabin itself. Inside this moving simulator platform are show elements including two AA figures (Captain Rex-RX-24 and R2D2), a video screen, a projection system, seating for 40 guests (with a guest safety harness synched to a "go/no go" operating system) custom fiberglass paneling for interior décor, acoustic paneling throughout and a "killer" sound system! (I'm not sure if it met THX specifications at that time) and finally, the "magic" that brought the entire cabin to feel like a very real flight experience. The Imagineering programmers synchronized the AA figures with the simulator cabin and the film, creating the first show/ride simulator experience in the industry.

Getting to the loading door would become the "new pre-show guest experience." Star Tours would introduce the latest in "queue" area guest entertainment. This added experience was the "set up" to the story and helped alleviate the "tedium" of standing in a very long queue line. You love those queue lines, right?

The show elements to be estimated in the pre-show consisted of; several AA robots servicing the parts conveyor belt overhead, the "Starspeeder" a full-size replica and an electronics repair room. The same ramp for the Adventure through inner space remained in the space and was used to take you up into the "launch area." The room represented a futuristic "Union Station" with background departure announcements, video screens with departure listings to the various planets and a variety of "supply" tubes across the floor and ceiling to represent heating, cooling and I suppose fuel lines. To create an atmosphere, "Vapor shots" would go off in places, of course the parts conveyor belt was constantly moving over head. As the queue line narrowed up and beyond the ramp, a wall ahead of you represented the loading doors of the Starspeeder you had just seen below. The ride "operators" would coordinate the line into the "loading doors" and with a "whoosh of air" the doors would open to allow entry. Each door was in line with the row you would sit in upon entering the cabin. Crossing that ramp I spoke of earlier wasn't even noticed. I don't believe many guests thought about what happened to it once the ride began. Once seated, "Rex" would advise you to fasten your safety belt and once the safety system indicated that all passengers were "safely buckled in, the ride system was a "go!" I recall that when I first experienced the ride, I got nauseas. I'm not a big fan of coasters and such. If remembered correctly, the ride was eventually "toned" down. I wasn't the only one who had experienced this "air sickness." I understood later that it had to do with the "horizon" line in the film. That coupled to some of the gyrations programmed into the simulator created the feeling. Just a memory, can't swear to it!

Star Tours became an attraction where I did not have much to do with as far as the budget or field costs are concerned. Dave Melanson, the project manager for WDI, worked through the Disneyland off stage staff for the project. That's just the way Disneyland operates. The ride itself, broke all records, was duplicated in Florida, Tokyo, and Paris. At a reported $30M +, it was the most expensive theme park attraction at that time-anywhere! The original Star Tours was closed in 2010, making way for "Star Tours – The Adventure Continues!" I've never seen it! And with perfect timing, as I finish my final read through before sending to the publisher, Star Wars, Galaxy's Edge, opens to the public tomorrow, June 1, 2019! I have come full circle!

As Star tours opened, I was beginning to hear rumors that the Paris project was ready to be given a green light. This was good news for me, because Steve knew that my number one interest was to be part of the team. And as my opportunities seem to work out most of the time, I was asked if I would join the team as the senior show/ride estimator. That was the good news! The not so good news was that I would be moving down the street to a leased building and that I would not be working for Steve Sock. We had heard rumors that the Studio (Michael Eisner) was going to build the project with a very different management approach. I was told by Steve that I would be working for a company called LMB (Lehrer, McGovern, Bovis). This would include all of the work for estimating, meaning that all would be quantity Surveyors (QS). I told you about these special estimating professionals in chapter two and now I would be working with the pros.

My introduction to Dave McQuilkin (and that's with an "I" at the end! as Dave would tell you!) our Chief Estimator for EDL, took place at the Glendale campus offices. It was a short introduction. Steve mentioned to Dave that I would be assisting him with all show and ride estimating. I don't recall how long it was between that introduction and the actual start of our work, but if I had to guess, maybe a month or two.

I remember that introduction. As I mentioned in part one, the standard Imagineering dress code was a Mickey golf shirt and jeans. Dave appeared in a $1,000 suit and tie and was every bit an "east coast" guy, who had worked at a major contractor called Bovis, in the New York area. His heavy Scottish accent was accompanied by kind of a devilish "who the hell are you" grin, and I could tell that he would be a very different chief than I was used to at Imagineering! This is not to say that he was gruff, or ever tough on me. Well, maybe a little, I needed a kick now and then. But that's ok! I would learn so much about being a chief estimator from his mentoring.

Up to the time we physically began to move our EDL team over to Chastain, there was a feeling of "separation anxiety." I felt it personally. I also didn't feel like it was the same cheerful place I had remembered from my EPCOT experience. I recall conversations with other EDL "transfers" from WDI that expressed the same feeling. But why were we picking this up? I think from what I remember, I had the distinct impression that we were going out on our own! Somehow, this new project was not going to be the same experience as that experienced during Tokyo Disneyland, or for that matter, EPCOT. There were a lot of rumors floating around, but what did I care? I was "on loan" to LMB with no offer or agreement to go to France. I just concentrated on doing the best job I could do.

I'm not going to get involved or go into the reasons or the strategy adopted by the studio to bring on a 3rd party contractor for EDL. If you want to know more about this, I suggest you read the book titled *Disney War* or other EDL research which can be found on the internet. The story I can tell you is from the time I started the EDL project in Glendale, (1986) up to my relocation to Paris and subsequent return in December of 1989. What I have are memories of how the Imagineering and LMB relationship started and where it was when I left. Both good and not so good. These experiences were a troubling beginning to what turned out to be a truly great theme park in Paris, France! It would only take five years, three years after opening day, to work out the bugs!

CHAPTER EIGHT

Chastain

Prior to actually having the EDL offices at Chastain, I would meet Doug Stapp and Dave at a small outdoor break area at the new Chastain building. The three of us would establish the budget for the project, meeting on Saturday's when it was quiet, to establish the scope of work (as we knew it) into the WBS format on excel. This was also to bring Dave up to speed on the design process and more to the point, the terminology of show and ride. Setting up a billion-dollar budget estimate on excel was easier said than done. And that was left up to me. With a potential budget of $1.8B, the format required all facilities, shows and rides with subcategories for all of the elements found in each land. To say I was weak in this area, is an understatement. It was another baptism of fire moment! Included in this spreadsheet were all the elements of the new project. They included themed retail, food and beverage concessions, area development and all backstage buildings for park operations. Each area or land would include "individual "tabs' within the master spreadsheet. Tabs in excel are essentially "pages." These "tabs" had to "link," one to the other, from the sub totals of each part of the project, culminating to a grand totals summary level page (tab) and ultimately to an executive one-page summary of estimated cost. I also included a notes column for each line item. Just behind the executive summary, a bases of estimate page (that nobody reads!) was also included. The notes column allowed us to point out the areas that were "soft" (meaning we had little confidence in that number) and if so, what our assumption was based on.

It would be the single, most in-depth excel spreadsheet I would ever set up! It would also have the most problems I've encountered in an excel estimate! I learned the hard way that unless all the tabs were synched correctly, all sub totals and totals could be incorrect! With the number of tabs created, and the manual "linking" of one detail to another, it was easy to make a mistake. And no matter how many times you reviewed something of this magnitude, your eyes played tricks on you. You really began to see what you wanted to see! It was a colleague at WDI that taught me how to use excel and minimize these issues. The idea is straightforward. In excel, everything you enter, can be printed or modified to print. You can "hide" any column you do not want printed. This makes it easy to add a column off the side that can be set up to validate the totals of each line item, for example. This allows the estimator to verify the amount with a quick review before it becomes a "link" issue. But as I note above, after looking at columns and numbers all day, it is very easy to miss the obvious. And I sometimes did! It's been a while since I've had to worry about this problem. Who knows? Maybe excel is easier to use? Personally, I don't care! I'm retired!

This routine of Saturday budget reviews with Doug and Dave were the most interesting and best experience in my estimating career. Between Doug's Imagineering and Dave's core and shell experiences, it was like having independent office hours with the best professors in the business. However, there was only one problem with the estimated budgets we were preparing for EDL. Our budget pass was "real time," not a factual representation of "what might come!" Imagineering was given a mandate to develop what is referred to as "a cookie cutter" design and that was the scope of work we prepared for the initial EDL budget document. Our "scope" used existing rides and attractions from Disney parks or "a blend or reconfigured version of them" as our basis of estimate. However, there was a different plan brewing behind the scenes from Marty Sklar and Tony Baxter. To give you some idea of the scope we were budgeting, here is the overall park at the time of corporate approval. There were 27 major projects in five lands: Frontierland, Adventureland, Fantasyland, Discoveryland and Mainstreet USA. The EDL lands were to be exactly the same attractions found at Disneyland or Walt Disney World. The Haunted mansion, Big Thunder, Pirates and Small World and

Pirates of the Caribbean. We had begun to hear conversations related to innovations and special cultural accommodations for the European guest. Main Street would still have its iconic street with horse drawn trolley cars, but the actual "thoroughfare" for the guests would be located behind the main street buildings. These were covered arcades with wide walkways, much like you might find in a modern shopping mall. Otherwise, the storefronts and the interiors would replicate Disney World Mainstreet.

The design intent, in development at that time, reflected this, in this early first pass. I had suspicions and reason to believe that the design intent was changing. However, Doug and I had "been around the block," so as the next pass progressed, we reverted to a "semantics" level version for EDL. Dave understood why we were doing this and helped us project costs ahead of the curve.! Knowing full well that what was mandated by corporate would soon be changed by the Imagineer's. I visited the various show producers for each "land" on a weekly basis. Based on my observations, EDL was not going to be anything like a cookie cutter design! In fact, it would be "lovingly Imagined to a cultural version of what the European audience would appreciate!" This of course meant "it will cost a whole lot of money!"

As our Chastain offices were getting near completion, observed by us on a weekly basis, it was time to think about the new space in preparation for the QS team coming from Europe. The leased building was a large warehouse type structure located next to the "5" freeway. It was a building with hundreds of thousands of square feet. Referred to as the "Chastain" building, (I don't know why) it was not located on or near any street called Chastain. Having met Dave earlier, he reached out to me to assist him in exploring the new space and setting up the new estimating office. There were still subcontractors all over the building, installing flooring, doors, HVAC and electrical. With an office plan, we found the space set aside for estimating. It would be a few weeks before we could move in as a team, which was fine because the LMB QS staff would not arrive in Glendale until the scheduled date of occupation.

In the meantime, I would visit the new space several times a week with Dave to explore. This is the appropriate time to "set the stage" for the "antics," I grew to admire about our new chief! Patience was not one of his strengths! I found this out on one particular visit to the new office space. Let me set the scene! Our office space was finally carpeted, utilities were ready, and Dave thought that we should just get in there and start working as soon as possible. The problem? There was no office furniture. Dave did not view this as an obstacle. On one of our exploratory tours, we saw office furniture delivery trucks come in and out of the loading dock area. We knew that somewhere in this vast warehouse, office furniture would be stored and eventually delivered to its assigned spaces. On one Saturday, after a long budgeting session, Dave said; let's find out where that office furniture is stored! You didn't argue with Dave! In the furthest back corner of the warehouse, there was a large quantity of office desks, chairs, file cabinets and everything you need for an office. As we roamed through the stacked furniture, Dave "picked out" his desk and chair and asked me what desk do you want? I said to Dave, I'm pretty sure there was a "hierarchy" or specific type of furniture to be provided to each employee based on rank. He asked again; don't you want a desk? Of course, I said! With that out of the way, we found furniture dollies and rolled our choices to our new space. Interestingly, I do not remember any security or other personnel in the building that day. Those that we did see were subcontractors and paid little attention. That afternoon, we had set up our desks and I remember looking over my shoulder for quite a while for the "office desk police" to arrive and confiscate my furniture! No one ever did, nor did I find out, how Dave managed to keep that furniture. I'm pretty sure that Dave's strong personality was something that Imagineering never had to deal with! As for the marked furniture for certain individuals? All I can say is I had a very nice desk and a comfortable office chair! I suppose "they" just had to reorder!

And the shenanigans kept coming! When the "Brits" finally arrived (and I say this with great respect because there were Scots and a token French lady too!) the atmosphere at Chastain took on an International setting. The EDL team management was set by LMB and WDI with; "land" project managers, Adventureland, Paul LaFrance, Fantasyland, David Todd, Frontierland, John Spencer, Fantasyland, Discoveryland, Tony Catton (joined by Larry Devin and Rick Gridley) and a Belgian gentleman whose name escapes me. The Quantity Surveyors (WDI estimating did not have responsibility for the project until early 1990) and eventually one other for show estimating (only in California) was David Lizzio. The LMB Quantity Surveyors team were David Mcquilkin, Chief Estimator, Michael Foulsham, 2nd to Dave, Larry Roy, Frank Cassin, Mike Szczepanski, John Hyde, Valerie, Andrew Newton, Larry Devin and Jean Michel Noalyht, all Quantity Surveyors. WDI estimating supported me with one show estimator who maintained his workstation at the main campus while in California. Each land was assigned a show producer. Adventureland was Chris Tietz, Fantasyland, Tom Morris, Frontierland, Jeff Burke, Discoveryland, Tim Delaney and Main Street, Eddie Soto. The entrance Hotel was under the design auspices of Wang Chao, the Chief Corporate Architect. The private architects, a team were represented by; Robert Stern, Frank Gehry, Stanley Tingerman and Michael Rotondi.

The morning of the arrival of the QS team, I entered the building at my usual time of 7:30 am. The QS crew had already been there for two hours which can be expected with the time difference. They had been relocated for the pre-EDL work in California.

Nothing new for this crew, most of their assignments involved International relocation. With my first cup of coffee that morning, I realized, I wasn't in Kansas anymore! Anywhere outside of the U.S., if you didn't know, most folks, really like strong coffee! Not just any strong coffee, but the kind where you sink your spoon in it and it stands up by itself! That kind of strong coffee! The automatic coffee machines were displaying "tilt" if you know what I mean? Anyway, you get my drift.

This new work environment was exciting and also very challenging. For one, my hearing is not great in my left ear. Between the French, Scottish and British accents, it took me a while to acclimate my sense of hearing to this new language environment. Then there were subtle, and not so subtle, terminology and practical issues related to our work. It took a while to understand "flude" for example. That's "flood" on this side of the pond! My biggest challenge was having to unlearn the U.S. Imperial measuring system and learn the metric system! It had not crossed my mind that everything was going to be in metric, but there it was. Another baptism of fire. Try that on the fly with deadlines you cannot control! Even normal office supplies began to be transferred out to the European standards. We went to A-4 paper (11.3 X 8.3) stock, binders that had a different ring locking system (to fit A-4 paper) and this stupid open circle on the binder edge which I never did figure out the use for! Our American printers, thank god, would accommodate this size and you can print it out if you like to compare. Then there was the work ethic itself. Of course, the LMB team came to work in suits and ties every day. They started early and worked late. Without a family to go home to, this turned out to be the same for me when I began to travel on business. During the work hours, the pace was intense, businesslike and "proper!"

And in the morning, first thing the French would come into my office and greet me with, "Ca Va" which is how is it going? And then shake my hand. It actually was a nice start to the day. In those first few months the LMB team had to learn what they would be estimating. Not the building structures, they were experts in all styles of construction, but the themed facades and the shows and rides. The FF and E became quite an issue later. They were seeing items in the interiors they had never experienced. Guess who they turned to? By default, I became the "go to" guy for everything related to show, ride and FF and E. It was now my turn to be a Carl Simmons or Loretta Hoffman and give back to my profession. These quantity surveyors were extremely bright guys and gals and willing students. It was a common everyday experience for them to ask me questions. So much so, I suggested to Dave that these folks should get a behind the scenes tour of Disneyland. Dave agreed, set it up and I became the designated tour guide.

We met at Disneyland early one morning a few hours before opening so I could take them through the dark rides and inside as many attractions as possible. Although the technology would not necessarily be the same, the sets, lighting, audio, water treatment systems and flume propulsion jet equipment operated in the same manner. We happened to catch Pirates at a downtime where the flume channels were drained for annual maintenance. I can tell you that there is nothing like the smell of that place with no water! Our DL guide also told us that there were many "disgusting" things left by the guests! I had one language issue with Valerie, our QS from France. On my tour I referred to the "show sets" as we walked around the various scenes. Not knowing French, I did not realize that what I was talking about had a different meaning in the French language. The word "Chaussette" means "a pair of socks!" there was a really good laugh by the group when I learned what I was doing by one of the Brits. Of course, these "blokes" spoke at least two or more languages! I suppose this is a good as place as any to say something about the language issue between the Europeans and the Americans. It's not so much an issue now, but even as late as 1987 I would be questioned by the LMB crew about Americans and their lack of other languages. I was certainly one of those Americans, but my explanation went like this. In Europe and the U.K., the distance between anyone country is very limited. You can literally travel to almost any country from Paris, in hours. And that's by car. In the U.S. of course, hours of car travel mean you are still in the United States. My reasoning being, except for maybe southern California, where Spanish might be useful, everyone spoke English! In Europe and the U.K, whether you vacation or do business, it's likely to be across the border, only a few hours away where another language is spoken. Knowing other languages is a necessity there. Not so much unless you travel Internationally on business, but even that isn't a problem. Because most countries have English speakers.

As our tour continued, we had lunch in the employee cafeteria at backstage Mainstreet. Being backstage was a bit of an eye opener for them. We'd see the costume characters taking their breaks. It kind of bursts your image of Mickey or Minnie sitting at a picnic table with their "heads off" having a smoke!

It was during lunch that the topic of having my Mickey Mouse credit card with its 35% discount came up. Being on the spot, I offered to purchase things form the stores for the entire crew. I think I spent over two hours at various stores helping each of them buy souvenirs. This became complicated when a few of the guys decided to purchase over a thousand dollars of jewelry. I have to say; I was a bit stressed about this, because I really didn't know them and would have a huge credit card bill due in 30 days. My angst, however, was all for nothing. I received either cash or a U.S check the next day. It was also the last time I did that favor!

Before I get into some of the more "interesting" office politics, I want to tell you that you cannot work with a team of "Brits" without a weekly pub night. They found one nearby in Burbank; an Irish pub called Buchannan's. This is where I learned to drink a "pint" of Guinness, or a Black and Tan or just a Harps! When I say drink, I mean you have not gone to a pub with this lot without a few pints. Not only that, I seem to recall that I could not get my money out fast enough to pay for a round. These Fridays became a way to release the stress of work and get to know one another. I have not forgotten the camaraderie and great times we had on Friday nights. The downside, and I'm not proud to say this, is that there were nights when I should have had a designated driver! But I was stupid and selfish back then! And hindsight being 20/20, I don't recommend it and recommend you always have a designated driver!

With the Disneyland tour completed, the LMB crew began to understand how everything worked. Not that the questions stopped, I began to see more recognition in their eyes when I explained something. As we settled into our new office space, the day-to-day routine would be "interrupted" now and then by things that bothered Dave. For example, our area had double door "pass thru's" from one adjacent space to the other.

It was obvious that the Imagineer facility planning group did not ask LMB for any input on Chastain interior space. Located adjacent to the QS group would be the PBA's. The very idea that the PBA's could just walk between estimating and whomever we would have on the other side of us, was not a concept Dave accepted. He had a very strong and different philosophy of how EDL was going to be managed under the

LMB banner. However, this was by the studio's mandate, but not exactly transferred down to the rank and file. In a situation like this, Dave's response was to move all of our four drawer file cabinets against both doors on either side! And as instructed, we did! For a while our space was very quiet. As the spaces next door on either side began to occupy, particularly at the outset, we'd often hear a "thump" and a "WTF" coming from the other side of the doors. This would be followed by a curious PBA staff member coming into the main hallway entrance to our space to see why they could not open their doors! We would just hold up our hands, making the point; don't look at us! How and why this remained throughout the California project work, it did. Every once in a while, there'd be a THUMP! We'd look up from our work, and each other and grin! Dave had his own way of dealing with issues such as this. And it would not be the last.

I should take a moment and explain the difference between a QS and an estimator. Quantity Surveyors provide the estimate for the project assigned. Following the estimate, they act as the administrator and the accountant for the project through opening day. These are the typical duties of the Quantity Surveyor and what they are trained to do. A QS does not have a PBA looking over their shoulder. This made good sense to me, but as I noted before, Imagineering uses the PBA's as a business practice. I mentioned earlier that the estimator and the project manager are the two people that know or should know everything that is in their project. At WDI, there is a "handoff" from estimating to the PBA's. It is just the way it has been since I worked at Imagineering. Not at all though, in the world of the International construction contractor.

Dave became our Chief Estimator for the entire Paris project and had come in from the New York office of Bovis Lend Lease, LMB. Dave was a tough, experienced and professional construction professional, but had no entertainment or Disney experience, much as the entire LMB staff. I would need to demonstrate my show and ride experience to Dave, to have any chance of ex-pat status in France. It was easy for the most part. Dave, beyond the "tough construction professional persona," was quite the empathetic and stand up "boss" anyone might want to work for. We became acquainted over the next few years, went through a few battles together (he always had your back!) enjoyed his friendship. God Bless you Dave and Rest in Peace!

Meanwhile, as everyone on the EDL team at Chastain was bringing the project to life, Studio management was placing the emphasis on EDL being the "model for saving money-both in its management, design and relocation." It was not going to be the "money machine" that benefitted those that had relocated to Tokyo, nor would it be a costly "new" design that gobbled up corporate cash! This statement available on the internet, is exactly what I heard in 1986. The reasoning behind this was that the relocation policy for Tokyo had been a profit wind-fall. We heard many stories from the Tokyo staff. Some said; they pocketed "thousands of dollars," because everything was (more than) paid for during their Tokyo relocation. Whether this was hyperbole on the part of staff we spoke to, without a doubt, many of us had dollar signs in our eyes thinking this would be true for Paris. It was excellent motivation for a while! However, this was not yet on my radar and I was considered "on loan" to LMB in any event. As the work progressed, Steve Sock at WDI finally found me some help. Tom Lizzio was hired and came over to Chastain to help. Tom's help was welcome but his experience in show estimating was limited. In fact, he really was a writer, and let me know right away that it was his first interest. That worked out ok, because Tom was interested in that earlier topic I brought up. The semantics of estimating. He would work directly with the scope writers, after we agreed on the appropriate terms. He went on to promote proper documentation procedures for themed project management and was editor on a project management publication. The Themed Entertainment Association (TEA), an international non-profit association representing the world's leading creators, developers, designers and producers of compelling places and experiences, is a great organization to get involved with if you are interested in the themed entertainment industry. As Tom and I continued our estimating process for EDL, we were motivated by the LMB quantity surveyors, to prepare accurate and detailed estimates. We were quite passionate about it.

It was the time on the Saturday budgeting sessions though, where my loyalty and skills in show and ride estimating made Dave aware of my abilities. So much so, that as the first year and half went by Dave began to drop hints about going with the staff to Paris. I saw this as an opportunity to expand my knowledge, plus get an all expense paid trip to Europe for my family. Hints turned into reality soon after. My new title was "Responsible Budget, Spectacles Et Maneges," which translates to Chief Estimator, Show and Ride. I would hold this title for the first time on any Disney project.

CHAPTER NINE

Ex-Pat; The Experience

This is going to be a particularly challenging chapter to write. It's going to come out somewhere between "bitchy" and "sure glad I did that!" Probably more the former, with the latter being the look at it from the rear-view mirror 30-years later! I had an opportunity to move to France with a young family and a spouse, who placed her 20-year teacher's tenure on hold! Seemed like a great idea at the time! Sure, there were unanticipated issues! On our part, and the companies. Relocating to a foreign country can have both an upside and a downside. However, when you are going through it, it seems like everything is a downside. Thirty years later, though, the upside outweighs the negative! I suppose that goes for most things in life. I try to live life moving forward and not in the rear-view mirror. However, dwelling on the positive, I would be remiss if I didn't thank a few people throughout this story, who were there for our family through the stress of the move. And it was stressful!

First and foremost is Thor Degelmann. Thor had the unfortunate experience of being assigned the relocation program in Paris. I met Thor mostly to "discuss" the negative and most stressful issues of my relocation. With the advantage of my rear-view mirror, I'll tell you that Thor is simply the nicest person in the world. Even with my "tantrums" in Paris, he remains a friend, doesn't hold a grudge and we talk about future collaboration together. Forgiveness. That's a trait we should all strive for! There was one other that deserves my gratitude. Yves Valante, my assistant at EDL (who you will meet later) was there for our family and became our "fixer" for many issues where only a "local" could handle them! Thank you, gentlemen! And without the support and love from my spouse and kids, I wouldn't have lasted half as long as I did!

Love you Guys! For you that want to be relocated, take these stories and think about your possible outcomes. I hope that the industry has changed, and from what I see on "House Hunters International," that seems to be the case. You'll be far ahead of me, who had to "live it" to tell this story!

By the time the offer to be part of the EDL team presented itself, about six months in, WDI had come out with an entirely new set of rules for Paris ex-pats. Unlike those for Tokyo, they leaned heavily in favor of the company. For example, "you could not lease or rent your personal property for the length of your commitment to Paris" on relocation. This is a big consideration when moving overseas. Consider the alternatives: leave your house vacant or move another family in to take care of it or lease it! And the answer is? According to the Tokyo team, leasing their homes was a huge plus!

Another policy stated that "personal tax requirements" would be taken care of by Disney. Disney hired one of the big 5 firms to handle all expat returns. Only later after our return to the states, did we find out that the returns over-inflated Disney's gross contributions to our individual circumstances. Everything was done according to the law, but it was not designed to benefit the employee. This new relocation package was not what I (we) expected. It led to the stress of the entire experience. Still, with all of the new rules, being paid to move to Paris was a once in a lifetime opportunity. What do you think?

As the full detail of the relocation program evolved, Alison and I had to discuss the repercussions on her career as a high school teacher and the family's well-being. The cultural implications alone were daunting. Our children (Andrea & Christopher) were 6 and 3 years old at the time. Alison had tenure (20 +years) at the local public high school. Being an only child complicated her decision even more! Just a few of the many things we had to consider. To further complicate the decision process, Disney wanted us to relocate to the West Side of Paris, the so-called "American side" where all U.S. ex-pats lived. English speaking International schools were on this side of Paris. This is where the company "assumed" everyone wanted to live. On the face of it, it appeared to be a good deal. English speaking schools, American ex-pats nearby, everything neat, tidy and the "same as living in southern California!" Initially, we were drawn in by the lure of being in the center of Europe and being near to the Imagineering team. However, living in the West side of Paris seemed like keeping everything the same. My commute was 30 miles each way in heavy LA traffic to WDI in Burbank. I'm thinking, what is the benefit of commuting one and a half hours to the East side of Paris where the Paris EDL offices were located? The offices were located at Le Pascal – Porte 7, 3 a 11, boulevard Georges Melies, 94350 Villiers sur Marne. My choice was either a crowded train ride (I was told that it would be standing room only) or a bumper-to-bumper commute across Paris. The same number of hours, only in a different country! Merde! I wanted none of it! I pleaded my case for the East side of Paris, closer to the project site. The travel folks at WDI thought I was nuts! Eventually, they approved my plan to relocate to the east side of Paris under my terms. With that settled, a house hunting trip to Paris was scheduled. Going into this we weren't naïve, (maybe in hindsight?) there would be challenges. Having decided on the "go" decision, we were determined to work through any and all issues. This is where the "fun" of reloca-tion really began. At least at the beginning!

As my luck would have it, I was scheduled to go to Paris and look for housing with Ahmad Jafari. I knew Ahmad through my prior Imagineering projects at EPCOT. Ahmad was the chief architect for the World Showcase Morocco pavilion. He is now a Disney Legend as well he should be! It turned out that we would be the first ex-pats assigned to Paris. Our spouses would accompany us! Alison and Ahmad's wife Malek. It's not very often you get a "free" all expense paid trip to Paris! It was our first trip to Europe. We departed from LAX (First class in those days) and arrived in Paris with our accommodations booked at "Le Grand Hotel." A five-star hotel in the heart of Paris near "L'Opera." While Alison and Malek planned our evenings in the city of lights, Ahmad and I set off to the Euro-Disney offices, about 30 kilometers to the east. We arrived by taxi at the EDL offices, introduced ourselves to reception and waited for "the Disney Magic to begin." When the receptionist looked at us with that "deer-in-the-headlights" expression, we knew something wasn't right! You could actually see her thinking; "who do I let know that two Ameri'caaans had just arrived from Cali-fornia?"

Finally, after a long wait at the front lobby, a (I can't recall her name) woman entered, introduced herself and asked; "what business do you have here?" We did a double take and realized we were in trouble. There was only one small problem. Glendale had not alerted the Paris office that we were coming. No one in Paris had a clue, nor were they interested in helping us with our relocation. We were caught in the middle!

Having a friend like Ahmad was a lifesaver. If it was just me, a "lowly show estimator," I don't know who I might have turned to. At Imagineering, just like in television, theatre or film, the "stars" are on stage not in supporting roles! Ahmad was one of their top architects. They messed with the wrong "hombre!" Clearly frustrated, Ahmad asked for permission to go to a private office so he could immediately call Imagineering. I remember this conversation so well! After some delay, Marty Sklar got on the phone and Ahmad proceeded to tell him what had just happened. In so many words, he provided the details of the introduction. Finished with that, he said the four of us were going to go enjoy the sights and sounds of Paris, while WDI figured out how to remedy this situation in the Paris office. If I had said this to Marty, we'd still be "street begging" for our return travel home! As I said, it's a good thing to have a friend!

Ahmad concluded his conversation, letting him know he could be contacted at Le Grand Hotel! Completely frustrated, we headed back to the hotel, getting our story straight to inform our wives. Once they understood that we would be having some fun and sightseeing for a few days, there was no issue. That evening began with a taxi ride just outside Le' Grand Hotel. Entering the cab, I was going to "show off" my extensive French lessons and asked the driver; "excusez-moi, por favor, parle angles?"

The driver, slowly turned his head to me and asked in perfect English; "sir, which language would you like to speak?" After a beat, the laughter was spontaneous! We realized the language faux paux (French & English) and the sincere delivery of our driver! We started our "holiday" with "le bateau mouche," a boat ride with dinner on the Seine River. Afterwards, a stroll down the Champs Elysees and some ice cream while watching the world pass by. We all enjoyed each other's company. Which resulted in a lifelong friendship. A bit of information on my French lessons. Being assigned to EDL, I was provided individual, daily, one-hour French lessons. I called the source to make sure I would have my lesson scheduled in the early hours of the morning. This was important, because I worked with numbers. I could not see myself going into a language class after lunch or later. My head would be swimming in numbers, and I'd be going into that "sleepy time" one gets after lunch. Alison will vouch for that. She asked me one day at home; why are you rounding our checking account to the nearest hundreds? Not realizing that working with hundreds of millions of dollars every day were affecting my personal life! Of course, I was completely ignored and was scheduled for a 2:30 PM appointment every day. I tell you this because the story above will give you an idea of how much French I learned while in Paris! Obviously not much. Today I call it taxicab French! After our first year though, I was always happy to have my daughter Andrea with me. I'd just pull her to the front and point at her as my personal translator!

So began our relocation house hunting odyssey in Paris. We waited for three full days for a response. In the meantime, we visited museums and cathedrals every day. On the third day (sounds biblical) the Paris office formally invited us to begin our relocation process. The treatment was a complete turn-around! It was evident they had been told to accommodate us and to do so quickly and courteously! Still, it was evident that being told to "take care of the American's was not something they wanted to do. This displeasure became apparent in many subtle ways over the course of the next six days. It was not a formal process or plan to show us local housing. They were "punting" and that is being kind. There were no introductions to realtors, they simply assigned one of their "go for" staff as a driver (a young Sri-Lankan). He had absolutely no experience or knowledge of Paris and its environs. Worse, he had no idea what an American family might want for a home. And for the most part, his broken English made it hard to communicate.

Using his personal vehicle, not exactly a new model, he stated quite frankly, he knew nothing of what he was supposed to do. He promised to give it an honest try. The results were never satisfactory. How could he? He came to Paris as a refugee, somehow landed this job at EDL and probably didn't have much experience with "housing." Let alone the standard of living of a typical American family. Put it this way, our expectations for a "home" were not even close! It would take another phone call to Marty and once again, Ahmad was promised that the next day we would have a local realtor to show us around Paris. Right! And I can speak French!

For Alison and me, our luck changed quite by accident. In the evenings, we would sit at the bar in the Grand hotel where the bartender, Bruno LaBoute, told us about an American style housing development on the Eastside of Paris. The homes, built by an American developer (Pardee Homes) were in the small village of Lesigny, about 26 kilometers outside of Paris. Lesigny seemed like it would be worth looking into. It was about 8 kilometers from the EDL offices. About a 15 minute, no traffic commute. at least we had an alternative if nothing productive came from the Paris office. Within a day or so we were given a tour (finally a real estate person was assigned to us) of the area and shown a property in Lesigny. The house, being built by an American developer, had an USA feel. This appealed to Alison thinking that it would help the stress of the relocation for the kids. It was also close to a main highway, had easy access to the site office and was surrounded by a huge forest. In its "as is" condition, it would require a new kitchen, some painting and other interior fixes. All within the budget allowance provided for my relocation. We loved the neighborhood, and without any other choice, it seemed like the place we could live in. I admit, though, we felt rushed and wanted to get home! We reached agreement with the relocation folks and entered a lease for our new home in the village of Lesigny! We also learned it would take several months for the interior remodel. We were told that we would be coming back to a temporary rental in the city of Vincennes.

With our housing out of the way and the end of our 9-day stay in Paris, we visited the Eiffel Tower and our last "expense paid" dinner at the Jules Verne restaurant. We also got to the top of the tower for that magnificent view of the city of lights! The night before, we had a wonderful time at the Lido De Paris, a very popular and well-known Paris burlesque dinner theatre. We could now go home while our new home in Lesigny was being prepared and make our travel plans. The day before we were to fly out, I began to have stomach pains and developed a high fever. Alison had to call the Hotel's house doctor and he confirmed I had a temperature of 101 plus. It was likely some sort of flu bug. We went with this diagnosis and departed for Heathrow the next morning. Alison, as I found out later, went to great lengths to "fib" about my condition to British Air. It seems they didn't want the liability of having someone so sick on such a long flight. Somehow, she convinced them that I would not be a problem (in fact I don't remember the flight) and found myself at home with a high fever and the symptoms of the flu! A day or so after our arrival home, Alison heard a "thump" upstairs (I was bedridden) and she found me on the floor passed out. She sent our son Christopher to a neighbor's home to fetch a nurse who just happened to live next to us. Our neighbor arrived and told Alison without hesitation, "Call the paramedics." I was very dehydrated and had a weak pulse. The next thing I knew, I was on a gurney with Alison and the kids watching, as the paramedics carried me down the stairs to the waiting ambulance. This was rather embarrassing with the neighbors outside, the sirens and all the commotion. At the hospital (fortunately our nurse friend went too) I was in the ER and the doctor insisted it was just stomach flu and I should go home. Thanks to our RN neighbor, who insisted it was something else, the doctor, reluctantly, had them do a scope of my stomach and environs, only to discover that they were filled with ulcers! I had a sever case of food poisoning and needed an IV and all sorts of medication. It was serious and I ended up in the hospital for several days. I learned to hate that IV, drip-drip-drip! No solid food just that damned I.V! Later, we put two and two together and came up with the "foie-gras" (that's duck liver pate) that I had eaten in the hotel's mini bar days earlier. Apparently, someone had opened that container, smelled it, and placed it back in the fridge. Let me be the first to tell you "Buyer Beware" be careful what you eat in strange countries! Finally, after a good week or so I was over my illness. I was back on task fighting for reasonable show and ride budgets for EDL.

As our estimating team came to its conclusion for the so-called "cookie cutter" concept, we began our preparations for relocation to France. Although this decision was premature (due to the ongoing design in Glendale) we were given orders to head to Paris as quickly as possible. Before we could do so, Alison had one hurdle, which was to get her school district to sign her unpaid leave of absence (which they did) for the period of time I would be assigned to the project. We assumed it would be at least three years. I worked on selling our two vehicles and leasing our home (Yes, I defied the policy) plus all the other things one needs to do planning an international relocation. Finally, in early summer of 1987, our family (Alison, Andrea, Christopher and myself) was set to go. To take advantage of the trip east, I scheduled vacation time and planned a family vacation at Disneyworld. We stayed in the Fort Wilderness trailers for five nights and had a great vacation. It was the families first visit to the site and my kids finally got to see daddy's "golf ball."

After a week at Disney World, it was on to Paris. The flight, Business Class for all, was a first for the family. Andrea went up and down the center aisle flirting with the passengers. At that time (Pre-911) the pilot would roam through the cabin and sometimes invite children to come up to the cockpit for a look at the plane's controls. At home years later, Andrea would discuss the various cabin parts of a 747 and her travels to France at school and parties. Just another day on a plane! Ho Hum! Sadly, the 747 has recently been taken out of service. It was a beautiful airplane, and I am sad to see it replaced by the airbus. You haven't experienced that plane unless you sit in the upper cabin and experience take offs and landing an extra 10 feet off the ground! When I was her age, I rode to California on a train. I couldn't tell you how to get to the next block, let alone the restrooms of a 747! That's a kid's life today. It was just a few years later that flying lost all of its glamor thanks to 911!

Upon our arrival in Paris at Charles De Gaul airport, there was no Disney greeting party, no guest relations representative with balloons and a riding stick saying, "follow me!" We were on our own. We all had large luggage as we should for International travel and proceeded to the rental car area. Disney "travel" had reserved one of those small European cars for us. Of course, no vehicle in the rental car's fleet could hold our luggage. So, I negotiated for a large Audi four door. I'd hassle with the expense later. We packed that car to the back window, filled the entire trunk and stuffed the rest of us like a clown car! We headed out of the airport and onto the French highways for downtown Paris and our hotel. A hotel we understood; we'd be at until our temporary apartment in Vincennes became available. Thanks to Alison's "navigational skills," the drive to Paris was uneventful. We checked into the Grand Hotel, a beautiful hotel just near L' Opera, the city's premier Opera House. The Grand was the same hotel we used for our relocation housing trip. A view of L'Opera was just outside our window!

During our first few days, we enjoyed sightseeing with the kids and stopped at Les Tuileries to burn off some of that "kid" energy. Les Tuileries also had a very old "hand pushed" carrousel which was the first we'd ever seen. It was a small carousel and the "operator" would walk around pushing and pulling the old machine. Very low Tech! Les Tuileries was also where I jogged during our relocation trip. Actually, it was where I vividly recall seeing the Eiffel Tower for the very first time as I turned a corner of the park! My first full week at the EDL offices was scheduled for the Monday after I arrived in Paris. Alison made her itinerary with the kids, to keep them occupied as best as possible. It would be tough living in a hotel with two kids, but she made the best of it. Each night I would come back to the hotel and we'd find a local place to eat, get ice cream on the Champs and enjoy walking around the streets of Paris. Everything was going as well as could be expected, when I was told that our stay at Le Grand would be over at the end of that first week. We were notified to move over to another hotel, more of an apartment, across the street from the Grand. It was a step down in amenity and a disappointment.

We knew prior to landing in Paris that our Lesigny house would not be ready. We would have to go to a temporary flat. This flat was in a small village by name of Vincennes and was about seven kilometers from the centre of Paris. Compared to our Pardee home in Lesigny, this was a modern flat, close to the city by train and fully furnished. Because it was summer, it was not much of a problem for Alison and the kid's as far as outside activities. There was a lovely park nearby and plenty of small village shops to window shop. School was still a couple of months away, giving us time (or so we thought) to move to Lesigny before the start of school. The local public French school to be exact. We soon learned that things don't happen quickly in France. The French will tell you that there is always one more piece of paper needed to close the deal! No matter what you are doing. Since our newly remodeled house was getting a kitchen makeover, floor refinishing throughout and a few other minor fixes, there was no way that the house would be ready to move into by the start of school. This put Alison in the position of having to drive the kids some 13 kilometers each way to the new school. Although I had little problem driving in Paris, I can't say that Alison was thrilled about it.

An interesting story about our flat in Vincennes. Just above our flat, the tenant always played American rock and roll. We were curious and finally met him in the "lift" where he told us that "he loves everything American!" He took us to his flat and the entire front room was filled with American blue jeans! He told us that it was his full-time business and could not keep his inventory ahead of the demand. The French love our jeans!

Our new home in the village of Lesigny was close to my office in Villiers sur Marne and about 20 kilometers outside of Paris on the East side. The delay in Vincennes lasted about two months until our house in Lesigny was finally declared ready for habitation. Over the next few weeks, I had to keep going to the office every day and that left Alison with all of the difficult things like registering the kids into a French school, shopping at Carre Four, the French version of a Costco, and getting the house in order. Of course, the newly installed kitchen appliances blew up the breaker box. There were leaks from the new plumbing and our California belongings had still not arrived.

Imagine this scenario. This being Alison's first relocation to a foreign country, (with little French language skills) answers the door for delivery of our California belongings. The delivery is completed, with French speaking movers, leaving a living room stacked to the ceiling with packing boxes with the remaining furniture left wherever it could. No one was there to support her, no one to help in unpacking, nada! In tears from frustration and quite overwhelmed., she called me, and I did what I could to raise the flag to our relocation department. When I came home that evening, I was quite agitated myself. I set up a meeting the next day to discuss our problems. My plea went un-answered. Only later, I learned that according to relocation, "we tried to "leverage the system" by bringing over our grand piano to Paris! It was on the manifest! We were dumbstruck. But there it was on the bill of lading, one grand piano. I suggested that maybe the paperwork is wrong. It was to be placed in storage, that we knew. I said we have nothing to hide, come out to the house and see for yourself! So, they did. Funny, no grand piano could be found! They also noted that the furniture had not been carried to their proper rooms. I think it was an I opener for them and finally we received some help to get the furnishings organized.

This, however, did not stop the relocation problems. We only brought furniture like our king-sized bed, because we were told that beds of this size would be difficult to find. That turned out to not be true. We knew that we could go through the Ikea catalog and order what we need, because we had a decent budget as part of our relocation package. Ikea, now popular in the states, sells furniture that needs to be "assembled." And of course, the items arrived, boxed and un-assembled. You can imagine (once again) the delivery with the entire living room filled floor to ceiling with Ikea boxes! My choice was, get help, or take a week off from work. Relocation said that they expected me to assemble the entire lot. After much yelling and screaming, and with Dave's unique way of persuasion, a crew to assist us in this assembly was sent over. Later I learned that Dave had told them he was going to send me home to assemble furniture full time and that all estimates for show and ride would-be put-on hold! As I said, Dave had his way of handling things. But I was now in a "do whatever it takes position" to help my family. There was plenty of grumbling by others too at that time. I admit, my frustration displayed itself, sometimes in a very ugly manner. I think back on this and feel bad that I let it all out on Thor! It wasn't just me though. There were other disgruntled WDI ex-pats! I probably was the most vocal "client." At the end of the day though, thanks to Thor, everything calmed down, we got the help we needed and today, years later, Funny how when you reach 70, things like this seem so unnecessary and insignificant in your life!

In the middle of all this we needed to get two very important tasks done to become "legal" ex-pats. One was our Carte de Jour and the other, a French drivers license. All ex-pats had to get a French driver's license.

Our first task was to go to our local "Prefecture" (an administrative office) where we would meet the local constable and sign our "ex-pat" papers. A relocation representative picked us up and drove us to the local office. Our documents included my Carte De Jour (work permit) and the families temporary residence status cards. The local officers treated us very nice and made the experience pleasant. Thanks to our French relocation representative it went off without that "extra" piece of paper the French always seem to need!

If only the driver's license process went as well! We would be in France for a few years, so a driver's license was mandatory. You will appreciate what you have here in the United States when you hear this story!

First of all, there was no French to English study guide. We had to learn everything in French and figure out the various laws by ourselves. Secondly, the French version of the DMV, I'll call them the FMV, would not compromise on how us ex-pats would complete the process. What this meant, is that we would be required to take the test in French with no translator to aid us. Further, no translator was allowed in the testing area. A distinct dis-advantage to be sure!

Eventually, with some "mouse" coercion, the FMV settled on a compromise. We could have a translator, as long as they stood directly in front of the projection screen and faced away from us at all times. I'm not sure what they thought the translator would do. Maybe we all had a crash course in sign language? The other requirement, only specific questions could be asked. Any attempt to get an answer from the interpreter and I'm sure the guillotine would have been brought out! Ce La Vie! I had prepared enough to actually pass the test and get my license, which is given for life by the way. Although, since then when I've traveled back to France, I would never acknowledge I have one. I don't want to take any chances if there are wants and warrants still there from past parking citations or that car I accidently sideswiped on the narrow streets of Paris! From my experience driving there, it's clear to me that they might want to consider having a few qualifying license renewals every once in a while! Getting the license also allows me the opportunity to tell you a very crazy story about bringing my personal car to France.

Our relocation package offered two choices of how we would get around in France. 1) a special rate "buyers" program was being offered for a brand-new Peugeot delivered locally. My view of the deal weighed heavily on the resale angle. I could purchase a new Peugeot for $30,000 US, but what was it worth in three years? Would anyone buy it? Or I could bring my personal car and the company would pay for shipping. My research indicated that there were less than a handful of 1987 Chevrolet Camaros Z-28s in France. GM was represented there with at least one GM dealership in Paris. Gasoline wasn't an issue and I thought, maybe I could sell this car for $40 or $50 thousand dollars at the end of my tour? Cars in France are very pricey, and my Camaro would be unique and almost one of a kind! Settled, I would plan on it. My Camaro didn't arrive until about two months later at the harbor located on the coast at La Harve. This port city is about an hour's, maybe a bit more in a slower car, from where we lived in Lesigny. I thought that maybe I would be the only expat to bring over an American car. This wasn't the case. One of our project engineers, Doug Le Blanc had the same idea and brought over his corvette with the same idea. Doug came with me to La Harve to see exactly what the experience would be for his car's delivery later.

Shipping the car was one thing, getting it passed the French version of a "smog and safety test facility" was another.

Once delivered to the port, my car went through a certified inspection process. Essentially, they prepared the car to meet all French laws. For about 6,000 FF, here is what they did. 1) changed the rear seatbelts to exactly the same seat belts except they were "made in France." 2) changed the headlights to "yellow." All cars in France have yellow headlights! 3) changed the flasher red light from the dash to the top of the steering column. And 4) using black masking tape, blocked out the lights on both sides of the car!

When we arrived, my Camaro was near the center isle of the vast warehouse. The hood was up, and it was surrounded by several warehousemen. The local representative told me that the battery was dead. This is also where I noticed that a very large dent was on the top of my right front fender. It looked like another vehicle ran across the top of the fender. I never did find out why, and I don't remember if we ever got paid by the insurance we had. The starter battery was wheeled over, and I showed the man where to attach the spring handles. By now, the front of the car had warehousemen circling the hood, with some of them actually leaning in to see it start. No one spoke English, but Doug and I did our best to let them know that they should not have their heads under the hood when it started. This type of American horsepower was just not available in France at that time. I sat down in the front seat, made one more attempt to clear the hood and finally just turned the key! The 330 HP small block started with that roar that only American muscle cars make and two of the men hit their heads on the hood, startled by the engine roar! I thought, now we're in trouble, but every one of them had a big smile on their face and were saying Oooo, La, La! Quite an experience. We left the warehouse and proceeded home to Lesigny on the "Peage." The toll highway in France is well worth the few Francs with the very smooth highway. Because the car had been sitting for a couple of months I decided to "blow it out!" There is no speed limit, per say, on the Peage, so I "pegged" that Camaro to the speedometer at 149 MPH! Doug and I were both surprised and loving it!

Bringing that car to France was a real kick. Driving it around France was never dull. Every single "little car" wanted to race. The police would pull up behind me, come up to my left side, then my right, then in front and look in their rear view! Usually with a thumbs up when they sped away. Once, I was caught in a vehicle check line. I wasn't able to get out of it and crept up as the cars were inspected one by one. At my turn, with my limited French, I showed my California Driver's license, let them look under the hood and they let me move on. All of them were smiling as I left! If we ever were feeling homesick, we'd take the Camaro into the city and park. It wasn't long before an English speaker would come up to us to ask about the car. When the April 1st snow and ice came, I drove to work and through our roundabout. Discovering the hard way that I had California tires, and not mud/snow tires. I did three 360-degree spins! Fortunately, without hitting the curb. Finding tires for an American car in France is not easy! I finally found them in that Carre Four Costco type store nearby. I had four shopping carts with a tire in each. The clerk at the checkout asked; "what kind of truck do you have!" Getting them mounted and balanced was an entirely different problem. I found a tire service, much like our Midas shops nearby. The owner dealt with me in person and we figured out that he could mount these tires for me. While I waited, he kept "eying the car." Seeing this, I thought I should just let him take it for a spin after everything was done. You know, to make sure the balance was all right. With a huge smile, he did. When he came back, he offered to trade, straight across, pink for pink slip his almost new BMW 5 series four door. I should have made the trade, but I didn't. In fact, I regretted this because I ended up not being able to sell it because it was never registered in France. It was shipped home and Alison had the honor of going through U.S. Customs to get it back! It was a very bad experience! While on the subject of cars, I did purchase a used Mercedes 400. I found it parked on the Champs with a for sale sign written in English. Long story short here, I made contact with the seller, a German and purchased it for 6,000 FF. It was kind of a scam. I had to drive with him to Heidelberg where he lived to pick it up and bring it back. I did not know that I would need transfer paperwork from France to do so. When I went through the border gendarmes, I had to argue that I was just going to visit my family in Paris. A script that the

German seller told me to say. In frustration, the gendarme let me though because we could not communicate! Of course, today, the EU has opened those same borders That Mercedes was a great family car. With only maintenance by a Mercedes dealer and a set of new tires, we drove on vacation to Brussels, Strasburg, the Black Forrest, up through the Rhone River, the French Alps and all four corners of France.

My American expat colleagues appreciated the decals (from three countries) I attached to my trunk lid. They represented Belgique, France and Deutschland. Or as the stickers displayed, BFD! Only the Americans got it! That car turned out to be a winner. I sold it when I left France to another expat for 6,000 FF. I heard it blew up some months later!

Even with all the hassle, the stress and the cultural shock, our family made it through the first year! I'm not going into great detail about all the things we did, as a family, but here's some of the highlights of living in the Paris suburbs.

The French school nearby was not unlike an American public school, except it was all in French! Kids are bullies everywhere we found out the hard way. Language problems began right away, with a conference with Andreas teacher. Learn French! So, we hired a tutor and that sped things along. Christopher was bullied for being an "Americaan" and lost his best neighborhood friend who had to move away! By the end of year one, Andrea was fluent in French and our neighbors said; "she has a perfect Parisian accent!" I would always push her to the front of me when we were out together to translate! Christopher, spoke a little, but he was just going on four years old. No impact yet on schoolwork. But I think he made it through ok, with Alison's help of course! Soon Alison enrolled Andrea into a ballet class. It was at the local community center and taught by a really nice woman by name of Carol Sellier. Carol had danced with the French Ballet! The end of the year recital turned out to be Marie Antoinette! Guess who was "Marie" as a child? Andrea, our blue-eyed blond from California! The other French girls in the cast were quite jealous as we learned later. Alison struggled with the language daily, and no one appeared, nor was it ever offered, to provide a tutor to help her assimilate into the culture. Only on her own, did she figure out the basics!

The very reason we went to Paris in the first place was to see France! And we did, plus many of the countries surrounding it. All of the typical tourist sites in Paris, of course. Every Sunday was a trip on the "RER!" That's the phonetic way we called the train that went into the city from a station about five miles from us. In the city, we'd go see movies, plays and the sights! The movie theatre offered English speaking versions with French subtitles. The one we really like the most was Disney's (Under the Touchstone Banner) Who Framed Roger Rabbit? That was funny because it was all about Los Angeles! One evening in Paris we went to see the musical "Cats." It was the first international tour and we had all seen it in Los Angeles. The audience just didn't get the story! The four of us did and we hooted and hollered and made the cast feel so good, that they literally started to "play" to us in the front row! When the cast came down into the audience, they congregated around us and ignored the rest of the crowd! They were ecstatic that we wanted to come backstage afterwards for autographs! They told us that we made their day!

We also traveled to many cities and countries surrounding France. That Mercedes I bought on the Champs, carried us to place like; Lyon, Brussels, Luxemburg, the Black Forrest, Duex Alps, Bern, Geneva, Lausanne and Bordeaux and many others.

Our first Christmas in Lesigny we strung up some Christmas lights, got a tree and all of us packed up for our trip back to Los Angeles to visit the grandparents. Our neighbors thought it was very strange to see colored lights on our house. By the time we got back from L.A., there were about a dozen or so houses that got in the spirit and added lights too. Many of the expats on that first wave felt that everything could have been much easier. With the experience in the rear -view, most feel like overall it was a great opportunity. I'll close with this. There were cartoons floating around the office to document the mood of that first wave of expats! I'd share that "reloca-tion" cartoon with you. A picture is worth a thousand words after all. But I don't want to be visited by the Mouse Police. All I can say about this is, Buyer Beware!

CHAPTER TEN

Le Pascal

This part of my story starts the second week we landed in Paris. I commuted from downtown Paris, to my new office called Le Pascal. We did not have GPS or smart phones at that time. You notice the street orientation first. Paris had never been designed for automobiles. The streets are narrow and the orientation confusing in its layout. It is very easy to "go in a circle." The "roundabouts," literally circles without stop signs, are an experience all by themselves. I learned to drive Paris by noting local monuments, not by street names, over my shoulder. I'd just keep heading towards a major object that I could see over the buildings (the Tour Eiffel, the Sacrecouer or something big) keeping the object off of my left or right shoulder. These were my GPS coordinates and how I learned to drive in Paris. It helped that the French stay on the right side of the road, just like us! I set out to find the Pascal office on the East side of Paris. With some minor miscalculations, I finally figured out the route and arrived about 45 minute later. Not too bad a commute, but that's from the center of the city.

Arriving at the new office, I met Dave McQuilkin and the QS staff. Dave made me feel welcome and assigned someone to help me with anything I needed to get organized in the office, and at home too! I was given a tour and shown to my new office. I found quickly that in Europe, they have been far ahead of us as far as accommodating the office worker and the green movement. Each building must have natural light for all employees. Thus, my office, although situated in the inside of the building, was one window away from the building's central courtyard. This allowed light to enter from both the outside and the inside of the building. At first the office seemed fine. Only later did I find out that the HVAC for the space was out of sync with the rest of the floor due to it being an add on! In the winter it was freezing, and in the summer, I sweltered in the heat and humidity. A more humorous aspect of my office was the sliding window added later to my left side of the desk. This was to alleviate the heating and cooling problems allowing air in the main hallway. It did, sort of! Weeks later, when our WDI project managers arrived from the states, they'd come up to my window and order take out! It became a running gag and I eventually put up a faux menu for everyone's enjoyment.

ESTIMATES TO GO!

- 100 FF - Quick estimate. – $1,000,000!
- 300 FF – Ballpark! – Right! Go to Dodgers stadium!
- 1,000 FF - Need it yesterday! – FU – Strong Letter to Follow!
- 5,000 FF – Penalty for saying – You're a project killer!

No matter what they did, I still was cold in the winter and hot in the summer! They never got the balance. And here I was with a team building a billion-dollar project!

"Murphy's Law," suggests; "it's not IF a problem will arise, it's when!" And with the designs changing in Glendale, the problem didn't take long to reveal itself. We were using "cookie cutter" costs for our original budget. Only a few months after we had left for Paris, Marty Sklar was successful in changing the earlier directive (from a cookie-cutter concept) to an entirely new Euro-Disneyland. Makes sense, yes? Send your entire estimating and project management team to Paris, change the rules and see what happens! All of the attractions, shows, rides and building facades changed completely to fit the new environs of Europe! This meant that everything we were doing in Paris, was obsolete! Obviously, this didn't make much sense at all. Knowing this I made my plea to Dave. I was "twiddling my thumbs" here in Paris and would need to head back on monthly business trips until the design team moved to Paris. There really was no other choice. He approved my travel plan for the next six months.

It was on my first trip back to Glendale, where I happened to land in the middle of a management issue between Imagineering and the Studios. I had to research this myself, and to clarify, this story is paraphrased from James R.

Stewarts book, Disneywar, and my personal observation at Imagineering when it actually happened. From the book, Jeffrey Katzenberg appointed Jeffrey A. Rochlis as the New Chief of Technology in 1987. Jeff came from Atari, a computer company, and he had a reputation for being the "terminator." He met his fate at Imagineering, according to the book, when he was assigned to "rein in costs!" Decisions implemented would be his infamous "triangle of success" program, and his failure to bring in "Pleasure Island," on budget. I actually attended the meeting where the Triangle of Success was introduced. I can't say that anyone I know was enthused! It's noted in the book, that Marty Sklar did not like this arrangement at all, and was quite vocal in his feelings to Michael Eisner! Marty was perfectly capable of running the place (Take EPCOT for example) and this "outside" control would only serve to disrupt the Imagineering process. If you need to understand the "behind the scenes" details of this story, the book is Disneywar, by James R. Stewart. Issues like this and much more are brought to life in a very telling story about the power in the magic kingdom. Check it out!

All of this happened during a business trip to Glendale from Paris. I was attending meetings specific to EDL. Remember, at this time there still was a "hands off" policy at Imagineering for the EDL project. It was pure coincidence, but I just happened to be passing by the very same conference room where a very significant meeting had just concluded on the new attraction for Disneyland called Splash Mountain. As I passed the conference room, the management staff (responsible for the flume ride) was just letting out. I knew many of the folks coming out, and wondered at the time, why everyone looked so down in the mouth. These folks looked like a truck had hit them! It was that obvious! I had never been to a meeting at Imagineering where I witnessed this kind of "dejection." We had heard rumors in Paris, that Splash had some production problems and was in scheduling trouble. I didn't know the extent of these problems until I came back from Paris and was enlightened by my estimating colleagues. They were on site at Disneyland for the installation of Splash Mountain and knew the issues firsthand!

This is the story related to me at that time and my revisit to an *LA Times* article published, April 30, 1989:

> Although they are not pointing figures, park officials are clearly disappointed. "We planned to open in January or February, and we weren't able to do it," said Robert W. McTyre, vice president of marketing and entertainment at Disneyland. "We're not in a position to say who was responsible. But obviously someone didn't think things out correctly."
>
> According to amusement industry insiders and former company executives, the problems are the legacy of a brief period of uncharacteristic cost- cutting at the Walt Disney Co.
>
> After laying off hundreds of its own engineers and support staff in the early 1980s, the company decided that Splash Mountain would use "off-the-shelf" technology customized to Disney's specifications. The company hired outside firms to handle the project management and and most of the engineering and construction.
>
> Disney got more than it bargained for. When executives took their first test rides, climaxed by a five-story, 45-mile-per-hour drop through a briar patch, they received a rude surprise. Splash Mountain, it seems, had taken its name a little too literally.
>
> "I got soaking wet one day and had to go out and change my clothes," said Tony W. Baxter, the ride's executive producer.
>
> Months of Redesign. Getting wet is one thing. Getting drenched is another. Disney was concerned some people would avoid the ride if it left them dripping wet. "The tradition of Disney is that nobody is ruled out," said Baxter. "It's a negative if somebody says, 'You guys go. I don't want to get all wet.' "
>
> To make sure that doesn't happen, Disney engineers have spent months redesigning the log boats that ferry passengers through a fantasy world based on Disney's 1946 film "Song of the South."
>
> The original eight-passenger logs were redesigned to hold only seven people in an effort to take some of the splash out of the mountain's grand finale. A lighter, fiberglass body was used in the new models, which were fitted with an underwater scoop to help divert water.
>
> Other adjustments were made to help stop the boats at the bottom of the final 45-degree plunge with the least amount of slosh.

"Water squirts out to the side instead of straight up into the boat," said Don Newfarmer, a ride engineer with the Santa Clara office of O. D. Hopkins Associates, the outside firm hired to handle development of the flume ride. Hopkins is no longer involved with the project, although neither side will discuss the circumstances of the break."

The article indicates the situation that was made to the public. My colleagues added a bit more to the story. The flume ride vehicles were also getting "stuck" on some of the flume trough curves. There was another issue having to do with "ride envelope." The ride envelope is a space on the engineering drawings, providing for a "safety" area for the rider. With arms outstretched, there cannot be any protrusion of any kind that a rider could touch or otherwise be impacted. Disney maintains a very high standard for guest safety. The issue related to this was the ride vehicles proximity to the HVAC ducting overhead. Apparently, some of the installed ducting was within this envelope, exceeding the ride vehicle safety specification. These issues, among others, from what I was told, had been addressed in the Jeff Rochlis meeting on Splash Mountain.

To my knowledge, no Imagineer had been treated like this before. It just wasn't the Imagineer's style of management I had experienced during the EPCOT project. Jeff would find out soon enough, just how much power Imagineering had with studio management. He was out on his "ears," so to speak, not long after this Splash Mountain tirade. Just a month later, I returned to WDI on another Paris-Glendale business trip and learned this news. One day I was invited to an "all call" event in the outdoor lunch area where a special event was to take place. This "special" moment was performed, in the parking area between the MAPO and WDI buildings. The parking area was set up with a small stage and a PA system. I want to clarify, no one knew what was about to happen. The skit began with two WDI actors portraying a very unflattering "faux" telephone call that concerned a certain executive and his termination. As the skit played on, we could hear tires screeching and loud engine noise coming from the far end of the parking area, about 100 yards from our location. We could see it was a corvette heading straight for us. The corvette skidded to a stop just in front of our crowd, when suddenly, a very agitated driver began cursing out loud at us, using "finger" language and throwing something out of the car onto the pavement in front of us. It was a "princess telephone," if I remember correctly.

Completing this, the driver raced out of the lot with tires burning rubber, all the while shaking his fist and cursing! It was very funny, but I couldn't relate to the skit since I had been living in Paris. It was explained to me afterwards that this was a re-creation of Jeff Rochlis leaving WDI on the day he had been let go by the studio. I'll never forget the laughter and this end to a very unusual chapter in WDI history.

Perhaps Splash Mountain's project team deserved critical attention, I can't say because I don't know the facts. However, yelling, screaming and threatening is never the solution. I've seen it happen quite a bit in the TV/Film industry. Disrespect is fairly common in these industries. It has never been part of my management style. After the event, and from other stories I was told, my thought was that Splash became a critical issue because of its tie to a pre/post-opening McDonald's/Coca Cola promotion. The ride issues had created a delay for opening day. You can imagine this creating a huge problem for both companies! McDonalds and Coca Cola with a warehouse full of (dated) opening day promotional collateral, and Disneyland's promotional tie-ins were now useless. All planned and ready in advance. I wondered; what does McDonald's or Coca Cola do with their costly campaign materials? According to the article in the Times, it was settled and has been a successful attraction for the park since opening day. And that's how I heard about this story!

Each month, I went back to California for a week, stopped over in Orlando for a week and headed back to Paris. I would take a shuttle flight from Orlando to Miami and catch an Air France flight direct to Paris. I would arrive in Paris on a Monday morning (7am) and taxi directly to Le Pascal. For the first couple of days back, I would "hit the wall" with jet lag about 3:30 pm or so and leave for home. This was a very ambitious schedule and completely wore me out. Besides missing my family, it was a waste of time and project funds. But at Imagineering, it's only money! By the end of those six months, I had almost given up on the whole deal due to extreme exhaustion. I recall turning the corner at the terminal on one Air France flight out of Miami. I saw the 747 sitting there as I approached the gate, stopped and said to myself I've had it, this is too much. However, I collected myself, boarded the flight and prayed that this nonsense would end. It would, after three more months of this very challenging schedule. The good news from this effort? Our original cookie cutter estimates caught up to the new thinking. The bad news? The project was now exceeding the original budget! Badly!

My task, much like on the EPCOT project, was to develop as detailed a budget as reasonably possible. I was constantly on the run attempting to stay up with the design changes. As my trip reviews brought in new versions of the attractions from California, and scope documents were updated, my "Paris" estimates needed to reflect the new information. Fortunately, the documentation process started taking shape in A-4 binders in California. The reality of it being just me and my computer was not going to work! This was my first frustration and the beginning of my learning curve on a foreign assignment. That is, learning to do everything by myself. Dave, however, was aware that I was overwhelmed, and set out to get me the support the project needed. The budget we had prepared before we left for Paris was practically useless. These trips allowed us to validate the project budget, increasing costs from our original projections by as much as 100%. The cookie cutter attractions (Pirates of the Caribbean, Haunted Mansion, Space Mountain) were essentially the same rides, but Paris became the opportunity to adjust certain scenes, and more important, fit the exterior facades of each attraction to the European environment. This became a particularly important issue with Cinderella's Castle. I had to agree with Tony Baxter on his point that Europeans grew up with real castles all around them. Euro-Disney had to have a Fantasy castle that rivaled centuries of such "Chateaus" found in Europe. Another attraction that couldn't simply be transferred to Paris was the Carousel. A Disney Carousel is already a one-of-a-kind historically accurate ride. Paris had to have a statement, according to Tom Fitzgerald, a show producer from my EPCOT days. Tom became the show producer for Fantasyland, with

David Todd, the project manager for WDI. The cost of this and other attractions would have a huge cost impact on the project budget and future relationships between show design and estimating. Reported years later and documented in books about Michael Eisner, the costs of the projects would be over $3 billion dollars. Very different from our original $1.8 billion target! This historic note put an end to the idea "EDL will be an original cookie cutter concept!"

The most significant challenge I had to deal with in Paris was the studios "hands off" Paris mandate" by WDI. As I said earlier, EDL was taken on by LMB, the main purpose "to allow" them to manage the project in France. Except for the shows and rides, which were my responsibilities, the decision for LMB as project management was due to their European experiences in construction. In any event, that was the stated purpose. In reality, it was a disaster waiting to happen! I'll tell you how it affected me. For one, LMB had no experience in mega entertainment resorts like EDL! I knew this, but it was a mandate by the studio. I had no choice in the matter. As the only Imagineer from estimating going to Paris, I was under a separate contract and "on loan" to LMB for my duration in Paris. This placed me in a real dilemma! To whom did I owe my loyalty? As an Imagineer, I wanted and needed the support of WDI. As an LMB staffer, I supported Dave and the LMB crew in Paris. For months I walked a fine line between the two organizations and realized that my loyalty to the project would stand above all else! I needed to focus on what was good for the project. And with the estimating work being done in Paris, WDI's hands off policy for estimating support was very problematic! I began to feel very alone as my faxes, phones calls and emails were being ignored after I arrived in Paris. It was only after my six months of traveling to Glendale, that I experienced, estimating's mandate by corporate. It was on one of those trips where then, Chief Estimator, Steve Sock, told me outright that he could not support the project anymore. He had been told to keep "hands off" and let LMB deal with it! This realization hit hard. I was the Chief estimator for all shows and rides for EDL with a staff of one! I had to find resources outside of WDI or I didn't have a chance!

I turned to Dave Holtz as a third-party estimating service. If you recall, Dave brought me into WED estimating and was now the premier estimating consultant for theme park attractions. Dave's lovely wife Conradine was also a seasoned Imagineer. Providing her talents as a consultant purchasing and installing "props" to Disney attractions, and other International theme park projects. Being alone in Paris with over $500M in attraction costs and no support staff, Dave would be a big help! I hired Dave Holtz Consulting to fill this gap and had him revise estimates on the Pirates Ride and Haunted Mansion, among others. I was happy for the support. Going to Dave was very helpful because his estimates were "golden" in attraction estimating circles and accepted without question because of their detail and quality. This alone took away a lot of the pressure.

It was six-months before WDI show design, production and project management arrived in Paris. We welcomed this change with relief and renewed energy. For the ex-pats already here, this was a two-edged sword. Many of us were still having great difficulty with relocation, specifically issues as basic as having a home furnished and set up! We wished them the best and helped as much as we could getting them orientated.

The main challenge for everyone, at least at the start, was the metric system. This often-caused great confusion. This and the exchange rate (U.S dollar and French franc) made for some interesting meetings! We finally settled on everything being in U.S. dollars, while the drawing packages remained metric. These two issues often created 'second takes' in meetings when estimate details were presented. How many square feet became a common question? That's $100.00 U.S. for 300 meters? We really had fun with this. All presentations to WDI staffers coming over on business trips had the same travel issues. The routine did not discriminate. Imagineering business travelers would fall asleep (due to their jet lag) sometime during the meeting. We could count on this and enjoyed the 'head bobbing' as they struggled to stay awake. We could laugh and share their pain because it happened to us on the other side of the pond during our trips. I've seen many a staffer from WDI do this. Even Marty Sklar was subjected to this "jet lag" phenomena. There's nothing like the sound of snoring to bring out the guffaws in a meeting. Sometimes we would "startle" the person and conclude the meeting as sort of a traveler's initiation. We always tried to have humor. Marty, for one, always went along with the fun! These events alleviated stress. Everyone was in the same boat, had enormous responsibilities and working 12 to 14-hour days!

There was another management meeting called by Mickey Steinberg. Mickey was our newly appointed Euro-Disney V.P., responsible for construction. With no permanent furniture installed, the meeting took place on layered gator foam table-tops with sawhorses for legs. These were not stable platforms by any means! The instability of these temporary tops set up an unusual moment. Preceded by his so-called reputation, everyone was nervous. He supposedly had quite a temper. Coming from the hard-nosed world of construction no one expected different. Everyone, me included, walked on thin ice not wanting to experience the "temper" of Mickey!" The subject of this meeting concerned the use of languages, other than English, on the ride graphics and in film content. A decision made earlier in California, that all shows and films would be in English. Mickey was attempting to get to the bottom of who had made this decision and resolve the issue. It was holding up the shows and costing money! Around the table, it was pointed out that we were in France and perhaps we should have other languages? I'm sitting there thinking; why wasn't this resolved in the beginning. Discussion ensued with topics that included park signage and subtitles for films. Listening to this, it was clear, I was experiencing what I call the Disney "attitude." I never saw this until I went to France. "We're Disney and we want it our way!" Believe me, this was noticed by our French colleagues. I heard this often from both my French and British coworkers. As the meeting progressed, Mickey was visibly agitated at the very fact we were even discussing this topic so late in the game. And to let go of that frustration, he slammed his fist down on the tabletop, which of course startled everyone. This moment was shattered by the physical circumstances of the setting. Gator-Foam (layered with two sheets) is simply a foam product about 1/2" thick. It is not anywhere close to plywood, which is a stable platform by comparison. As Mickey hit his fist onto the table, everyone's bottled water popped up into the air about 12 or so inches above the table, all exactly at the same time. As if it were a scene in a cartoon (in slow motion) every participant managed to grab their own bottle before it returned to the table. At that moment everyone froze in their tracks, looking at each other to see what was to come next. With great relief, even Mickey couldn't hold back his surprise and amusement at this outcome. Mickey started to laugh at the absurdity of the situation, and we all realized that Mickey was not quite the hard-nosed guy we had heard about. The decision for languages was held off for later, although eventually the park included both English and French in the park.

This is as good as place as any to interject another memory of that Dave Mcquilkin personality. The Le Pascal offices had assigned parking for all executives. Dave, being one of them, had his space in front near the main entrance. We were up in the office one day and Dave came in fuming! Someone had the audacity to park in his spot! For anyone else, it would be reported and perhaps a note would be left on the windshield. This is not Dave's method of justice! He simply left his car parked covering the rear of the suspect vehicle and came up to the office. The fun part of this story was when the office loudspeaker system announced; "will the driver of the vehicle blocking the parked car, please come to the lobby!" Not one of us would dare turn Dave in. We just looked at each other for the better part of two hours and smiled, before Dave finally went down and moved his car! We never did find out who the guilty party was.

As our workload increased with activity in Paris, Dave began to understand that I desperately needed support. My first hire was a very sweet woman from Vietnam. Her name was Le Hang. She had been one of the boat people from Vietnam and I was really glad to have her in the office! I assigned her to be my assistant responsible for setting up a computer tracking system for show and ride costs. Her language abilities (She spoke fluent French and English) really helped, and she was a very diligent member of our growing team.

The second member of our team was a French local by name of Yves Valante. The hiring of Yves was an act of "stealing from

another company" on my part. My first meeting with him
actually began where he worked. He was the Project Manager
of show set construction at the largest scenic construction
facility in Paris, called Ateliers Ouvriers Reunis. Translated,
this meant workshop! With my need to get help, I decided to
visit the scenery construction shops. This particular shop was
the largest at that time and had an excellent reputation. Once
there, Yves, being the one that understood English very well,
became our tour guide. After the tour we all sat down with the
owner and his daughter, Odile. Odile as it turned out, married
a colleague of mine from NBC studios who went to work for
Imagineering too! Small world!

The scenery shop was quite impressive. Not only did they
service L' Opera, but the Moulin Rouge and the Lido night-
clubs as well! Yves was very smart! I could tell he had his
theatrical "chops" and decided to make a move to get him at
EDL estimating. I took an opportunity to pass him a note with
my telephone number and a request to see me. And he (thankfully) took me up on it! I'm thinking it took several weeks, but
I was fortunate that he decided to come aboard. He became a
very good coworker and also a great friend to have in France.

Staffing just kept getting better. One afternoon, Dave called
me up to his office to meet a very young man, named Aaron
Haas. Aaron, had come to Paris on vacation (with the hope
of working on the EDL project) and with conniving and per-
sistence, found his way into Dave's office for an unscheduled
interview. My kind of guy! Dave liked his "hoots-pa" and called
me up to meet this young man. After meeting Aaron, Dave took
me aside and said you need another assistant correct? I did of
course, but this seemed a bit unorthodox, after all, we had just
met! However, both Dave and I had what you would call "a gut
feel" about Aaron, hoots-pa and all. He seemed honest and
passionate and it would sure save us a lot of time searching
for a candidate! I knew I could show him the ropes (he had
just graduated with a University Degree in Construction management) even though he had little construction experience.
Long story short, we made Aaron an offer and he became part
of our EDL show and ride estimating family. Aaron turned
out to be a real asset to the project and particularly of great

help to me. Our estimating organization could not have been accomplished without him! He really understood computers and picked up on the various show and ride elements quickly.

The Paris office was very quickly becoming the center of activity for Euro-Disney. The organization included Imagineering project managers and LMB project management staff. The studio finally was beginning to understand that LMB could not do this project alone. Dave was always supportive and helped me in getting my signature as part of the authority to approve show and ride requisitions. This added step in the process was needed as part of a "checks and balances" process. I was applying what I learned from the QS team and my experience of managing $12M of scenery a year at my NBC job! The process we set up handling these requisitions, was cumbersome to say the least. It was not on computer and had to be validated and logged into the A-4 binders for each attraction. This process, if had to set it up today would all be done by computer.

My EDL documentation set up was an entire wall of A-4 binders, one for each show and ride for the entire project. There were five lands (Main Street, USA, Fantasyland, Adventureland, Frontier land and Discovery land) and each of these lands had anywhere from five to seven attractions. Not including the exhibits or themed retail that also required show and ride estimating. Combined it was over fifty separate estimating projects. Our wall of binders was a work-in-progress, with a daily barrage of cost implications for each document we logged in. Organizationally, these binders contained individual tabbed dividers, providing us with fairly quick access to project related estimates, cost to date issues and their scope! Not exactly a computer, but for 1988 a pretty nice system. Each day, our team analyzed all incoming information for shows and rides. This then would be entered into our excel spreadsheet program by Le Hang and Aaron. The system was set up to revise the estimates as new information was documented.

This team managed volumes of written data, validated requisitions and maintained the estimated costs of the project. The office crew maintained the functions of documentations and review while I kept abreast of what is known as "design creep." This is a term used on all projects at Imagineering. Essentially it is the difference between what the estimate was based on and what had changed during post design. Hence, design creep! The Imagineer's had their own faux vigilante group called the "design police" in California!

Working in Paris at Pascal was a great experience. Pascal was just off the A-4 highway and about 15 minutes from my home in the Village of Lesigny. My workday was extensive and averaged 12-hour days, six days a week, but I came to love the French work style and in particular, the extended lunch time. The French lunch is one of their big meals of the day. Sometimes it was hard to choose. (I know you have your pity towel out for me right now!) In our building the lunch facility was a company subsidized affair with wonderful haute cuisine available for everyone. It was not only cheap; but the food (expected by the French employees) set a new standard for us ex-pats.

There were also a variety of choices not far from our office. We could walk to a shopping mall called Noisy La Grande for fast food including McDonalds (which was an absolute must once a week for us ex-pats) and Burger King. Besides the Pascal cafeteria, our favorite café restaurant was the Restaurant De La Marne. Situated next to the Marne River (a tributary that connected into the Seine) the LMB staff had discovered a small cafe with superb cuisine and a river view. There was always wine and beer for lunch which did not help my "lack of a nap time" in the afternoon. The cafe was a struggling restaurant that 'grew up' thanks to the Euro-Disney project. When we first began to eat there, the menu was somewhat limited. The crowds were not there, and it was not yet on the EDL map for food choices! We really enjoyed the tables just outside overlooking the Marne River. In the two years I ate at this cafe, it went through a complete interior re-decoration. This by the way, is why Disney searches for new park properties under assumed names and with great secrecy! If Disney is buying property, the values surrounding the development just go up exponentially! The owner of Restaurant De La Marne, who always treated us like royalty, knew we would spread the word to our colleagues at EDL. An interesting part of the experience was watching the owner's son as waiter. He was maybe 8 or 10 years old and would come to the restaurant every day at lunch time to help his dad serve. I never observed any child labor law enforcement by the way. This became the life at the office for the EDL project. That is until the reality of what was happening back in Glendale finally had a change of mandate by the studio!

CHAPTER ELEVEN

The Lights Go on in Glendale

As we continued salvaging the transition from "cookie cutter" to new park design, a process that lasted for approximately 9 months, I received a call from Glendale from our Director of Finance Jim Thomas. Jim called to say said that the hands-off policy (Recall that Disney corporate had left LMB to their own management of EDL) had been removed by corporate and that he was coming out to Paris with his new V.P. of Finance, Andy Mandell. The stated purpose was to help us get things on track and moving forward. After nine months on my own and no return emails or phone calls from WDI estimating, you could say; I was skeptical!" Being nice, I let him know I would welcome any help I could get from WDI. Within a couple of weeks Jim and Andy came to Paris and invited me to meet them for dinner. Jim didn't speak to the past, but said they wanted to understand how LMB estimating was doing on the project. I sat there listening quietly to their story about WDI coming to our rescue. I thought for a moment and with good management technique, repeated what I understood was now going to happen with their help! I'll paraphrase what I said to them; so, we have been left here in Paris, resigned to our fate with LMB management. And now, after 9 months of being on our own, help has arrived? Do I have that right? WDI (the cavalry) is now going to come and straighten all of this out? Their answer, of course! I responded, ok, that's good and very much needed. But allow me to tell you the current state of our project, if you don't mind me being candid? Jim said, that's what we want! I said, it's a cluster fuck and almost completely off its track, and quickly bleeding profusely on the way to a major budget bust. I didn't mince my words. I went on. There is no design control that I can see, and from my view, the LMB executive project management has no experience in theme park construction. I'm glad that Imagineering has been given the green light to take back the project!

Jim seemed to be in shock. I don't think that he was ready for me to be so blunt! But at that point I had nothing to lose and everything to gain! We continued on the topic of what to do next. I suggested he get the support we need, to Paris, yesterday! Starting with estimating, followed by project management. My comments had just verified what they already knew back in Glendale. Jim and Andy promised that help was on its way and that was a promise kept. Within a few weeks, Steve Sock, Mike White and others arrived for extended business trips. As we plowed through the budget and estimates for the next several weeks, it was both exhausting and fun at the same time. I didn't see very much of my family because of this, but at last I was working with the talent for show and ride that understood what we needed done. Dave's QS team on the facility side, were spot on with the budget process and management thereof. It was the show and ride areas that suffered simply because there was only one of me and my three new assistants. All rookies!

Besides all the new help, perhaps the best part of having the Imagineering colleagues in Paris was their expense accounts. I can't lie! All meals were on them and of course, I showed them the most expensive places to eat. There were also benefits. Not just me, but other ex-pats took advantage of the hotel dry cleaners. We'd just hand our dry cleaning over to them, and they'd bring it back clean! Dry cleaning was very expensive there! Knowing that no expense would be spared, and that our expense reimbursement requests were not going to be questioned, made life easier. As expats, most of these "expense items" were not available. The expats seemed to all feel the same. We had been deserted, left on our own, and had a lot of pent-up frustration. Taking advantage of small things like the dry cleaning, was only one way of getting back. However, it was not just the expats. We saw other Imagineering staff on business trips that spared no expense either. Adding full unopened wine bottles to the dinner bills for example. Once around the celebration of French Bastille day, I had dinner with a few Imagineers, and a couple of very expensive souvenir bottles of "bastille" labeled wines went back to their hotel!

I was there with staff that joked about it. I am not condoning this type of action, just stating the facts and how we all felt about it. Good thing I confessed. I feel better!

But it was also very hard work! It was not a waste of nine months. My staff's organization of the individual document files and the entering of all show and ride estimates into the WBS system made the job much easier. However, we still needed to analyze and evaluate a new EDL budget. This is where I revealed my creative semantics estimating technique to Jim and Steve! As I learned from my work on EPCOT, my EDL estimates had budget line items for show and ride elements that didn't necessarily exist anymore. With only the three of us, and the flow of information as chaotic as it was, it was simple to leave in or change line-item details in the show and ride estimates. Sometimes it wasn't on purpose! Just too much information and not enough staff to organize it. I was really the only one who had all of the information stored, and it was all in my head!

In practice, before the cavalry showed up, EDL show and ride estimating maintained the current cost of the project for each scope of work. Estimating's budgets were used to compare cost to date (CTD) and reported as such, in all project budget updates. All of this under my team's management. In other words, we controlled the flow of show and ride cost information. A film for example, might be deleted for an attraction. Or an AA figure or piece of show action equipment was deleted from the scope. Anything might and was changing since we left Glendale. Even I could not keep up with this flow of information traveling back and forth for six months. This same process was used in the "core & shell" estimating, except with many more components. With the late change in design, we were always at a disadvantage. We were completely aware that a project budget of over $1B, the level of scrutiny or review was not high. Especially between cost and design. There was simply too much to track! The show producers knew what changed, the project managers knew what changed, but no one person, excepts me that is, knew the line items in the budgets were in our hands! Dave and I knew there were only a couple of places where the budget could have this "rainy day fund." And that was in show and ride!

Getting back to the help from WDI, the process of identifying budget items were reviewed. We dissected the attractions budgets and where I could, revealed my rainy-day funds. Many of these items were actually no longer in the scope of work. I was now able to demonstrate, that for show and ride, EDL's budgetary problems were not as bad as previously thought. At least as I understood them. I remember the looks around the room as I'd interject; "this may not be what it appears to be," as if something magical was about to happen!

Eyes around the room would get very big and a slow smile would appear on the faces of Jim and Steve. They'd respond, "What exactly do you mean by that?" I'd thumb through my A-4 binder and show them my documentation for a scope deletion or change, and how the current budget didn't necessarily reflect that scope change. This went on for weeks. When all was said and done, we had saved over $100M for line items that were no longer in scope! These "savings" however, were somewhat of a trade-off between what we now knew as the reality in show and ride, and the very significant cost overruns on the rest of the non-show scope of work. There is no doubt in my mind that without the savings I had created in show and ride, the overall project costs would have been much worse. We had guessed at the time that there was at least a $1B problem. Little did we know that later it would be reported (in recent biographies) that the entire project grew to $3 billion to $4 billion depending how overall costs were presented a few years after opening. Seems like I wasn't the only one not knowing what was really going on! In regard to my creative line item estimating, I won't suggest that Jim and Steve were especially pleased as executives of Imagineering. However, I know that on a personal level, they understood the circumstances and that the outcome could have been far worse. With the "cavalry" on board, and the budget re-calculation completed, the project began to take on more positive vibes and employee morale began to turn in a positive direction. This process included a substantial increase in meetings and accountability for each department. Frankly, it was just nice to have some colleagues I knew in France and their support!

With this renewed interest by the studio and the support of Imagineering, the project took on a new life! A very critical meeting soon after this infusion, was scheduled to review the total project budget by Frank Wells, then President of the Walt Disney Company. Not too much of a surprise to us because we were aware that Frank was the "green eye shades" to Michael Eisner's "idea man" relationship. Everyone was asked to have a complete detailed project budget prepared for this review. The meeting would include all of top LMB and Imagineering management including project managers, show producers, production management, estimating and accounting. A conference room was required to accommodate approximately one hundred Euro Disney staffers. It was a "big" meeting! There was a general feeling that this would be a 'comeuppance' meeting with the guillotine ready for anyone ill prepared. At least that, is how many of the French felt was coming. Everyone was stressed, particularly the French. However, they seemed more concerned about how to dress in the presence of Frank Wells, than they did about the review itself! Not a revelation, since everyday was a fashion show at the office in Villiers sur Marne. Euro-Disneyland work attire in Paris was far different than the casual golf shirts and jeans we wore in Glendale. My own collection of Yves St. Laurant suits would later become donations to our favorite charity when I retired in 2012. Since the meeting was going to focus on the entire budget for the project, there was also concern that the meeting could take several days. Many believed that a budget of over $1B, could not be reviewed in a single meeting.

Meeting day arrived, and the conference table had a seated staff of over forty, with standing room for everyone else. It was like a summit meeting for the heads of state in Europe. I was one of the more fortunate ones (I thought being seated was better than being a standing target) and we waited anxiously for Frank to make his appearance. Interestingly, I had met Michael Eisner a few times for the project in Glendale but had never met or actually seen Frank Wells in person. Frank entered the conference room and the French and Brits looked shocked! Frank Wells, the President of the Walt Disney Company was in a white T-shirt, jeans and a pair of tennis shoes. Added to this, the EDL staff were still getting accustomed to the use of first names as a greeting. Frank put that to rest with a "Frank" Mickey badge on his T shirt! This was a "class thing" in France, and it took me some time getting used to it! Little did I know; this would be a precursor to my meeting George Lucas for the first time. Of course; that's another story! Understand that the power players in the entertainment industry are not "the suits!" It's the people in jeans that you have to worry about! Just imagine the French and Brits reacting to this breech of fashion protocol. Mon Dieu!

Franks began the meeting explaining that he was here to sort out the budget status and would do so by asking specific questions. He mentioned that he would focus on particular elements of the project as a way to "test" the integrity of those budget items. Of all the possible elements he chose, he started with toilets! I wondered why Frank focused on this area of the budget. I realized after an hour or so of questioning, that he had a specific objective. As he went through the budget of all on-stage and off-stage toilet facilities, he learned in great detail how all budget areas were constructed. Perhaps more importantly, he began to understand what the design and construction goals were for the project. For example, he discovered that the toilets were going to be American Standard, imported from America. His response to the staff was? "Don't the European's have toilets?" A fair question. The operations specification was American Standard, he was told. They knew from their vast experience at Disney parks what the quality needed to be to withstand the rigors of use by millions of guests, 14 hours a day, seven days a week! Frank asked, were toilets made in Europe of less quality than those made in the U.S. of A.? Haven't French toilets held up to the test of time? Didn't toilets go back as many years as they did in America? Merde! He closed his query on this subject simply by stating the obvious. Demonstrate to me how the quality of French toilets is any different here in Europe! As Frank continued his focus on toilets, it was obvious that he used this methodology to get a sense of who knew their responsibility and who did not. It was easy to pick out those that had not, from the deadly silence in the room and the perspiration beading on the person's forehead under direct questioning. Under Frank's spotlight, one thing you didn't want to do is stumble on any question! After about two hours of Frank's in-depth education on toilet costs, the meeting was abruptly adjourned. Frank's message was clear. If you can't defend toilets (representing a small percentage of project cost) you can't defend the entire project budget. We left knowing that our budget needed scrubbing with an eye towards saving costs. If that meant changing equipment originally slated to come from America, so be it. We had our direction. I recall that for days after the meeting, Frank's casual dress code was far more important to the European staff than the importance of reducing the project budget. Imagine, arriving in jeans and a "T" shirt to a formal budget meeting in Europe!

Sadly, Mr. Wells died in a helicopter crash in 1994. He was the "cost" guy to Michael Eisner and I admired him very much.

This operational philosophy also was evident at one meeting in Glendale during my six-month catch-up tour! The topic was scenic murals (or drops in the theatrical vernacular). In the meeting I learned that all scenic drops for EDL were to be produced in California and Florida. I asked a stupid question. Why not in France? They invented it! I'm sure there are scenic artists in Europe that would be far cheaper? The response? Only Disney artists could achieve the quality desired for the park. Really? That was news to me. The real reason for this decision I learned later, was investment capital kept the Florida and California shop in business. Why not keep as many staff working in the U.S.? I really couldn't argue with that logic, but it does go to Frank Well's line of questioning. Why can't we locate these same items in Europe?

The project was moving forward, and LMB, an experienced construction management company, held a different view on project management than did Imagineering. This was an entirely new philosophy, and the Imagineering show producers and project management were introduced to a strict policy on budget control. The handling of project budgets was handled much differently in Paris and I was under strict orders to adhere to the policy! Here's how all this scrutiny affected me in Paris.

Dave came into my office one day and informed me that Mickey Steinberg had called a meeting to get to an understanding of the Carousel budget and my role in "keeping the budgets from the show producer," Tom Morris. First though, I want to address the elephant in the room. As Imagineers, Tom and I had our responsibilities to the project. Being "on loan" to LMB as I mentioned, placed me in a tenuous position with my fellow Imagineers. Tom was absolutely correct in bringing this to a conclusion with Tony Baxter and Mickey Steinberg. On the other hand, I could only do what was asked of me by Dave McQuilkin. Today it seems like a nonsense and an unnecessary issue. But each of us were correct in the action being taken at that time. For me personally, I felt bad that it happened at all, and should have gone to Tom afterwards and shaken hands. I didn't and I regret that. Today of course, after 30 years, one can only laugh at the circumstance!

It began with a budget review with the show producer Tom Morris. The attraction under review being the Carousel project. I was told that Mickey heard I had "held back" the Carousel budget "close to my vest." Meaning, I was reluctant to share any budget information. True, I did keep the budget on my desk and informed him that I was under orders to not provide copies. I prepared to defend our policy, the department and myself. It was a critical meeting, and I was now placed in a defensive position. One never likes to have to do this, but when you are backed into a corner, well, you just have to defend yourself! Dave McQuilken sat next to me for support with Mickey to my right at the head of the table. Across from us sat Tony Baxter and Tom. Mickey started with a story that set the tone for what was about to happen. It's a management technique I have used to this day and give credit to Mickey for this wisdom. Mickey reminded us of our goal to come to an agreement of what had transpired between us in the first place. He related his strategy in the following manner. I'll paraphrase. We are here today to get to the truth. In this meeting we will have Tom's truth, and then there is Carl's truth. The truth I am interested in, is here right in the middle (gesturing with his hand between us at the table) and that is what we hope to accomplish today. He asked Tom to relate his side of the situation. Tom said that he had come into my office for a meeting and asked to be informed of the budgets for various Fantasyland attractions, in particular, the Carousel. He said that I had discussed the budgets but did not let him see any of the documentation to support those budgets. He stated further that I had held the documents away from him so he could not see the information. Tony was here to support Tom (and from his view rightly so) to see this practice stopped, and for all budget information to be made available to the show design team.

Mickey then asked for my side of the story. I explained; I was sorry that this issue had reached this level. I began by relating that on the day of our carousel budget meeting, I had provided all budget information, which included all attractions for Fantasyland. I told everyone that Dave McQuilken controlled all budget information (per a management directive) and that there was a process for obtaining this information. The process was simple. All budget information was the responsibility of the "lands" project manager. It was their responsibility to disseminate this information to their team. Our responsibility was to make sure that all project managers had updated reports and full copies of any information, relevant to costs. Which we did! As required, I would be available to discuss anything in the budget to clarify or revise any issue. The issue of budget control and security was critical for the project and Dave had established this control methodology in Glendale at the start of the project. This directive was partly in response to an instance of failure to retrieve a duplicating task at a copy machine outside the estimating department office in Chastain. Someone had left a copy of the entire Euro-Disney budget on the copier. Dave's reasoning was simple. Budget information could be provided to outside contractors and vendor's giving them an unfair advantage during the bid process. Thus, as much as show design wanted their own budget copies, they needed to go through their Imagineering project managers. It was a decision that was out of our hands. I noted that estimating would always be open to meeting with show design and that this is exactly what had happened at our Fantasyland budget meeting with Tom. The next thing I brought up had to do with a tactic known as a "bluff". Before I tell you this part, I must emphasize, there is one very important thing you must never do when you bluff! Never bluff without being able to follow through, except in cards! A practice I learned from my EDL experience and use to this day!

I delivered this statement to Mickey. I said my assistant Yves Valante had sat in on the meeting in question with Tom per my request, to take minutes of what transpired. This was a common practice I used for any meeting where budgets where discussed. Concluding my statement, I reminded everyone of the cost information request process and noted (for Mickey and Tony) that Yves was sitting just outside of the conference room, ready to come in (with or without me) to relate his version of that meeting. I had done this as a precautionary measure. Finishing this thought, Tony responded that it would not be necessary for Yves to come in and that he would follow the policy. We all thanked Mickey and he adjourned the meeting. As I left, Mickey told me; "I have my eye on you." Dave reassured me that Mickey meant it in a very positive way and further, that I had handled the situation professionally. I've often wondered to this day, if only things had been different!

There is no doubt I was under a fair amount of stress prior to this meeting. Actually, I was sweating bullets! What with Mickey's reputation, I wasn't sure of the outcome. But after the meeting, I was convinced that all he wanted to do was make sure that we all had a grasp of our responsibilities. It seemed to me that if you could hold your own with Mickey, were prepared and spoke the truth, there would be no problems. If you came unprepared or didn't know what you were doing (showed any weakness) he would come down on you hard. I took away a good lesson that day, specifically, how to set the proper tone for a "non" confrontational meeting. Thank you! Mickey!

It was just when I felt that I was getting into the rhythm of the EDL project, that my circumstances changed. Many more Imagineering staff came over to help straighten out the various problems, and the work seemed to grow more intense and the hours longer. Although this helped the project, it didn't do much for my home life. Adding to my stress, after one full year and a half of relocation, we were over the relocation hump and finally settled in. I should have known! The minute I feel "settled in" everything usually changes. This proved true once again, with the delivery of a letter, in early May, from Alison's school district in California. For some unknown reason, her school district rescinded her three-year leave of absence agreement and changed it to one year. Her choice was to come back for the fall semester or give up 20 plus years (of tenure) in the California school system. This meant that Alison and the kids would need to be back by August for the new school year. Since my EDL project commitment had a three-year end date, I was faced with a difficult decision. I knew that Alison couldn't lose her tenure, and on that we were in agreement. But leaving the project at this stage, when everything was turning around, left me in a quandary. She has always been the rock in our family. Her tenured position teaching was permanent and allowed her to be home for the kids. My career, had always been "project to project." Allowing me the freedom to follow my "gut," and move around every five-years or so! This news was a complete shock, and a serious impact on our plans to stay in Paris for the next three years.

For the interim, all we could do was for me to stay in France and let Alison return to her job. What else could we do? The thought of being in Paris for another two years without my family was too much. Business travel is one thing, long term separation was another. I don't have the personality or the desire to live with the latter!

I worked out an arrangement with Jim Thomas to stay on the project for six months. This would provide enough time for someone to transition into my responsibilities. Even six-months was hard for me to do. As a professional, I could not leave Imagineering in this difficult position. My replacement, whom I will leave unnamed, was not perceived as a friend to my staff. This came from a luncheon week's earlier, where I introduced him to my staff after the "cavalry" arrived! During that lunch, the topic of language was discussed, and he stated out loud; I think the French need to learn English! Not the diplomatic move I was expecting. No question he was the right estimator to fill my position. And under the circumstance, the only one available to or willing to relocate. My staff expressed their displeasure at this change, and I felt very bad about what they might experience. I have never heard one way or the other how things turned out! As part of my six-month "extension," I had also worked out a travel deal to return to California at least once a month until my tenure in Paris ended.

Before Alison headed back to the states, we had to give notice to our tenants in California. They had signed a two-year agreement, and fortunately, we had a 60-day notice of lease termination clause. Alison would live with her mother for a time, not more than 6 miles from our home in San Dimas. The good news was that we could not have had better tenants. They would call me and ask if they could add new curtains to our family room or install a new sliding shower door. At their expense! They understood our situation and agreed to the notice. Who could ask for a better lease experience?

My situation was a very big deal for Imagineering and LMB. So much so, that Jim stepped in personally to see what he could do to keep me on the project. When Alison came back home that summer, Jim had her come out to WDI to see if he could persuade her otherwise. It was a valiant attempt, above the call of duty, as far as I was concerned, but he could not resolve the issue. He called me later and told me that he tried, but nothing was going to change. With that door closed, I proposed a plan to move in with one of the Imagineering expats. I could leave the house in Lesigny and open it to another expat. Relocation found an expat from Florida, assigned to the park's rockwork construction. It was a two bedroom flat near the west side of Paris in Vincennes. This would be my new home for the next six months.

It was my responsibility to transition every bit of knowledge in my head, organize the A-4 ring binders for each attraction, and make sure that the new Chief Estimator could hit the ground running. Thanks to Aaron, Le Hang and Yves, a revised computer spreadsheet was completed bringing everything current with the design level before my departure! It was a very long six months, ending with only two of those California visits.

Leaving EDL, was the most difficult career move I have ever faced. My emotions were all over the place. On the one hand, my obligations to family were pulling me home. On the other, my responsibilities, especially with the feedback I was getting from my staff, was stressing me out! I was second guessing my decision every day. My staff made it more difficult, when they invited me to a luncheon to say goodbye. I still have the "Mickey," they gave me, a hand painted crayon cartoon with a suitcase and their personal goodbye messages!

Flying home, just days before Christmas was both exciting and sad. Landing at LAX and seeing the family changed my attitude quickly! Alison had moved everything back into our home and had settled in after her one-year leave. A new Chevrolet suburban had been purchased, which I saw for the first time. It was great to be home, where another relocation adventure awaited!

But first, the week after New Year's, I met Jim Thomas and to be clear, what he had told me in Paris was still true. That there would not be any work for me at WDI if I came back. No new projects had been approved; all of the work was now concentrated in Paris. This I expected. Fortunately, I learned that you don't sit and wait for opportunities. I had responded, months earlier, to a former Imagineer who was now heading up a new group at Industrial Light and Magic (ILM) in San Rafael, California. On my first trip back after my six-month notice, I flew up to San Rafael, to meet the general manager for a newly formed design group to be known as "LucasArts." This group I would eventually refer to as "Imagineering-North." The design group was established to create new shows, rides and attractions, much like Imagineering does for the Walt Disney Company. The position I interviewed for, Director of Project Management, was for a new theme park project in Kapu Cay, Hawaii. At the time, I didn't think about why this group had been formed, but developed my opinion later about a year in to the work. In any event, I returned to Glendale, not knowing if I would get the job, but felt that the interview went well. My Chief Estimating experience was a plus! A couple of weeks before Christmas, I was contacted by the GM and offered the position. I would start my new position after the new year! It appeared we would be relocating up to Marin County, California! But as you know what's coming, that's another story!

CHAPTER TWELVE

Dues Paid (Plus Biz History)

I include this chapter to note that in the business of show, when you see someone who "has made it," it's not usually an overnight success! Reaching my position at WED as a show estimator, fits in this category! I had paid my dues, and I believe to this day, it is what Dave Holtz saw when he hired me at WED for the EPCOT project!

My 40-year show biz career started at Clokey Productions. I started as a model make for the Davey and Goliath animated television series. "Hey, Davey!" (couldn't resist!) This was my first job and it happened when I was in my second year at Citrus Community College.

My model making and theatrical life actually began at California State University, Los Angeles. I was the Production Manager/Shop Supervisor for the School of Dramatic Arts. "Drama" being the appropriate word here as my life and career has experienced plenty of it!

I had zero motivation to do anything in high school and for a brief period afterwards. It was the 60s and my energy focused on girls, surfing and love-ins. I had not gone to college yet but spent a year in Hawaii surfing and drinking. When I came back home, I worked at Chevron as a "Gas Jockey." During my off-time, I often joined my best friend (since 2nd grade/still is!) Steve Mikulka at the drama department at California State College in Pomona. Why? To meet girls of course! This volunteering lasted for two years at the Cal Poly drama department. It was also the beginning of my interest and career in live theatre.

This is also where I met Alison in the main stage "green room." Meeting her changed my life! I met Alison before there was even a hint of going to college, I knew immediately that this was the girl I wanted to end up with! In fact, on the second date I proposed. Alison though saw things a little differently. With my proposal, she responded correctly, that the disparity in education and motivational goals between us was a problem. Not exactly the kind of response I was looking for. But she didn't say no. Instead, she offered a challenge; "Get an Associate Arts degree (at a minimum) and she'd think about it!" I accepted the challenge! Of course, it makes all the sense in the world hindsight being 20/20. Alison was just completing her fifth-year teaching credential in English Literature. And me? I was still pumping gas full time at a Chevron station! The challenge then, became the basis for me to get serious about my future. I did not realize at the time; we were going to spend 50 wonderful years together – and still counting!

It was an awakening of sorts for me and I was fortunate to find it. Some never do! Long story short, I completed the challenge and graduated from Citrus Community College. With an Associate Arts Degree in Physical Education!

Completing my first year at Citrus, I segued from gas jockey to my very first job in the entertainment industry. I started show biz as a model maker at Clokey Productions. Art Clokey being the producer of Gumby and Davey and Goliath.

As I completed my AA Degree, Clokey was winding down with Davey and Goliath. I decided to move on to Cal Poly to pick up my bachelor's degree in Theatre Arts. This same year, I had a scare with the draft where I almost had to go to Vietnam! That cost me one semester. Fortunately, I didn't have to go because of an old football injury to my knee. At Cal Poly, I didn't want to be an actor (I really hate to be on stage). My interest was in scenic design and technical theatre. It was backstage that I had put my efforts into as a volunteer. I found out to, that my model making skills at Clokey Productions would come in handy. I was not much of an artist (in the sense of sketching and drawing). But my professors welcomed my model-making skills to fulfill my requirements in my scenic arts classes.

Among the models I built, my favorites are a Kabuki theatre stage, (demonstrating how this form might fit on a proscenium stage) and a working "half view" section scale model of the Drottningholm Palace Theatre. This model demonstrated what is called "the wing changing" system, complete with a practical working system. "Wings" in theatre terminology are the side masking panels for stage left and right. The "wings" on my model slid on roller frames located beneath the stage, (with the wings extended up above-through slits in the stage floor). These were manipulated by physical labor, exactly the same mechanism used to raise a ship (a windlass) anchor! The model demonstrated the moving apparatus (on and off stage and underneath). Interesting where life takes you. Just two years ago we went to Stockholm and I ended up giving the backstage tour at the very same theatre! I first learned how stage rigging hardware and its terminology developed while at Cal Poly. Much of it came from ships crews that volunteered their "shore time" to local theatres. These "mates" had created stage rigging from their crew experiences on sailing ships. Terms such as "man the fly rail, clew off the line, batten down the line, reef that drape and rig up those lines," among others, were common terms for a working crew on a sailing ship!

Cal Poly has a reputation of "learn by doing." The course work provided a hands-on experience in technical theatre. We used the latest manual dimmer boards, lighting fixtures, audio and rigging equipment. I'm not shy about throwing in a little theatre history when the opportunity presents itself. Theatre lighting technology has developed over time from what was known as "a piano board" to todays computerized models. A "piano board", slang for an entire wall of dimmers, was "operated" by several technicians! In 1903, the Kliegl Brothers installed 96 resistance dimmers in the Metropolitan Opera House in New York. Imagine a wall of dimmers with 96 individual handles! The term came from the way the technicians had to operate, or "perform" the up and down movement of the 96 handles. Hands, feet or all at once! Whatever it took! You may also recognize the term "Klieg" lights since I've brought up the Kliegl Brothers.

If you want a good laugh, (considering it was 1968) I can claim the assistance of a computer student's help on my thesis show! (Cal Poly being one of the few schools that required a thesis project to graduate-essentially a master's thesis). He used "punch cards and tapes" which were "fed" into the computer as the "program." There was only one problem. A lighting dimmer system capable of translating that program to the lighting equipment didn't exist! Now I feel really old! However, technology had arrived, and everyone believed "if it came out of a computer, it must be correct."

Working through my two years at Poly, I worked 16 hours per week in various theatre jobs, carried a full 12 to 14 units per quarter and spent 24/7 at the theatre department. The one job that I really enjoyed was working in the box office. This is where I learned publicity photography and film and print development in the dark room.

It was the spring of 1968, my department chair suggested I go to graduate school. This idea had never crossed my mind. I had to discuss it with Alison, since it was another few years of part-time work, not to mention, I didn't think I would be accepted. But I did take him up on his offer. "Mac" (our department chair) introduced me to the Theatre Department Chair at Cal State University, Fullerton. At this meeting I was assured that there were half time jobs available right away starting in the summer before my first semester. This provided relief for the job requirement part of the decision. And because it started my first semester, it gave me a head start with orientation to the faculty, staff and facilities. I could not believe I would be a grad student. Just a few years earlier, I was a gas pump jockey. Things were changing fast!

This also about the time that Alison and I tied the knot! I guess I demonstrated I could stick to my promises. We married in 1970, the day after Christmas! Don't ask about the date. It's a long story!

Alison continued with her secondary education teaching English Literature and she also took over the Drama Department. She also picked up her master's in English Literature from Poly! We were a team for many years at the high school. Alison directing and me doing sets and teaching the students stage craft. My work there was very beneficial because I could design anything I wanted! Alison just need the floor plan. I call those years my scene design immersion!

We also did one summer stock tour together. It was for the City of the Angels Opera Company. There were five different operas performed for the City of Los Angeles Community. Six nights every week. A new set up every night and only four of us on the crew. Our day began at 1 PM and ended usually at 2 or 3 in the morning. Plus, an hour's commute each way. It's a good thing we were very young!

Cal State Fullerton started me out as theatre manager for the three campus theatres. I was also a teaching assistant (in my minor area of television production) and a shop assistant building scenery. All of this fit into my "jump in and do it" style that became my pace for years to come. All jobs were on campus and contributed to my overall knowledge of theatre production. I always tell people that I started with a broom in my hand sweeping the stage. All of these experiences became invaluable later on in my career.

My crazy but very talented graduate advisor was Todd Muffatti. As my scenic design advisor, he was a superb model maker in his own right. Todd was a graduate from the prestigious school of theatre at Carnegie Mellon University. A top theatre arts University. His classes were always fun, informative and unpredictable. I recall looking on with envy at his many slides of architectural styles, all taken by Todd in the many foreign countries he had visited. Little did I know that my career would take me to many of those same countries and so much more! I hold much respect and appreciation for his guidance during my two years at Cal State.

Like Cal Poly, only with a formal written thesis requirement, I completed a production design for my thesis design project. The play was "A View from the Bridge", by Edward Albee. Not my first Albee play. I had worked on "Everything in the Garden" as assistant designer at Cal Poly. This production added to the over 30 plays I had designed or constructed between acting as my wife's scenic artist at her high school, Cal Poly and finally at Cal State. Los Angeles. All before I went to WED. Physically producing the project was fun. It was the drudgery of the written justification part of the thesis I didn't care for at all! The department wanted $25 words, philosophy and inner-personal sensory psychology.... da, da, da, da da, duh! The truth? "My design just felt like it fit the script!" The theatre gods interfered, and a job offer out of left field, would force me into doing the damn thing on the road!

It happened in the spring of 1973. Just six weeks before opening night of A View from the Bridge. I'm in the scene shop, my shop supervisor taps me on the shoulder and mimes phone call! Scenic shops are very noisy! I go over to the office and a deep voice identifies himself as Chuck Corson. He asks, would you be interested in being a production stage manager for a summer job at Busch Gardens in Van Nuys? The show is a Mark Wilson Production. Could I come in for an interview? I'm thinking to myself, "Mark who?" (This became a running joke later in the park shows) Confused to how my resume got into his hands, I agreed to the interview. All I knew at that point is that I never applied to a Mark Wilson Productions!

At the interview, I learned that Chuck had called an old buddy of his at Disneyland looking for stage managers. My resume, sitting on his desk, was the result of my attending a seminar with Alison some months earlier. It was 1972 to be exact. We attended a seminar at the Disneyland Hotel. Alison, being a full time English teacher, was invited, and I went along because there was going to be a presentation by Disneyland Human Resources. I saw the opportunity and I handed my resume to the HR Director. I left thinking nothing would come of it. Fortunately for me, this one did! Don't get too excited! It wasn't the ideal show business job just yet! Remember the elephant joke and the circus? (A man works at the circus taking care of the elephants. Rather, he has to clean up after them. Day in day out, until months become weeks then years. After a while, he's sick and tired of cleaning up elephant dung and he started to complain. He hates what he's doing and lets everyone around him know it. One of his coworkers overhears him grumbling and says, well, if you don't like it, why don't you just quit? To which our hearty circus man replies: "What and give up show business!?")

Soon after the seminar I was called for an interview at Disneyland. I was asked to join the graveyard shift clean-up custodial crew. Literally, steaming up chewing gum on the side-walks. I learned at the time of my interview; the "mouse" did not allow facial hair of any kind. I had a pretty cool handlebar mustache that was sort of my "trademark" at the time.

I asked, why would I need to shave if there are no "guests" in the park during the hours I would be working? Their reply, it's Disneyland policy! I declined and told them that my spouse would divorce me? I wouldn't shave off my "stash" for the Mouse! You can ask Alison!

Which brings me back to the Chuck Corson interview. Chuck said the show is called Showtime America and there was also a Magic show to be produced by Mark. It was a very short interview. It was as if he had already checked out my background and made the decision! He wasn't giving me any time to decide. I thought of everything that would have to change; finishing my thesis production design, work full time at a job 50 miles from home or school, and wrap up the written thesis section of my thesis all at the same time!

Accepting the job, it actually extended my graduation two years! My decision created one other "educational glitch" that was beyond my control. Because of the additional two years to complete my written thesis, Cal State Fullerton would transition to a University. This changed my degree from an MA to an MFA program. The MFA program was essentially what I had completed, but because of the delay, I received a Master of Arts in 1975. My theatre education taught me to organize, plan and execute. It also prepared me in that what I was going into was a stressful business. But stress in the theatre or any form of entertainment is a given. As they say, "What and give up show biz?"

The job started immediately, paid $200.00/week (a tidy sum in those days) and I became the stage manager for Showtime America from the first audition until the closing performance at the end of summer! This job was what would be called a "summer stock" position. But what an opportunity!

I learned of Chuck's history with Disney and who exactly Mark Wilson was later on! I also learned my resume had come from Chuck's replacement at Disneyland, who had Chuck's old title of Director of Entertainment. Chuck had called in a favor, needing a stage manager for Mark's new shows. It was that earlier visit to the Disney teacher's seminar that started it all. Proof that you should never underestimate where any opportunity may lead you!

On my way home from the interview, I realized the position was going to be problematic. I was already busy enough, but this job meant I would be crazy busy for the next four months! At 24 though, with my adrenaline working overtime, working in the industry I'd trained for would be a blast! Later on, I would tell friends, my career experience was like "being on a Carousel." Constantly reaching for that brass ring! And somehow, I would manage to get it all done. That's show Biz!

Showtime America is what is known as a "park show," meaning a production specifically produced for a theme park. In this case, Busch Gardens in Van Nuys. Busch Gardens was primarily a brewery. The "Garden" setting outside and adjacent to the brewery was for the public. It was a prime example of "bait & switch" marketing, and it worked. The public could tour the brewery, walk around the man-made lakes and enjoy the various tropical birds, swans, the flora and fauna free beer samples. Can you say Budweiser? With theme parks all over southern California upgrading their rides and attractions, Busch had to step up its game! So, management decided to transform its park by adding live show venues and other amusement park rides. Showtime America and Magic became the parks new productions, to open for their brand-new amphitheater. But I'm getting ahead of myself. Who the hell is Mark Wilson? And for that Matter, who knew there was a theme park next to the Busch brewery in Van Nuys? Like you I'm guessing, I didn't know either at the time. The San Fernando Valley might as well have been the other side of the moon for this San Gabrielite! However, I quickly learned all about the new park, and of the tremendous talent and contributions Mark Wilson made to the World of Magic.

With the amphitheater under way, the physical aspects of the productions, including costumes, props and sets were being readied. It seemed I spent most free afternoons hopping from one shop to another. It was during this effort that I was introduced to John Gaughan! John created and constructed almost all of the illusions and equipment for the world's magicians. Going to his shop was a special treat because you never knew who you might run into! I met David Copperfield there for example. John also had his own version of a security alarm in the shop. There were two locations with "open hanging cage platforms" for his half a dozen Macaws. They were very, very loud! John said that only once did someone attempt to come in after-hours! John's number one master carpenter was from England. I loved the work they were doing so much; I almost became an apprentice to him. It would not have been a bad career decision. Just different.

And of course, Showtime needed a cast. Mark brought on a very talented choreographer by name of Anita Mann. Who he had hired for other MW Productions. My first impression? What a gorgeous lady! First impressions aside, Anita was a very warm and loving person to work for! My work would benefit greatly from her suggestions and kindness throughout the entire experience. So, the first order of business was a "cattle call." An audition was held for dancers, male and female, at Mark's Chandler Street, North Hollywood studios. This area is now known as the North Hollywood Arts District. Hundreds of hopeful dancers showed up, and it was my job to help with registration, organization and whatever else was needed to keep the day moving. Anita put them all through their paces and it was a fascinating display of talent and not so talented performers. It was here that I learned that this is a very tough business. I also noted the difference between a classically trained dancer and one without that training. Something unexpected happened to me as well. Many of the auditioning talent were very "friendly," eager to get my attention. The Dancers tried everything in their power to get a "leg up" so to speak, for a chance at one of these positions. Little did they know I had no say so whatsoever in the decision!

It was a very long day of auditions and it was now up to Anita to cast the show. Within a couple of weeks, rehearsals started in a dance studio located in North Hollywood. It was here that I began my role as stage manager for Showtime America. My first task was to layout the stage floor dimensions with colored stage tape on the studio floor. This, a replica in size and shape of the actual Busch Amphitheatre stage. The choreography began and the show started to come together quickly. Showtime had a very talented cast of ten: five boys and five girls. Since the show ran seven times a day, seven days a week, it needed "swing" dancers that could allow days off for the troop. This brought the total cast to twelve. Dance rehearsals, a new experience for me, were fun to watch, but it was my responsibility to learn the show quickly and assist the art director with the set construction, prop procurement (fake pistols for example from Stembridge Rentals) and the logistics of getting it all to Busch in Van Nuys. This is when I met the art director for Showtime, John Shrum.

John was a very talented art director from television. Mark knew John from his work at the Magic Castle in Hollywood, where John was the original interior designer. (Mark was the headliner for the opening of the Castle and a board member.) I met John again later at NBC studios where I was the Scenic Operations Manager. John was also the art director for Johnny Carson. John is honored to this day in the entry lobby of the Castle with a special plaque. He had this very deep "whisky voice" and helped me with sourcing some of the props I needed for the show. With rehearsals under way, using the pre-recorded music track created in Gold Star Studios in Hollywood, it all started to come together. It amazes me to this day how fast the dancers pick up the steps of the choreographer. The dancers are maybe a half a beat behind the choreographer, duplicating the exact same steps in real time!

The show itself was a musical history of vaudeville up through modern times to the mod 70s. At Goldstar Studios, it was my good fortune to meet the owner's Dave Gold and Stan Ross for a "pick up" recording session for the soundtrack of Showtime America. Another first for me. I wish I had a list of the studio musicians at that session, but this is the scene as the recording developed, for the specific purpose of "laying down" the "tapping" soundtrack for the dancers. (The dancers performing live for seven shows a day, were not expected keep the exact tapping in synch with the music track) So, Anita and her dance captain (Her name was Marilyn and a tall gorgeous blonde) performed this "tap lay down" on a piece of plywood, on the floor, together in front of the studio musicians. Microphones were placed on the floor in front of the board to record their taps. As the musicians recorded, Anita and Marilyn tapped away performing the same choreography that would be used in the show. What I'm sure they didn't count on was the show (it was all male musicians sitting in front of them) and this I will never forget, was the wide-open eyes of the musicians as Anita and Marilyn tapped away! I'd say their reactions were particularly "animated" during the "wings" sequence. (The "wings" in tap dancing, is when the dancer "fly's" off the dance floor while the dancer "leans" forward") For tap, it's one of the most difficult steps to perform and is designed to "bring the audience "out of their seats." Imagine your arms up in the air and one foot leaving the floor at a time while the dancer leans forward at the waist. Kind of like a horizontal, vertical jumping jack with a swimmer's butterfly stroke thrown in all at the same time. Gentlemen, I'll leave this one to your own "mind's eye." I can honestly say that after this tap session, the men in the room felt like they needed a cigarette! Please no letters! It was 1973!

As opening day was now getting closer, I had to move out to the park to complete preparations for final dress rehearsals on the new stage. The stage construction was not done, the set, lighting and sound systems were also not completed. Responsible for these tasks were Keaton Walker and Brian Bartholomew. Keith and Brian were Las Vegas and television veterans providing art direction for shows such as, Julie Andrews, Cher, The Emmys and many others that are all part of entertainment history. I was in awe of their presence and wanted to do everything I could to make sure they noticed me. I was able to do that successfully one evening with Keaton. I managed to get his attention one all-nighter backstage and asked him his opinion on some of the scenic drafting designs I had done in college. Keaton graciously looked them over and I recall exactly what he said. " These are very precise and well-done drawings; how long did it take you to do them?" This was my moment to shine and I thought to myself, wow, he likes me, and he really, really, likes me! (Wait a minute, that's a Sally Field line-I'll get to her in a moment) I said, "Mr. Walker, these took me many days to fine tune and execute." His reply; "to make it in this business kid, you need to do this quality of work in hours, not days," and he left. A showbiz lesson to live by!

With construction behind and the show scheduled to open in three days, I did what any self-respecting theatre person would do. I stayed there and worked twenty-hour days, sleeping where I could, when I could. Heck, when you're twenty-something it was just a matter of doing what we had to do. The curtain goes up no matter what!

Finally, Showtime was ready and scheduled for 10am in the new to Busch Amphitheatre. Maybe a bit early in the day for a musical show, but it was what is known as a "soft opening." Meaning, there was some flexibility. But of course, everything did not go as planned. The lighting and sound systems were just not quite there yet! Nonetheless, the audience, having filled the seats by 9 am, was getting restless! The delay was becoming a real issue and we did not want to disappoint this first audience.

Our secret weapon took control. Don Frantz, a true showman saved the show! And now is a good time to introduce you to him!

Don was our company manager and responsible for both the showtime and magic shows in the amphitheater. Brought in by Mark from Hershey Park, Pennsylvania, Don was the Director of Entertainment at the famous Hershey's Chocolate Amusement Park! He had come in just a few weeks earlier where we first met outside the theatre. And immediately we hit it off and the laugh fest began. I'm not sure it has ever stopped. His bio speaks for itself, but the two of us literally started together in 1973 and have been friends ever since. I'll share a few stories later, but for this purpose, this is where I truly saw the real Don Frantz in action. Armed with a squirt gun and his own wit, Don walked out onto the stage in front of five hundred people and "vamped" (improvised) while we resolved the problems. You'll have to trust me on this, but it takes a lot of "Hootspa" (Meaning to have energetic nerve or to be feisty without violence using humor) as they say and Don with his jokes, his antics and his squirt gun, was able to keep the audience at bay until we were ready to go. All of that hard work paid-off and both Showtime America and the Magic Show opened to great reviews and ran through the summer 1973 season.

Although it became tedious in some ways (Try doing the same show, seven times a day, seven days a week) I learned that being a good stage manager also meant being a good "motivator." Sometimes I would grab the dancer's fingers when they came close to the "wings" of our stage. Sometimes I would "hang" upside down in the "wings" as they came off stage and sometimes, I would throw in the time tested "rubber chicken" at an inappropriate time, just to break up the monotony. The cast got back at me only once. I found myself "on-stage" as part of the cast. They dragged me out and all I could do was play along. I was quite embarrassed. I have always been a "backstage" kind of guy. I also found other ways to occupy my time and fill the long routine of the day. Because the production aspects of our show were put together at the last minute, I had time for plenty of fine-tuning! The kinds of things that could be done to make the show better technically. Take the show lighting for example. I don't remember the LD's (Lighting Director) name, but I do recall that he came from the film biz. In theatrical lighting, you don't see too many 10k's. A 10k is a size of light fixture typically used on film sets. It is a huge fixture with 10,000 watts of lighting power. Two of these, one on stage left and one on stage right were placed within 15 feet of the stage. They not only took up space (They're about 24" in diameter by the same depth) but they were bright and hot. The cast complained about this which is why I started here. The original design also had "9" lights. Nine lights are exactly what you can imagine. A series of 3 lights in 3 rows, one on top of the other. Again, a great fixture for film or television, but not normally used in live theatre! So, with time to spare in-between shows, over the next several weeks I adjusted the placement of the 10k's, the 9 lights and also the fresnels and lekos. (Fresnel, named after a French physicist, because its stepped lens. A light that provides a "wash of light". Leko, slang for Ellipsoidal, a long range, focused light.) In the process I made many adjustments to both the "gel" colors, light levels and many of the light cues. I also revised a few things on the up-stage wall of the set and spent hours figuring out why the audio system wasn't doing its job as designed. Once completed with my adjustments, it was the same show-but different! I recall Mark came to one of the shows about three weeks after opening and I sat with him in the amphitheater. Mark kept looking over at me asking, "What's changed?" The show looks really good! I explained to Mark that the original show had a few "minor problems," problems that I took upon myself to fix. It was a risk

I knew, but it paid off with Mark bringing me on board after the Busch Shows for a three-year run at Mark Wilson Productions. I'm fairly sure why there were so many technical issues. First the theatre itself was not ready for us to have dress rehearsals. Perhaps having film/TV designers creating for the stage wasn't a great plan? Whatever happened, I took it on and tweaked the show to make it look as good as possible!

While at Busch, there is one story I really have to share. It came about from a crew problem with the 4th of July fireworks show, also produced by Mark Wilson Productions. It happened on the 4th when the "powder" guys (the crew that assembled and fire off the fireworks) decided to get sick and were unable to come to work. This left only one powder guy to assemble, place and run the show! As you might imagine, this was a very big problem for the 4th of July. Busch had advertised this heavily and they were expecting a record crowd for the show around the famous Busch Park lakes. I was not aware of this until Don came up to me at one of the very early breaks between shows and said, "Come with me, we're going to assemble fireworks." Confused, I ran with him to the back lot where the powder guys had their building set up to prepare the show. Both Don and I were quickly introduced to the assembly process. This went on throughout the day and for me it was between shows. As we finally finished the assembly of the fireworks, we carted them off to the lake. We noticed that the banks surrounding the lake were quickly filling up with guests, setting their blankets and holding their spots for the nine pm. fireworks extravaganza. No pressure, it was only about 6PM!

With the stage shows out of the way, we realized that we were really cutting it to the wire, pun intended. We now had the task of getting the assembled fireworks into the lake. Of course, neither of us were dressed for a swim. But troopers that we were, we rolled up our jeans and waded barefoot into the water. OMG! Remember the ducks and swans I mentioned? Guess what is at the bottom of a lake where ducks swim? Duck shit! I remember the crap squishing through our toes and both of us looking at each other thinking-shit! Well, you know what I'm going to say, "and give up show biz?"

The pressure was on and we had to complete the preparation and make sure that the fireworks went off at 9 p.m. As we got closer to 9 the crowds around the lake began to clap and shout, "We want fireworks, We Want Fireworks!" I'm sure they could sense something was wrong. What with two guys wading all around the lake in front of them, in the dark, smelling like, well never mind!

Under this kind of pressure, we would attach each floating rocket assembly with its two wires, one-at-a-time, to the previously staged wires in the lake. We finally finished about fifteen minutes after nine and waded to the center gazebo in the center of the lake. It was from here that the fireworks would be "set off" to the music track. Today, all fireworks shows are programmed and set off by computer. In 1973, there was a board, literally, which had nails attached to one side and another nail on the other side. The "operator" would simply touch between the two nails and complete the circuit. Thus, the fireworks would be electrically charged and go off. All by hand and choreographed through the actions of the operator. Fortunately, although late, the fireworks went off, and the audience around the lake erupted into thunderous applause! We had done it! It was only after the show that the operator told us that what we had just done was extremely dangerous. Only licensed power guys knew the safety rules for handling black powder. We had no such license and went blindly, troopers that we were, to get the show open! At this point all we could do was laugh. Both of us ended on the banks of that lake, soaking wet, duck shit on our legs, laughing as hard as we could for a very long time. It was a great relief from the stress and the unknown dangers we had just experienced together. We truly became "brothers" in arms that day and remain so to this very day!

Since we are going to talk about theme park development in this book, let's look at a little bit of Busch Gardens desire to expand in the 70s! The Busch Park in Van Nuys was simply an extended "park setting" where visitors could stroll around the man-made lake and have a free beer. Until the new amphitheater and a few other attractions, it remained much like it was designed to do. However, as Busch saw its audience grow, a bigger plan was put in place.

Corporate decided to build and open a new "themed" area to attract more audience. The theme was a western style town with a few new attractions such as a film, shops and of course-free beer! And they invested several million dollars to make this section work. There was only one minor problem. Do you recall the "free beer" samples I mentioned earlier for the park? Well, the new western town was to be no exception to this marketing tactic. A great idea, but "someone" had neglected to notice that the new section of the park was "just outside the existing city boundary of Van Nuys." So, how did this affect the new area you ask? Well, there was only one main entrance to the new area. And because of the boundary noted above, a license to drink beer in the new area was not given! Security guards at the entrance, politely asked you to "finish your beer" because it was not allowed in the new section! This is what is commonly known as a "cluster (**&^%$)! It wasn't resolved at least, by the end of that summer to my recollection.

This lack of planning seemed to be the status quo for the operations management as well. For example, the general manager of the Busch Park wouldn't or couldn't (due to lack of funds she said) provide our shows replacement lamps for our show light fixtures. Although this was in the contract for them to do so, it never happened. As a dedicated stage manager, I found out (don't tell anyone) where they kept their supply and managed to keep the show lighting operational! Note: Read and know your contracts!

After the summer season closed, I acted as Mark's technical manager. As Don and I learned, Mark being a nocturnal person, worked into the wee hours of the morning, it wasn't uncommon to be called by him at three in the morning. Hello, did I wake you?

In any event business trips came up suddenly and became kind of a joke at home. "Carl, where are you going this time?" asked Alison as she rolled over and went back to sleep. For example, Don and I were sent to Mexico City to negotiate a new venue for both parks shows on a trip requested by a producer from Mexico City. He asked Mark to provide a couple of park shows at an aquarium venue just outside the city. Mexico City because of its geography is located in a natural bowl, which holds and prevents bad air (Smog) from escaping. I don't know how it is today, but then, the air pollution was terrible. I thought Southern California was bad at the time, but it was the first place I'd been where the citizens wore surgical face-masks. It was that bad. We arrived at the venue, which actually was an old and tattered tent structure. As we walked down the dirt floor aisles, our first clue of what we were getting into was the main power supply. "Power" consisted of a heavy-duty cable snaking its way across the ground, thru small puddles of water and ending up "attached" (really just a bare section of wire-bent as a "U") draped over the nearest utility power pole just outside the property fence. The lighting "board" for the stage consisted of an electrical breaker panel, which was located in a van parked inside the tent with its rear double doors facing the stage. Meanwhile, several poor dolphins were swimming in three small above ground tanks in front of the main stage. They'd pop their heads up and look at us as we went by, appearing to be pleading for help! It was so sad! From a show lighting perspective, all one did to light the stage was simply turn on the circuit breakers. Woooompff! Instant brightness! Everything came on with no capability of dimming for subtle light cue effects. On top of this the current "show" with the Dolphins, performed among other "live" stage acts. We didn't ask what kind of acts. The Dolphin tanks, I might add, had questionable filtration systems and God knows what kind of care these animals had.

The final insult to this entire fiasco were the cast accommodations. We were shown one very low-end apartment building nearby, but the producer wanted our cast to live in very small trailers backstage. Like a gypsy camp! Trailers that also looked like they were over 100 years old. They were in the same place out behind the theater tent, placed within the confines of the electric power cable snaking throughout the yard. My worst enemy would not have advised me to live in or perform in this venue. We advised Mark that this was a "no go" and headed on back to the states.

Back home in Hollywood, all was not lost! Mark and Chuck had negotiated a deal for two shows in Houston, Texas at the Astroworld Amusement Park for the 1975 summer season. The same productions we completed at Busch Gardens in 1973. Astroworld had just been purchased by Six Flags and is known as a "scream park" (a park that has many roller coasters and thrill rides). By contract, Six Flags was to build a temporary air building for the two shows. An "air building" is just an inflated building with turnstile type doors so the air won't escape. Large fans are used to maintain a constant pressure resulting in the building acting as a "balloon." It was a popular temporary structure during that time. However, it wasn't an appropriate building for the Houston climate. We were fairly successful in getting back our original cast for Showtime, with a few exceptions. One of our better male dancers had a bit of a problem. He was required to shave off his beard! (where have I heard that before). In the end, he relinquished his position, and we were off to Houston for the summer. Much like before at the Busch show, we had many problems in getting the facility ready on time for rehearsals before opening night. I had been there for several weeks by then and when the cast walked into the building one week before opening, they were in shock. Everything was in disarray. The audience seating was being assembled, (they had just delivered it because it had been delivered by rail to the wrong city) the stage set, rigging and lighting were only half completed, and the audio system was mostly in the box. Everyone wondered if there would be an opening night anytime soon. If you know the WED/WDI Park openings this is a familiar theme!

So, those of you interested in the business of show, I offer another prime example of the kind of dedication it takes to fulfill the dream! I, along with several other crew members and our Astroworld staff, literally stayed up for three full days and nights to get that stage and facility ready for opening night. I wish I could say that I did this without any help with drugs. That wasn't the case. Somewhere about day two, I was really dragging and wasn't sure if I would make it without some sleep. One of my colleagues "happened" to have what they called "whites," I guess it's was a type of caffeine or something stronger. I honestly didn't ask. All I knew was I couldn't take a break and had to get that show opened. The tablets did their job because I made it to the third day without any sleep and we were able to turn over the stage to the cast for rehearsal on late morning of the day of opening night. There was a side-effect to those pills, a story that turned out be quite funny as I look back on it. Several of us went outside to get some fresh air. It was a beautiful summer evening in Houston with the stars out and a welcome relief to the stuffy and humid air of the theatre bubble. (the A/C still wasn't working) The next thing I remember, and this is two days later I think, we left to have breakfast at our hotel (The Shamrock Hilton, which sadly, has been demolished) with our crew. I remember breakfast and that's about it. The waitress had to wake us up at our table because we all had fallen asleep. We left forgetting one of our colleagues who went "MIA" and was found later; still sitting on the toilet in the men's room, sound asleep. If you can imagine, "Sir, please wake up, you seem to have fallen asleep on the John!"

Later that day after about six hours sleep, I made it to the invited guests only pre-opening and the show went fairly well-for a dress rehearsal! Our efforts had paid off and the shows were set for the summer at Astroworld, Houston, Texas. By the way, Chuck Corson came through to check on things now and again and introduced me to some great restaurants in Houston. Don Frantz did the same and helped us keep up morale. Morale was important because most of the cast had never been away from home. Add to this, the weather in Houston was very humid and rainy compared to our beautiful dry Southern California. Astroworld (originally built on swamp land) already had high humidity and 90 to 100-degree temperatures. Constant sweaty palms and body sweat made everyone uncomfortable and lethargic. I suppose that's why the nightlife in Houston is very active after 10 p.m. It's really the only comfortable part of the day in Houston in the summer. Our show building didn't help that much either. Although it had air conditioning, the AC didn't work all that well for the space. On some evenings, we could swear that we had our own mini thunderstorms on the ceiling above!

If heat and high humidity weren't enough, how about a flood! I'm not lying; we all got to experience our first flood in Houston. When it rains in Texas, it really rains! Not the wimpy, drip we call rain in California, no, rain that comes down in buckets, closing down freeway over-passes-real rain! On that day, the rain started coming down like there was no tomorrow. It was in early June and I had to pull over on the freeway because the freeway overpasses looked like waterfalls. You could not see through them. When I did make it to the park, the first thing I did was inquire with park management if they were closing the park. Nope, partner, "It's just a little rain." We'll think about it and see if it gets any worse! Since I was the day-to-day company manager, I noticed that the grounds around the park reached "ankle level" on the guests. Still no shut down! I started to look for shelter for the cast. The only thing I could find was the executive conference room over at the management offices. These offices sat up on a bit of a hill. I told the management staff that this was where we were going wait out the storm, and that there would be no argument. I had to look out for the safety of all these kids. As it turned out, it was a good idea. The storm got worse and Astroworld management finally closed the park to the public. Sadly, from my viewpoint in the conference room, I could see my one-year-old Dodge Dart Swinger (that Alison and I owned) and the water inching halfway up the side of the car doors. I knew we were in trouble! Everyone in the cast was very nervous! When the rain finally subsided, and the water drained away, everyone was safe, but many of the kids wanted to go home. It took great effort to boost morale to settle down the cast. Another aspect of show biz not taught in the theatre arts classes!

While our "bubble" theatre was under construction, so was the construction of the "Coney Island Cyclone" a new wooden roller coaster. Astroworld had promoted this as the biggest and fastest and without a doubt it was a very scary ride! It was rated number one in the United States for many years after its debut. For my purposes, and to demonstrate a bit of my knowledge on ride development, I used to sit outside and watch the construction of this coaster and enjoyed watching the last few weeks of testing the ride vehicles before opening day. Testing went something like this. A group of about sixteen men would split the tracks, eight to a side of the track. (of the steeper inclines that the coaster vehicle would have to travel). They would send the coaster off to the first chain driven hill and once it left that first hill, the rest was all gravity. So far, so good! However, are you aware of the "fine-tuning" that needs to take place to align the tracks? The tracks are aligned to reduce "friction" to a point that the coaster train could do so on its own momentum. Thus, as the coaster train came up the steeper hills, the crew, already stationed on each side, would "manhandle" the train up and over the "hump." This was done over and again until the alignment was worked out and the coaster train was operating smoothly throughout the system. From my perspective, it was interesting and got more so when they started to add, "sandbags" as weight to mimic the human riders that would eventually ride this crazy coaster. So here I was, relaxed, taking a break and watching this alignment process, when I begin to notice "something" flying off the coaster as it rounded some of the turns. These "somethings" were the sandbags that were loaded into the train. I started to get a good idea of the speed and "g" forces that the Cyclone marketing "hyped." It was very impressive. I have to tell you here that I am not a big fan of scream park rides! I hadn't even considered riding on this thing. However, our management staff friends at Astroworld were, well, what can I say? Cowboys. They needed bodies and invited us to come over to the Cyclone pre-opening day and ride it. Don happened to be in town, and I don't think he was a big coaster guy himself. In fact, he said so. But those cowboys persuaded us to get on the ride. Oh my! I remember we were seated on the second train and I know I was scared to death! As for the ride itself, between Don and I sliding into each other, bashing each other side-to-side, we came out of the ride with bruised hips. We were a matched pair of black and blue! It was a violent, fast and after it was all over, an exhilarating experience. They tell me that they "slowed" it down a bit later because it had exceeded the "G" forces specified. Thanks for that, cowboy!

There was one other really memorable event that took place while I was in Houston. Again, road experience offers the best learning curve! It was the year Mark was to be given an award from the International Society of Magicians. The event was to be held in Philly, where Mark would perform as the honoree. I had nothing to do with it. However, Don called and asked me to get on a plane and come to "Philly" to help Mark and Nani. They needed a stage manager! I was on the next plane. The program was held at the Walnut Street Theatre. One of the original "hemp" houses. There's that sailor talk again!

The theatre was built in 1809 and the building read like a who's, who of theatrical history. It was host to celebrities such as George M. Cohan, Groucho Marks, Katherine Hepburn, Marlin Brando to name just a few. A "hemp" house in theatrical terms, is a "scenery fly" system that does not use a counter-weight system like they use in today's theatres. This theatre used sandbags to "weight" each line as they were loaded with scenery, lights or whatever was required for a show. If you could see this system, you'd swear you were looking up into the rigging of a large square-rigger. During the "rigging" process for Mark's act, I went up into the "fly lofts" where I had to communicate our needs for the show to the crew. These guys were strictly union types and gave young guys like me the "rookie" treatment. At the end of the day though, they helped me with all my rigging needs and as a special treat took me to their private "break room" which is a story in itself.

The rigging crew break area was a large room situated off of the "fly rail." The fly rail is where flying scenery is hauled up and down off the stage floor and tied off "at the rail". A stage level rail where they used "battens." Entering the breakroom, I witnessed an entire collection of Playboy Magazine! Each wall papered with Playboy Magazine covers, starting with the very first issue in 1953 to the latest publication. The stagehand that gave me this tour was obviously filled with pride at the collection and proudly walked me through each edition. I had never seen anything like it since. (Sadly, the Walnut has told me that this wallpaper no longer exists another piece of history lost to political correctness)

So, this show was my very first professional live "cue call" I had ever done. Sure, I had done close to 1,200 Showtime America and Magic Shows at the parks, but this was an inter-national audience consisting of magicians with Mark Wilson as the guest recipient of the award. Was I nervous? You bet your bippy! With only a short walk thru rehearsal, I prayed that everything would go as planned. I made my way up to the light booth at the rear of the house, met the light board and audio operators and checked my headset "com" line. (Short for communications line) I was ready to "hurl" my guts out I was so nervous. The guys in the booth tried their best to calm me down, but it was now time to do or die. I didn't intend to die. I called the first queue and the main act curtain opened, the lights went up and Mark and Nani did their big illusion to open the show. The magic, choreography, and the costumes were spectacular, and the audience loved it. The next sequence was set for Mark to perform some "close up" magic for the audience. My visual "cue" was Mark taking off his jacket. That was my cue to close the main act curtain so Mark could perform in front of it. As I stood their frozen to my spot, I didn't remember this visual prompt! Mark covered for me well, made some joke that appeared to be part of the act, but I knew that this was directed at me. If Mark could have said it straight, he might have said, Carl! Wake up! You're supposed to close the curtain here and give me a "spot" for my close-up stuff! Yes Sir! Point taken.

Fortunately, the audience never caught on to the mistake and Mark's closed his act with some very wonderful close-up magic. It was my privilege to "call the live show" for Mark's performance. Lesson learned! And as soon as we had packed up everything, I left the theatre promptly for some fresh air!

So where do you go when it is 1 o clock in the morning, and you are on the road? Maybe here is where I take a moment to give you a heads up on the road experience? Road shows are not all fun and games. Very rarely do show schedules allow for rest and relaxation. Theatre is a 24/7 business and demands a total commitment. This includes giving up holidays, weekends and other special events like family! It's a choice one makes like anything else and you have to decide if it's worth it. I often saw the sights in the cities I travelled to at off hours. We simply did not have time to go to local sites like a typical tourist. That doesn't mean I missed these kinds of experiences. For example, in Philly, I saw the Liberty Bell (outside the room where the Declaration of Independence Hall was signed) at two a.m. in the morning. On the positive side, there were no crowds. In kind of a strange way, the street lighting coming through the window made my observation into the chamber, a one-of-a-kind experience. The actual Liberty Bell was encased in heavy glass in 1976 and was in a park setting in front of Independence Hall. I understand it is inside today. Another strange coincidence happened on this trip. We stayed at the Bellevue Stratford Hotel. It was just after we left, that the first case of Legion Aires disease broke out at that very hotel! That was good fortune for us!

Once back to Houston and my normal duties as production stage manager, I made it a point to visit the audience during the shows to check out not only the show but to pick up on what the audience might be saying. It was during one Magic show I happened to sit behind a family. I sat there and observed the show for a while, but when I was about to leave, I overheard the "father" telling his smaller children, in step-by-step detail how each "illusion" was performed. I was shocked! I could not believe his children were having their "magic" taken from them. It was the first (and last time) I ever did something like this but felt strongly about "the magician's secrecy oath" I had taken. I leaned forward and told the man he was destroying his children's world of fantasy. He didn't like my comments very much, but as I returned backstage, I hoped maybe he would let his kids have a childhood. I'll never know how that all worked out, but I sure felt better!

Our two shows were operating fourteen times a day, seven days a week. As the summer came to an end, so did our run at Six Flags Park. I packed everything up to store in an on-site warehouse at Astroworld and came back to Los Angeles in late September. I flew back to Houston in December to load up a rental truck to bring back all of the show's scenery and props. It was on this trip that I learned the importance of checking the weather of the place you are traveling to. (for you would be road warriors) It didn't cross my mind that Houston, with its high summer temperatures and humidity, would be cold in December. It was! Houston was 28 degrees when I landed, and I had not packed any warm clothes. Dumb! Showtime was a personal record in stage management for me. I figured out later that between the two summers of Showtime America alone, I had stage managed over 2,500 shows! Working for Mark also involved the planning of new shows. Our next adventure was to get ready for a new magic show in Orlando, Florida. This show was scheduled to perform in a brand-new theatre (here we go again) in a new park called "Circus World Showcase." Near Orlando Florida.

Circus World Showcase was a venture created by the Feld Brothers (Kenneth, who I would meet later in my career at Industrial Light and Magic/ILM) and opened in 1974 with a 27,000 square foot "look alike" circus tent structure. Located in Haines City, the building was large enough for the 3 Ring Circus acts performed by the Barnum & Bailey troop which the Feld's now owned. The new park included an "Imax" theatre and a new theatre for Mark's magic show, which was next to the IMAX space. The IMAX format created by Canadian's Graeme Ferguson and Roman Kroitor. This format started as "multiscreen" (Cinerama, a three-camera system was introduced by Fred Waller in the early 50s. Disney's Ub Iwerks, with Eastman Kodak, felt it could be a full circle and introduced it to Disneyland in 1955) in 1967 and through their technical creativity, evolved into the IMAX format (a horizontal 70 MM Format) in 1970. The Imax film, produced specifically for Circus World, was of course, all about the circus. Go figure! Besides the super large screen format (72'0" X 52'8") there was this very large film projector in the booth. This projector supported by large "film loop" cabinets "fed" the projector. The film (at 70MM) was twice the width of the standard 35 mm format and moved through a "jewel like" mechanism past the lamp of the projector. Remember this was the early 70's and this was a very spectacular way to see a moving image on a screen. Speaking of the screen, the film was viewed in the Circus World facility standing, on "raked" foot platforms with "lean rails." What all this means is that everyone in the audience was very close to the projection screen, watching lions, elephants and other circus acts this close was a really fun and different film experience. The IMAX theatre created only one problem for our show and that was "audio bleeds". Movie theatre sound systems were just coming into the "boom box" format to fit the larger screen format experience.

My main focus was adding new stage rigging to this new performing space for the magic show. We had a few weeks to do so, where I had some break time and the privilege of walking around the circus grounds "backstage." It was a special thrill seeing the various animal acts rehearsing, the clowns practicing and the general hubbub of the circus back-lot. It was a very special privilege to meet Axel Gautier, who was on-site training the elephants at that time. It would be years later where we visited the Barnum Circus Museum in Sarasota, Florida, that I was able to close my "connection" with Circus World in a "memory book" located in the museum.

My main purpose at Circus World was to assist in the installation of "fly rigging" for the show. One illusion, known as "Azrah," required the new rigging. This production became my first adventure of cross country driving to deliver scenery. It also provided an opportunity for Alison and me to drive as a team. It was spring and we couldn't pass up this chance to see the southern states from the road, together. We planned the trip so we wouldn't be in a rush with plenty of time to stop and see some of the sights along the way. I wish we had taken photos because Alison (whose day-to-day driving vehicle was a 1600 Datsun sports car) soon learned what it takes to be a "trucker." At best, it's very uncomfortable and perhaps the worst, we didn't have satellite radio, so we listened to many bible belt stations along the way! But troopers that we were, we went with the flow and feasted at the best truck stops along the way (not kidding) and learned how to "draft" up close behind the big rigs (only once being "dusted") for speed. Dusted being a big rig driver's revenge tactic for drafting too close to their rigs! Can you say, "Diesel exhaust?" By the way, if you have never crossed Texas in a truck, I recommend-Don't! At just over 1,000 miles, it seems that you will never, ever get across the state of Texas!

The week had been an adventure for us. We had traversed the road from California to Orlando by truck, stopped in New Orleans overnight, for oysters, and dessert in Pensacola on another night for key lime pie! What is more important, we had done it together. That was the best part. Arriving in Haines, Alison departed, (by air) two nights later. We just had to go to Disney World! Chuck Corson arrived and treated me to dinner at a Hyatt's restaurant outside of Haines. Chuck was like that, always taking you to lunch or dinner at someplace special. He seemed to know all the great places to go no matter where we were. This dinner though, is where Chuck introduced me to Bass beer. Just two guys drinking beer and getting to know each other. I understood later on that he had a son about my age, perhaps we bonded because of it? At least that's how I felt.

The following day after spending the night in my new "head-quarters," a Holiday Inn, I drove the truck across the street to where Circus World was located. Pulling onto the site, it was as if I was right in the middle of that famous MGM movie "The Greatest Show on Earth." There was a variety of animals in various stages of their training. Clowns, well, being clowns. And a practice trapeze rig in full use with performers training! An entire wonderful circus rehearsing right there in front of my eyes. This new park would be known for its signature building, a very large structure that resembled a real circus tent. It was cavernous in volume, fully large enough to hold a classic Barnum and Bailey three-ring circus!

Very near this main building, was our loading dock used to offload into our theatre and also the Imax theatre. Talk about starting from scratch, our "theatre" consisted of a stage platform with the same "lean rail" raised audience platforms as the Imax. The room itself was built like a silo. A bitch of a configuration to add the required new theatrical rigging for our show as we soon found out! To understand the complexity of this space, imagine a room, shaped as a decagon (a 10-sided room, with a conical ceiling) starting at 45 feet from the stage. A very odd room to rig a theatrical fly system! I was there to meet an art Director by name of Bill Bohnert.

Working with Bill was a lesson in stage rigging that I never came close to learning in college. Working with a famous Art Director like Bill, was amazing! There was virtually no wing or upstage space anywhere. The stage itself measured about 20'0" deep by 40'0" wide. Downstage, the audience drop was about four feet, stage to floor. Circus World decided to place the dressing room (one room for the cast) under the stage. We learned quickly that the stage deck itself was a major problem. The deck was made up of 3/4-inch plywood (one single layer) and had a "spring" to it. This floor was great for dancing but did not provide a solid surface to handle a 40"0" tall rolling scaffolding, let alone a choreographed show!

Our main task was to provide the rigging for the shows "flying scenery" and illusions. The real problem with adding this rigging system started with the 45'0" ceiling. How the heck would we get up there? If you recall, I described the audience section as a "stepped" platform with "lean rails." There was a minimum "aisle" in front of the stage, but not wide enough for a "mechanical man lift." So that was out. Our only choice was to build a scaffolding system that would go to the height we needed, plus that could move both up and downstage, and left and right onstage as needed. We set up the rented scaffold and went about "marking" the ceiling for our "unistrut" rails. Unistrut is a "U" shaped rail system with a specific type of "hanger hardware" that slides along the inside of the rail. Very much like today's track lighting. At any point on the rail you can "lock" the hanger in the position required. The Unistrut rail itself, was to be attached to the "I" Beam ceiling rafters creating a type of "grid system" directly over the stage. So, understand this image. Bill and I, (it was just the two of us) 40'0" above the stage ready to hang the unistrut. Where's OSHA when you really need them? Very methodically, Bill, used a "plumb bob" to "mark" the stage floor below, matching its corresponding hanging point from the unistrut above. We started "upstage" hanging the first unistrut rail at the point where the conical ceiling was at its lowest. At the beginning everything was fairly easy to reach and although it was tedious work, we slowly progressed the assembly. However, I failed to mention one small detail. Do you remember we were doing this work 40'0" above the stage on a scaffold with wheels? The wheels didn't help stabilize the scaffolding, but they were not the root of the problem. It was the "give" and resultant "bounce" of the 3/4-inch plywood stage floor. This "bounce" magnified itself until it reached the 40-foot height of the scaffolding platform, causing the scaffold to "sway" back and forth. It did this all the while we were on it. And sway we did! For twelve hours a day or more, we worked on top of that rolling scaffolding to attach the stage rigging. The constant swaying finally became too much to bear. One afternoon (I remember this clearly) Bill and I looked at each other simultaneously, scrambled down the scaffold and hightailed it out to one of the outside loading docks. We lay down on that solid cool concrete, a huge contrast to all of that constant motion and a very welcome respite. It was almost better than drugs! We lay there, for some time, just peering up at the clear blue Florida sky, with its fluffy white clouds, Whoa! Wait a minute! The fluffy white clouds were also moving! It was like being on a boat for hours at sea.

We kept at it though and finally after several days of rigging we came to our last unistrut rail. Of course, nothing is ever simple, and this rail would be the hardest to attach. The last rail was "downstage" of the scaffold and just-out-of-our-reach. We both attempted to reach out over the railing of our scaffold platform, but we didn't much like hanging over 45'0" of dead airspace. Neither of us were that crazy! However, we were in the Circus, right? There had to be somebody out there who could perform this unnatural act of high wire, dare devil craziness? And "somebody" was there for the asking. He was a supervisor responsible for the maintenance of the facilities (I wish I had his name to give him the recognition he deserves) and It just so happened that his previous line of work involved climbing to the top of radio tower antennas and high-tension utility towers! Just to change the light bulbs. We had found our guy! Surely a mere 45'0" was nothing to this seasoned and fearless climber of towers of terror! Once we showed him the issue, he said no problem, glad to help, and scampered up the scaffold. Tools in hand and while leaning (almost at a 30-degree angle) and holding on to the scaffold railing by (literally) one foot, he attached our last rail and hangers successfully to the very top of the cone ceiling! Bill and I could have kissed the ground he walked on and offered to take him to dinner as a thank you. Nope, "just part of the job and glad to do it!" Now that's true Circus mentality. The show must go on!

The next nine stories, I've titled them tell them individually, are all part of my "Dues Paid" experience!

Burger King. Using his "celebrity" as the "hook," MWP (Mark Wilson Productions) had an account with Burger King. I spent some time with Don coming up with ideas for "giveaways" at their retail stores. It was an interesting perspective to figure out how to turn Burger King hamburger wraps, straws and other Burger King packaging into Magic Tricks. Mark also introduced the traveling "Burger King" promotion. MWP had five vans for as many locations nationwide, they performed, from school to school, doing a little magic show and handing out free burger coupons. The show, complete with "The Burger King" in costume and a throne, played to thousands of kids and was a very successful marketing campaign. Don was responsible for this event to and learned "sleight of hand" very quickly so he could teach the five area "Burger Kings." The idea being that the children would go home; "Mommy, Daddy," I have a coupon for a "free" hamburger at Burger King." Of course, the adults and other family members did not. The same idea applied to Apple later. Except those kids grew up with that brand imprinted in their minds and were programmed to buy a Mac product. I love American Capitalism!

Big and Little Snuffy. There was one event that is very special to my experiences at MWP and that was the National Fire Week Safety Campaign. Mark had contracted to "kick off" this National event with a "Magical" fire truck called "Snuffy." Snuffy was to be constructed using a standard golf cart chassis and was designed and built by John Gaughan, Master Builder of Illusions and stage equipment for the world's magicians. I met John for the very first time at his shop in Glendale, CA. It must have been 1973. The shop, a very large expanse of old warehouse located near the railroad tracks along the Los Angeles River, was John's studio and storage facility. As the full-size golf cart version of Big Snuffy progressed, Mark wondered how he would be able to achieve the same experience of a talking Snuffy in the smaller studios in places like New York City. Big Snuffy was to appear on numerous television programs nationally, and Mark needed a fallback position for the unique studio access problems. Remembering my experience with model making, Mark asked; "Could you produce a working, drivable model of Big Snuffy?" I said, the issue wasn't the build, the real problem was the limited time. We had less than two weeks before Mark kicked off the event on national television in Miami, Florida. I was a trooper for sure but didn't think I could pull this one off by myself. I asked Mark to give me a few hours and I'd get him an answer. My "go to" guy was Doug Beswick, although it was several years later from the time, we had worked together at Clokey. Doug, due to a downturn in the effects business had gone back to his "roots" as a metal fabricator. A career he could have easily excelled at! He had a working metal lathe shop built in his garage in San Fernando Valley and was fabricating special orders for various manufactures. As I broached the idea to Doug, his eyes lit up and with some trepidation, agreed to the task and the schedule. That's the "lure" of the show biz bug! There's always "one more exciting project" to tempt you away from that normal 9 to 5 job. Our first task was to create something on paper, duplicating little Snuffy from the full-size version to an 18" high model, measured at the boiler stack. We decided to use an available gas-powered remote-control racecar chassis for the basis of our model. Thanks to Doug, he thought about the various surfaces we might have to drive on and calculated the torque required for the drive system. We anticipated driving little Snuffy on carpet, asphalt and tiled surfaces. Carpet would give us the most trouble as I would discover the hard way, later. We had to figure out how we would do the "custom" wire wheels. Fortunately, we found the wheels in a catalog and ordered them for express delivery. Doug and I broke up our tasks to facilitate the very limited schedule. I took on all exterior features while Doug concentrated on the drive and "show action" systems. Specifically, little Snuffy's moving mouth on the grill, the turning headlights as his eyes, and his firefighter's hat that needed to flip up and down. This was one of my toughest assignments to date in the short span of my entertainment career. It was also not the first time I would be asked, "to pull a rabbit out of my hat." Pun Intended!

Little Snuffy slowly started to take shape. Doug's idea of converting to electric power took care of any noise issues in the television studios. Each of the show action features was powered by a small electric "servo" motor, that mechanically moved these features left to right, up or down, or gave Snuffy the ability to drive forward or backward and turn left or right. All of this was accomplished by remote control. Imagine fitting all of these functions into that small chassis! With Doug's consummate professionalism, and his technical skills, he did an absolutely fabulous job of creating a very functional little Snuffy. While Doug completed the chassis, I created Snuffy's fire truck body. Starting with the boiler, I hand turned the top from bass hardwood. It was glued in layers and turned on a wood lathe. The boiler stack is a Quaker Oats cereal box, covered in faux leather. The rest of the body was made from bass hardwood, except for the fenders that were plastic. We cut the plastic into strips, put the pieces in an oven to bake over a round wood form and voila, curved fenders. A bit of shaping on the sander and they were ready for paint. This was Doug's idea, in case the model hit something, they would "pop" off. Good thinking, as I would later learn. Several coats of fire engine red paint were air sprayed from Doug's small model sprayer, with Doug's kitchen oven providing "heated drying" between coats. The finished model stands about 18" high at the boiler and was about 24" long by 8" wide. The evening before my red eye flight to Miami, I tested little Snuffy on Doug's concrete garage floor, having less than an hour to practice with the remote functions. I hand carried Snuffy in a custom road-case built by Anvil Cases, a well-known manufacturer of "road show cases" for rock musicians. It had a foam liner that turned out to be a wise choice for the amount of abuse it would take on the road over the next two weeks. Leaving Doug with my very grateful appreciation, I was happy to learn that this event seemed to coincide with the industries resurgence in special effects. Not that Doug needed any new credentials! It's simply a feast or famine business! Sometimes you have to resort to plan B! Please have a look at all the fantastic contributions Doug made to the industry in the acknowledgments!

I arrived in Miami the next morning and went straight to Mark's hotel suite. The first thing Mark asked; does it work? With confidence, I answered, absolutely! I took Snuffy out of the case and placed it on the kitchen area floor and immediately drove little Snuffy into the baseboard of the kitchen cabinets. The plastic fenders worked as designed! I assured Mark that this was planned for and that I could glue the broken piece back on in minutes, having brought a full road kit for such emergencies. I moved little Snuffy to the carpet where it was a bit safer. The model did OK on the carpet, but not great. Fortunately, there were no carpeted surfaces in the studios for the rest of the trip.

Snuffy's debut was on a live morning news program. I don't recall the program, but it was very much like the Today show but on a local level in Miami. The news anchor would interview their guests out on a concrete deck setting, with a lovely marina as a backdrop. Big Snuffy was not on the set. As the news anchor interviewed Mark, I had to maneuver little Snuffy onto the set around Mark's (and the anchor's legs) and stop the model at their feet. Somehow, I did just that. Mark picked up little Snuffy and placed him on the table between Mark and the host, with little Snuffy's grill facing camera. Following a script, I "remotely" controlled little Snuffy's actions as he spoke, looked around with those cute little headlights and tipped his firefighter's hat appropriately. Everything was going well. The interview concluded, and Mark placed little Snuffy on the stage (concrete patio) floor and waved goodbye. On camera, everything looked fine. Off camera, I lost control and drove little Snuffy straight into a low stonewall! I never saw Mark's on-camera's reaction, but wish I had that tape! Fortunately, the fenders did what they were supposed to do and there was little damage. Fire Prevention Week Kick Off started in Miami and would take us to New Orleans, Chicago and ultimately to New York City. Big Snuffy's debut was also in Miami. The "gig" was a photo op (that's slang for Photographic opportunity) in front of the Miami Herald building. Big Snuffy was to "appear" by driving up to the main entrance portico on the street, followed by Little Snuffy. I'll set the scene. Imagine a street full of traffic and parked cars under a very large building portico supported with tall Corinthian columns. Waiting under the portico was the press waiting to start the "photo op" for the kick off of Fire Prevention Week. Enter Big Snuffy stage left. The crowd got it right away. It's "magic," no one is driving big Snuffy as it enters the scene, pulls up right in front of the press and say's "Hello, I'm Snuffy and I'm here to kick off National Fire Prevention Week!" Yes, that was the point. Big Snuffy was built with a "hidden" driver located in the boiler of the vehicle behind the driver's seat so that it would be magical! Look closely, there's a viewing port just above and behind the seat on the boiler for the driver's window. Larry Anderson (the actor) was the driver for big Snuffy. Larry came up in the magic biz as a street magician. I saw him many times at Mark's studio in North Hollywood, but I did not get to know him. Larry was an assistant to Mark on the television show, "The Magician" with Bill Bixby and went on to host Game shows such as "Truth or Consequences" and other television series such as "Days of Our Lives," Driving big Snuffy was just "a gig," that young actors did to pay the bills. It's all part of the "dues" one pays to stay in the business. As big Snuffy held the stage with his interview with the press, Little Snuffy was ready to drive up to and in front of big Snuffy for his own press debut. I was a bit nervous doing this, driving a small model onto a real street with moving cars. Everything looked so big compared to little Snuffy. Once parked in front of big Snuffy, the little guy was introduced and was quite a hit with the press. Too bad I don't have any records of this photo op. From the Herald building, we went on to introduce Big Snuffy to a middle school. The idea being that the children would be assembled on the asphalt playground in anticipation of big Snuffy's arrival. Big Snuffy would drive up magically and stop directly in front of Mark and the children. He appeared on cue from behind a nearby building performing several high-speed loops around the asphalt playground as we waited patiently for Big Snuffy to come up to Mark. Here's what happened. At a much higher rate of speed than rehearsed, Snuffy had to make the transition (between the grass and asphalt) on the playground area. As Snuffy was about halfway across that threshold, there was a very loud bang, accompanied by sparks, flying out from under Snuffy's chassis. We didn't know it then, but the height difference between the grass and asphalt pavement was several inches. The problem was underneath the chassis. Snuffy's brake pedal assembly (which dropped through the chassis floor two inches) didn't allow for this transition! Oops! Larry had successfully left the brake pedal mechanism at the scene! He had no brakes! We knew something was amiss, but we still had no idea why Snuffy was flying straight passed us making large concentric circles! Finally, Larry managed to stop Snuffy just as planned in front of Mark! And that's what happens in live show!

Big Snuffy was the prototype and had moving headlights with eyes, a set of lips that moved and a firefighter's hat that "flipped" up on command. Inside the boiler tank, Harry sat comfortably as the driver and used a Public Address system to "speak" as Snuffy."

As we drove our rental van on to New Orleans, I should tell you, both "Snuffy's" were transported by none other than Don Frantz and me. That's correct, a four-city tour, with Don and me as co-drivers. What? And give up show biz?

Here is what the agenda looked like:

- MIAMI (Day 1) Miami Morning Show Miami Herald Press Junket
- NEW ORLEANS (Day 2) Miami Middle School Presentation
- CHICAGO (Day 3) Bozo, The Clown TV Appearance
- NEW YORK (Day 4-5) ABC Morning Show, TV Appearance, Wonderama Show, TV Appearance, Captain Kangaroo, TV Appearance.

Here's a few other highlights. After New Orleans, we packed up both Snuffy's and set off to Chicago. Our next gig was in twenty-two hours. On a "sane" day, the 1,376 miles is a 23-hour trip. That would be a four- or five-day vacation trip with a family. Since we had no opportunity to stop because of this strict deadline, we ate many Burger King hamburgers, and took turns sleeping in the back of the van (between co-driving). I'm not sure on what leg of the trip, but I remember waking up in the darkest hour of the night and yelling out to Don; "Don! Don! Are you awake? I don't want to die!" Perhaps it was a bad dream, perhaps not. I'll never know, and Don doesn't remember either. There was also a side trip on our run to Chicago. Have you ever been on a long road trip and kept running into the same freight train or big rig? We managed to parallel the same freight train for days. Just for diversity, and a way to break up the tedium of all that driving, we decided to stop and pick up some fresh fruit and see if we could toss it up to the engineer! We located a very large wheat field next to the tracks ahead of the train. The engineer had no clue as to why these two maniacs were running alongside yelling and scream- ing. For us, it was a blast! We ran alongside the slowly moving freight tossing apples and oranges to the engineer and crew. Once they realized we weren't high-jackers, they thanked us with a long series of whistles, a friendly wave and disappeared on down the tracks. This exercise really made our day and had the side benefit of waking us both up for a good number of hours. With time to spare we arrived in Chicago and moved on to the tasks of getting the Snuffy's ready for their appearance. On our agenda was their appearance on the "Bozo's Circus" television program at the West Bradley Place studio. The program, which had been on-air on WGN-TV starting in 1961, was in various formats for many years! Bob Bell, as Bozo, would play the character until he retired in 1984. This was another piece of television history to add to my list. During our stay in Chicago, we spent two nights at the Palmer House hotel. Billed as the "oldest operating hotel in North America," the Palmer catered to likes of every U.S. President since Ulysses S. Grant. Coincidently, my family came to California from a city located on the "South Side" of Chicago called Calumet City. Calumet City was where the bulk of my "East Coast" relatives lived. You need to understand that coming from California, we think of anything outside of Arizona as the "East Coast." Calumet or "Cal City" as it is often referred, was the home of some famous gangsters in the 20s and 30s. Do you remember "Al Capone"? Yes, our family came from "Cal City," home of booze, broads and gangsters." Being Polish, I don't think that any of my relatives were "made" guys as far as I know! Our last stop for the Fire Prevention Week, was New York City. If you have never driven into New York City, it is the best way to get your first view of the skyline. Coming into New York City made LA seem like a town. Using the Central Park adjacent "Essex House" hotel as our home base, Mark's appearances in New York were numerous. The main shows were Captain Kangaroo, the ABC Morning Show and Wonderama.

Captain Kangaroo. I grew up with the "Captain" as a child of 50/60s television. Meeting him (Bob Keeshan) and Mr. Greenjeans (Hugh "Lumpy" Brannum) was a huge deal! Here's some television history. Bob Keeshan played "Clarabell the Clown" on another 60's television show. Do you remember "Howdy Doody?" Those of us in the baby boomer's generation know that show well. Mr. Green Jeans who shared the Snuffy Segment with Mark Wilson. I remember standing next to Mark, the Captain and Mr. Green Jeans, discussing the cues for Snuffy's entrance and exit. That is a very special memory. I also recall Bob Keeshan coming out from just beyond the set, placing his famous "hair" on the top of his head, just before that meeting. Another childhood memory dashed! The script called for Mark to call in "Little Snuffy" and introduce Fire Prevention Week. It was good to have Snuffy. the model, because as I said earlier, the New York studios were challenging for the full-size golf cart version. The main problem was the majority of television studios were "vertical," meaning that almost everything had to be brought up to the studios in freight elevators. Big Snuffy definitely did not work at this studio. I drove Snuffy in "on cue" from off camera and maneuvered him around Mark and the Captain's feet. Mark picked him up and placed him on a "hay bale," where the" interview" ensued. This is a photo of Snuffy on that hay bale. One of my treasured keepsakes, along with the script, of the experience.

ABC Morning Show. Our next gig in New York was Mark's appearance on the ABC Morning show. It too represented a real technical challenge for big Snuffy. Broadcast, "live" at their Times Square Studios, the show made its debt in November 1975. Our first problem was getting big Snuffy into the studio. We carted Big Snuffy around in a van as I mentioned earlier, and the ABC studio was our first challenge with small corridors. We parked the van outside the studios-one loading door and were met by four New York Union grips. These guys were "thugs" from the local and we had no choice but to let them handle Snuffy. "thugs" is still the best way I can describe them. It was @#$%$# this, and $%&^%$# that and how the #**&^% hell do you think you're going to get that @#@$%^^ thing out of there without a @#$%%& ramp? This continued from the lift out of the van all the way down the loading ramp and into the studio. Welcome to New York City!

Here I was just a 20 something, laid back Southern Californian, running into a brick wall. To this day I don't know how we finally got them to move Snuffy, but somehow Don and I (I'd say it was Don's Golden Tongue and his East Coast background) got them to lift big Snuffy out of that van. Believe me, I had never heard such swearing in all of my life. These guys made sailors seem like golden-throated orators! Fortunately, during all of this cussing and swearing, only one fender broke off as big Snuffy was "manhandled" down a very narrow ramp into the studio. Since I was concentrating on the technical repairs and getting Snuffy ready, I have only a brief "visual image" (in my head) of Bill and Stephanie interviewing Mark and big Snuffy.

Wonderama. Our last appearance for Mark was another children's program, called Wonderama. Another long running children's program that began in 1955. Running through 1986, the show had various hosts with Bob McAllister holding the longest job as host from 1967 to 1977. I remember the show as a child, but it was not on my list of favorites. Big or Little Snuffy were not making an appearance on Wonderama. This time Mark was to perform one of his "illusions." This is where it gets interesting. I have mentioned before that all of us connected to MWP were tied to a nondisclosure and confidentiality agreement. On Wonderama, Mark needed to rehearse with his magic assistant's, and we located a side area of the main studio for that purpose. We went to great lengths to make sure that the entire area was "secure" from "prying eyes" wanting to learn the secrets of magical illusions. Mark and cast rehearsed the illusion several times and all seemed to be going well. That is, until one of us (I don't remember who) happened to look up and notice a "viewing window" reserved for the parents of the children attending the show. If I recall correctly, the viewing window was at least 24'0" high and designed to "look down" on the main studio floor directly over the children's seating area. Another magical-Oops! The parents watched Mark rehearse the illusion, making his young assistant "disappear." Without giving away the secrets of magic, let me just say that the young woman needed to be very agile and quick!

Television Appearances. Mark and Nani appeared on a few other historic television shows during my tenure. My roll at the time was essentially a "go-fer" (as in "go for this, go for that") bringing props (in particular, pigeons) and illusions to the television studios. Do you recall "The Sonny and Cher Show?" Yep, Mark performed on their show. I can remember standing off to the side as the studio audience watched Sonny and Cher (in their "mod" costumes) on stage at CBS studios on Fairfax.

Last but not least, there was the Merv Griffin show. Merv started as a "crooner," with a style like Perry Como and Jack Jones. Besides his own daily television talk and variety show, Merv Griffin Enterprises created very famous television game shows. Wheel of Fortune was one of the most famous and is still on today. Wheel became one of the regular productions I took care of later on in my job at NBC Studios. I really hated that wheel! It seemed to break down every day. I met Mr. Griffin several times. He was one of the friendliest celebrities I ever met in the business.

Magic Castle. Founded by Milt Larsen in 1948, the Magic Castle was a very exclusive "Magic Club" created specifically for the magical arts. Located just below the Yamashiro Japanese Restaurant (former Japanese Consulate) in Hollywood and above Hollywood and Highland), the Magic Castle is an exclusive private club built into an existing Victorian Mansion. When I worked for Mark, it was very difficult to get into the Castle. It is much easier to get a guest card today. The guest card is an "invitation" by a member and allows you to attend with another couple. After pulling up to the valet only entrance up the step driveway, you enter a small foyer and are greeted by the hostess. After paying your cover charge, the hostess asks you to turn around and face a wall of books. You are asked to say the magic word, and once you guess correctly, the wall of books slides open exposing the main bar area. Sitting at the ornate bar, your stool might "magically" rise and fall" enhancing the effects of your drinking. There is also a grand piano "played" by a ghost by name of Irma that "speaks" to you in song. I'm not kidding. You ask Irma (the piano) a question and the response comes back by way of a music selection that clearly answers your question. It is a great effect and a real crowd pleaser; still is. Mark Wilson was one of the first magicians invited to help get the Magic Castle off the ground in the early 60s. He was also on the Board of Directors in the mid 70s. Milt has built this very unique venue that has grown into a multi-million-dollar business, now with its own hotel. As an exclusive and private organization for International Magicians, the Castle offers a library (The book archive is fabulous) and a place where magicians can rehearse and hone their act in front of a paying audience. The Magic Castle provides a showcase for many up-and-coming magicians, and a place for established professionals to mentor this talent. Many a celebrity honed their magical skills at the Castle including Johnny Carson, David Copperfield and Harry Blackstone, Jr. just to name a few. Mark opened The Palace of Mystery to inaugurate the largest theatre. I was there in the audience when Mark finished to a standing ovation. The Palace was a huge hit, and it operates today as a wonderful room to experience big illusions. If you ever happen to get an "invitation" card, please don't pass up this once in a lifetime experience. Oh, and say hello to "Irma" for me!

South Pointing Chariot. Connected to all of this, but an event that happened after Mark's tour in China (after I had left) is an interesting story and ties back to my model making career, Don Frantz and my tenure at Imagineering. Don, having gone to China with Mark during the tour, came upon a historical event tied to 3rd millennium Chinese history. During a rare break in the tour, Don visited a museum and came across an ancient machine called "The South Pointing Chariot." Don called and asked if I would be interested in building a model of this device. Although I was full time at Imagineering, I said yes and immediately called Doug Beswick. Doug was my "go to" guy for this sort of problem. I went over to Doug's home in San Fernando, North of Los Angeles, with photos and Don's history of the chariot. There was no schematic or "how to" plan of the gear arrangement, but Doug said he would take a "stab" at figuring it out. Not two days later, Doug called us back to see what he had accomplished. He had built a working prototype of the chariot, figuring out the mechanics in less than 24 hours. We sat in amazement as Doug ran the "rough" model around us and the stick figure on top, maintained its original direction! No matter how the cart was turned, if you began with the figure pointing south, it stayed south! Doug had unlocked the "secret" and we had a working model. Based on this model, we all decided to build another one, this time as a highly refined model for possible sale to high end collectors. The finished model, as seen in the photo, was constructed out of a Brazilian hardwood and finished with a scale model of the "Emperor." This maquette of the Emperor was not sculpted by any sculptor, but by a Disney sculptor by name of Adolpho Procoprio. Adolpho was Blaine Gibson's assistant at Imagineering and I approached him to do the sculpt for the Emperor. I brought this up on a visit I had with Blaine Gibson in 2009, having met him in his retirement community in Santa Barbara for dinner. Over a couple of weeks, the three of us completed the chariot and as you can see, it turned out beautifully. Once completed, we had high hopes of producing this version for Executives, as sort of a high-end desk toy. I used to take the South Pointer on business trips. I'd pull it out of its special case on the plane and start playing with it. In no time at all, I was the center of attention, and passed out several business cards to possible clients. I did this often and finally, this one fellow from Arizona called and ordered one! We only sold one. It was to a scientific instrument company in Arizona (I think). We never did keep any records of that and to this day, still have only the original prototype in our safe-keeping. In any event, in my research for this book, I recently spoke to Adolpho's son, Rueben who owns a sculpting design company called the Masked Avenger in Burbank, CA. Sadly, Adolpho passed in December 2018! Adolpho would never take a time for that sculpt of the Emperor!

I look at all this and still cannot believe it all took place in the first 20 years of my entertainment career!

CHAPTER THIRTEEN

Rear View, at What Cost?

Looking back in the rear-view, after writing this personal history makes one reflect. When I started to put this all down on paper, I had some idea that I could recall these events. That turned out to be a half-truth. I was surprised how father time distorts your memories. So much so, I had to go back to my archives. The year-end tax returns, my personal collection of Imagineering memorabilia and of course the internet. How did we get by without the internet in the 70s and 80s? Fortunately, I am blessed with a pretty good memory, and thus far, don't have dementia, at least no one has made any accusation I am aware of! The easy part was writing the story. The hard part was accepting the organization and scheduling of the events. Which brings me to this part where I have to look inside and face my own motivations for telling this story.

The question, of course is, "At What Cost?" The answer is complicated! Let's consider two possibilities and their impact on me and my decisions to work in the business of show!

- EPCOT could be viewed as a split decision. Half the studio's responsibility to Walt's dream, and half the studios responsibility to its shareholders. I don't think you can fault the studio for blending the two and proceeding with the project. Perhaps it's not the true realization of Walt's dream, but in my opinion, the park is a success on both. As a matter of cost, EPCOT was developed from a largely conceptual idea in relation to budget. This is simply how mega-projects develop. As the project moved forward from its "high concept" stage, with the wonderful Eye Candy provided by Herbie Ryman, a sense of budget was developed and refined as the design went through its phases. Somewhere, somebody at the studio, decided that the project moves forward at the budget provided. That budget may or may not have been completed by estimating. Real estate development projects can move forward based on the concept and a projection of the IRR or Internal Rate of Return, or the THRC predicted by recognized experts. I cannot say which method was used for EPCOT because I wasn't there. Probably both! However, by the time I came on-board, the project was funded at approximately $1.8B and was in full development. The Disney Company of course, makes decisions on projects like these because they know that the brand is solid and "if they build it, they will come!" What does this have to do with the cost of the work and its workforce?

Staying with the EPCOT example, those of us fortunate to have worked on the project, just had to keep the project moving forward. Once committed, the project was never in jeopardy of being cancelled. There was too much at stake. For those of us on the ground, it was organized chaos and everyone simply "got along, to get along," to make it happen. Everyone had stress! Estimating was constantly trying to keep up with the over running costs. The project managers were doing their best to manage the accelerating costs of both the facility and show and ride. The show producers simply designed, and Marty backed them up! And well he should! The proof is in the finished product! I suggest it was really a gathering of forces; design, project management and estimating, that worked together as a team, while the studio kept the money coming! Hopefully, somebody at the beginning of it all said; Well, it's all a prototype. I suppose that it will just cost what it costs! Today, this team represents the best Imagineering had to offer, they stepped up to the plate and hit a home run!

- EDL is an entirely different model. It began with two strikes against it in my opinion. 1) The studio mandated that it would be a "cookie-cutter" of Disneyland attractions, transferred to Paris. This is exactly what we were estimating when I started on EDL. 2) The studio directed an outside independent project management team (from Europe) to be the project manager. This is exactly the case when I was hired and assigned as "on-loan" to LMB. In fact, my salary was paid by LMB. Just the opposite of EPCOT and in a foreign country to make things more complicated. Compared to EPCOT, the stress felt by most employees I knew, was off the charts. Me included! Certainly, the relocation package and assistance did not work for those of us who came to Paris on the first wave. The lack of support once we got there, taking our focus off our work and directing it towards problems on the move itself, didn't help anyone. This combined with the language issues, the professional disagreements between Imagineering and LMB on site, and the complex procedures of the Bureau D' etudes, (for simplification-code review agency) became our problem. Going back to my "somebody, somewhere," comment above, this project changed to "somebody, somewhere, didn't think this through!" There are many examples to support this idea. Little things like ride packages going out to bid, piled high into a stack of "legalize" 16" high. I recall one meeting where somebody said, "we'll never get a bid based on these documents!" Then there were the initial policies that ignored the cultural habits of the European audience. No wine in the park? Fast food instead of sit-down tables and service? English only on the rides? It was a recipe to have Bastille day repeated from French history! Yet, better late than never as they say, the mouse cavalry came to save the day one year into our relocation! This all documented in numerous books and articles if you wish to pursue the details. Not exactly a home run because it took a full ten-years to straighten out EDL to the success it has today!

In my view, this all comes down to the decisions one makes in their career. My industry of choice was the business of show. I dislike the term Show Biz because it is too easy an explanation of what happens to people in the business.

The Business of Show seems to be all-encompassing. Not a simple "throw away" statement. But a true statement of fact of the trials and tribulations everyone goes through after taking care of that elephant! For myself, I started at the bottom with a broom in my hand, sweeping the stage. Through perseverance and a lot of help from others, I did good! And this story was just the first half of my game!

Finally, I have thought about what my career might have been with the mouse, had I stayed on in Paris. That thought left me years ago and I have peace with that decision. It was the right one. The business of show goes on, because there is always an understudy right behind you to pick up that elephant crap! If you become complacent, the show will just pass you by! You learn that much of the business is still like the old studio system! Just get on the lot and pound on doors. No one is going to come begging you to be part of the company. My path, interrupted by a situation beyond my control while in Paris, was devastating-at least for a while. Yet, through my early discussions with WDI, I knew that the work was in Paris, and that there were no guarantees of a job in Glendale. Instead of playing the pity card, I became pro-active and found the opportunity working at ILM, starting when I came back to the states. That's how the business of show works! It's true; when one door closes, another one opens! If not for this circumstance, I would never have worked for NBC Studios, Scenery West, or George Lucas, or the Renaissance Pleasure Faire Corporation. All companies that stretched my skills and my abilities to cope in the business of show! A little Barnum and Baily hoot spa goes a long way in this business! As the title says, there is a Cost of a Kingdom. What might it cost you? How much is it going to cost you to stick to your goal? Not to be too philosophical about it, but it's a question only you can decide, no matter where your career path takes you!

It's said that it's not the fall, but how you get up from it! If that's the case, I am the prime example of "I've fallen, and I can't get up!" LOL, I trust my experiences at Walt Disney Imagineering, offers some insight about the business of show. Just remember that old circus joke about the elephant.

Acknowledgments and Appreciation

This next section documents the many contributions and talents of the most influential colleagues I worked with and for in the business of show. When I started in theatre arts, I had no idea I would meet and work with so many talented people. Every one of them have made an impact to their craft and the entertainment industry! More importantly, my personal growth in the business happened because of their mentoring. These are the people I worked side-by-side, sometimes 24/7, through some very stressful productions. I am grateful and fortunate to have shared their friendship! It's been fun looking up their more recent contributions, remembering the great times and writing these short biographies for your enjoyment. It's also been sad to find that some are no longer with us! It's also a startling realization for me, that this only covers my work from 1973 through 1989. Yet, it still excludes my work at NBC Studios, ILM, Scenery West, and the Renaissance Faire!

Mark Wilson Productions

Mark and Nani Wilson. In Texas, in the 1960s, Mark was a rising star on Texas television with his own television show called Alakazam! He was a master illusionist moreover was highly entertaining in "close up" magic especially in card tricks and sleight of hand. Mark and his beautiful stage assistant and spouse Nani Darnel were taking the magic world by storm and deservedly so. Mark introduced choreography into his act; something that wasn't being done at the time and the rest is history. His television show was inventive, colorful and ran for five years and was syndicated in 1965. You might also know the show, The Magician" (1973) with Bill Bixby. Mark was the advisor for the series and by the way, those are Mark's hands in all the close magic scenes. There is so much more to say about these two very special people. If you love magic, have a look at their website and read all about their contributions to the World of Magic! What else can I say? This is where it all started, and I am forever grateful to them both!

Chuck Corson. Chuck started as an apprentice in 1956 at Walt Disney Studios in the casting department. He had begun his career with Fred Waring, the famous choral director, as a stage manager. He toured with the 40 plus cast and crew, set up the stage lighting and was the production stage manager. He then moved to Los Angeles, receiving a job offer from CBS television. A job which went away by the time he had arrived. In his search for work, the Disney studios hired Chuck as an apprentice in the casting department. Here he worked with the Mickey Mouse Club and Zorro. It was at the studio where his boss, overhead a conversation and learned that Chuck had been the production manager for Fred Waring) This is how he was called upon to use his stage lighting skills for a one-night Disney Big Band event at the Hollywood Bowl. The production stage manager was Tommy Walker (who Walt hired in 1955 and who later produced the fireworks shows for Disneyland and the U.S. Olympics). Chuck and Tommy Walker produced the first Disneyland Big Bands at the Hollywood Bowl. The show featured Benny Goodman and can you guess who? Tinkerbell! Yep, it was the introduction of Tinkerbell, flying and waving her pixie dust wand over the Hollywood Bowl! But maybe you didn't know that the first Tinkerbell was a 74-year-old ex-circus performer by name of Tiny Kline! The "flyover" was a hit, and this was the first time Tinkerbell flew in public! This is the event where Chuck moved from the studio to Disney live entertainment and television. Chuck produced what are known as Disneyland traditions for both "Night and daytime Entertainment". Walt called this "Atmosphere Entertainment" and it was at Disneyland and later, the Magic Kingdom in Florida where live entertainment got its start! Walt saw this new form of entertainment as a distraction from the "boredom of standing in lines for the rides and attractions". And so, it began with a small group called the Dapper Dan's! This "Barbershop Quartet" had been performing at a lesser known venue when Chuck found them, made an offer they couldn't refuse, and Disneyland history is born! However, Walt wanted more than just daytime entertainment. Disneyland during its early years was a daytime park, just like all other amusement parks around the world. The idea that a park guest would give up their dinner hour with the family was not accepted by Disneyland park operations. Security issues in a park that had no lighting after hours was a major concern! Walt though had a different idea and saw the possibilities!

This task fell to Chuck Corson. With his previous ties with the big bands from his touring days with Fred Waring, Chuck thought that the big bands would be a perfect entertainment for Disneyland. Walt approved, new performing stages were built (Plaza Gardens and 20,000 Leagues) and Benny Goodman became the first Big Band orchestra to play at Disneyland. The Benny Goodman Orchestra was only the first. There were many other performers such as; Al Hirt, Count Base, Pete Fountain, Louis Prima, Peggy Lee, Harry James and Mel Torme! (Imagine?) Chuck also created the fireworks show (with Tommy Walker) complete with Tinkerbell Flying over the park at the finale! Tink would "light" the show from atop the Matterhorn and "fly to Adventureland! I remember this well. And if these credentials aren't enough for you, how about as assistant Director of Pageantry, producing the live entertainment for Olympics at Squaw Valley, the 84' Olympics in Los Angeles and Lake Placid, New York! How many theatre people get to do that? I was living the dream! The thread of my mouse connection officially began with Chuck Corson in 1973! He became my mentor, and I would say a "father" figure at the time I worked for him. I miss him very much!

John Gaughan. John is an American manufacturer of magic acts and equipment for magicians and is based in Los Angeles, California. His style of work is classic illusions, not based heavily on machinery and technology. Great illusionists have noted his work, such as David Blaine, who has several times called him "a magical genius".

He has built illusions for famous magicians such as Mark Wilson, Alan Wakeling, Criss Angel, David Copperfield, David Blaine, Simon Drake, Doug Henning and The Doors, among others. His team of master craftsmen are responsible for the construction of dozens of major acts for stage magicians. He also has constructed a replica of the 18th century chess-playing machine, The Turk, which often tours chess conferences.

Gaughan created David Copperfield's flying illusion, which is notable for its graceful motion and unencumbered appearance. Gaughan holds a patent on a method for creating the illusion of flight A collector of magic history, John has several pieces in the Smithsonian that he has made or restored. I had the honor to meet John several times while working at MWP. On occasion, there would be other world-famous magicians at the shop having new illusions created. A chance meeting with David Copperfield comes to mind. Interesting how life threads you along its path. Later, I would build the scenery for two NBC Productions starring David. I used to work late and recall one very late evening meeting David in the studio hallway simply walking about by himself with his thoughts to himself. Watching his taping to a live audience was both thrilling and a great memory of my early start in the magic business with MWP. John, besides creating all of Mark's illusions, also created a "one-of-a-kind" prop for Mark Wilson Productions for a National Fire Prevention Week Event. Using a standard golf cart chassis, John and his team created "Snuffy". Snuffy was a "magical" boiler type fire engine that seemed to drive along without any visible driver. This is where my model building experience came into play for MWP. Building the "scale model version" of the Big Snuffy! John was and is a true gentleman and was quite fun to be around!

Anita Mann. Besides being drop dead gorgeous, (OK, I'm of the older generation! LOL) Anita is an extraordinary directory and choreographer. Anita's career began in 1966 with the Monkees television show. Anita's background was incredible by itself; for instance, it was her job to be Nancy Sinatra's "double." Just some of her professional credits include Here's Lucy, The Bobby Darin Show, Cher, Muppets Go Hollywood, (plus other specials for the Muppets) Solid Gold and the Lemon Sisters.

She has also danced and choreographed Elvis Presley and Michael Jackson! She also had her own headline show in Las Vegas! How about that! Anita was awarded the AFI Lifetime Achievement Award (A Tribute to George Lucas) in 2005 and has been awarded Emmy's for her television specials. A of bit irony here is that I worked for George later on too! You met Anita in my MWP story. I spoke with her just a couple of years ago and she is still the nicest person I've met in this business!

Don Frantz - Don was the Director of Entertainment for Hershey Park and he was responsible for creating the Christmas Pageant on their main stage. Don used to tell me all about that production and the problems he had "staging" camels, goats, donkeys and all manner of a vast menagerie" that he added to the event. The menagerie was a huge hit. The "pageant" became an annual Christmas event for years to come. Don has a lot more to offer and has contributed new events such as "The Amazing Maize, Maize" (a corn-field themed maize participatory event nationwide) and the "Walking tour of Historic Broadway Theatres) in New York City. Don went out on his own as an Independent producer and also with Chuck Corson, produced the massive fireworks display in New York City for the countries Bicentennial! Don also became an Associate Producer for Walt Disney Theatrical and was part of the team that created the very successful, first theatrical production of Beauty and the Beast on Broadway. I went to New York and saw that production and you could see the little bits and pieces that Don brought to the production. Following that record-breaking Broadway hit, don also was Associate Producer on another Disney hit, the Lion King! Off Broadway, he Produced the hit called "Disenchanted!" This very funny and irreverent musical is a satire of the Disney Princesses, now playing to an international audience. I invite you to visit his web site, townsquare productions.com, to learn more about the events and performances Don has created. Don remains active and has taken his talents to China where he is producing live theatrical and theme park productions! He remains my number one best bro from the time we both started in show biz in 1973! By the way! That's F-R-A-N-T-Z!

John Schrum - (1927 - September 10, 1988) was an NBC Television Senior Art Director. John Shrum was born in Los Angeles, CA and attended the Chouinard Art Institute. Upon graduation, he became involved in the advent of television at KTLA-TV studios. This led to John's move to NBC Television as an Art Director.

John Shrum was Art Director for Ralph Edwards' *Truth or Consequences*. He was the original Art Director for *Days of Our Lives* when the legendary NBC soap opera went on the air in 1965. Shrum also served as Art Director for other NBC television specials including the Emmy Award winning *Alice In Wonderland*. Later John became Art Director for Johnny Carson and *The Tonight Show* on NBC, when Carson first came to Burbank, California for a West Coast broadcast of the nightly hour and a half show which followed the NBC Eleven O'clock News each evening. So, impressed with Shrum's work was the TV Host that he asked the Network executive to make him a permanent part of *The Tonight Show* staff. Shrum won an Emmy and numerous nominations for his work on this show.

Away from NBC, John collaborated with Milt Larsen on the entrepreneur's world-renowned Hollywood private magicians club The Magic Castle, Mayfair Music Hall, Santa Monica, California, and the grand deco Variety Arts Center in downtown Los Angeles, California. I met John at Showtime America where he was the Art Director. Later on, as the Manager of Scenic Operations, I had the pleasure of working with him again on the Tonight Show! John was truly a character and had this wonderful "whiskey" breath laugh! I miss him!

Bill Bohnert. Bill is a television art director and perhaps is best known for his work on America's Favorite Video's, among other television favorites. He shared many stories with me when we were working together at Circus World, but I think his work on "The Ed Sullivan Show" was of the most interest to me. Particularly because one of those shows was the Beatles first "live" appearance. I remember watching that show on live television as a teenager. Bill and I installed the theatrical rigging ifor the Magic show at Circus World. We shared something in common. Both had started with a tool belt on! He is a consummate professional and it was a privilege to work alongside him!

Alan Wakeling. He worked as a demonstrator at two magic shops in Los Angeles, the Thayer Magic Company and the Magic House of Charles. He was also employed by magic inventor and manufacturer Merv Taylor. A chance meeting with magician Roy Benson in the early 1940s gave Wakeling the beginnings on an idea for a routine with billiard balls, which later became something of a signature piece for him. For a while he did an act with long-time friend Marvyn Roy, who later went on to be known as "Mr. Electric". Wakeling gradually became a regular performer at clubs in the Los Angeles area, doing a range of acts with titles such as "Rhapsody in Blue" and "Hollywood Cowboy" as well as the "Fan Act", which he began performing with his soon-to-be wife Helen shortly before they were married.

Wakeling worked as a performing magician until 1966 when he was offered a behind-the-scenes job with Mark Wilson, who had recently become famous across America for transforming magic into a successful format for network television. He served as Wilson's creative director for many years, contributing to Wilson's television shows, including *Magic Circus*, as well as to live productions in Las Vegas and major venues around the world. He also contributed to the work of other famous magicians including Channing Pollock, John Daniel, Marvyn Roy, Norm Nielsen, Dick Zimmerman, Peter Reveen and Earl Nelson.

Channing Pollock said of him: "Alan is a one-of-a-kind genius. I see him as one of the best kept secrets in magic, someone who was so good at what he accomplished that you'd want to keep him a secret". Among Wakeling's inventions is at least one distinctive version of the *Sawing a woman in half* effect. One version of this illusion, which bears his name, takes certain elements of the first ever sawing trick performed by P.T. Selbit and incorporates them into a new and very effective illusion. However, while Wakeling performed and perfected that variant of the effect, the origins of the so-called "Wakeling Sawing" have been attributed to another magician Virgil Harris Mulkey (aka The Great Virgil), who first performed it in 1942. A version that is fully attributed to Wakeling is the *"Double sawing in half"* routine for Channing Pollock. Among the illusions he devised for Mark Wilson were *Backstage, Girl Through Glass, The Spiker,* and *Excalibur.* He was also responsible for Wilson's *"Circus Act"* routine, which involved the *Gorilla crush* illusion. He had a passion for creating new model trains cars and we spent some time going over his latest models while at MWP. Alan acted in the capacity of consultant to MW Productions and was responsible for creating "big" illusions for Mark's shows. I remember Alan as a gentle man, with time to spare for advice!

Walter Gibson. Of special mention is Walter Gibson who was Co-author of Mark Wilson's book on Magic. A lifelong magician, he worked under the pen name of Maxwell Grant. He created the character of Lamont Cranston, a mysterious crime fighter with an alias called "The Shadow." The Shadow was an immensely popular radio program in the 30s. Neat radio history, yes? This was of special interest to me as my minor in my graduate work was television production. At Fullerton, I used to be a TA for a professor that taught Radio History. One of the highlights of that class was bring the students into the main stage theatre and dimming the light to almost total darkness. I would play the old radio shows, Jack Benny, Fibber McGee and of course The Shadow. The students, although not as entrenched in the Internet and such in the mid-70s, were still part of the television generation. They went crazy discussing the various "images" each of their fellow classmates had for the same piece of audiotape. It just shows the power of the imagination.

Keaton Walker. Keaton was the Technical Director for Showtime America. I knew he was a professional but, had no idea of his background! I asked him to review my drafting samples from graduate school and he said to me; how long did that take you? I said a few hours. His reply was, a nice drawing, but you need to be able to do that in less than an hour!" Keaton's work in the industry is extensive. Just some of the television specials he is credited for his work as Art Director include the Annual Screen Actors Awards (1996-2013), academy Awards

(2002/2003), Big Brother (2001), the Julie Andrews Hour and the Many Sides of Don Rickles.

Brian Bartholomew. Brian was the art director for MWP at Busch Gardens for Showtime America and the magic Show. Here are just a few of his professional credits as Production Designer; David Copperfield Specials. This is Tom Jones, Osmond Family TV Specials, 28th and 31st Primetime Emmy Awards, Cher TV Special, The Julie Andrews Hour, Kraft Music Hall Presents, Barbara Streisand TV Special and most recently, The Voice.

Cinesphere

Byron Bauer. As the department head for stage lighting and audio services at Cal State Los Angeles Drama Department, Byron became a mentor and a great friend. As production manager for the department, we worked together on many theatre productions. His talent in scenic painting, stagecraft and of course his technical abilities in lighting and audio were well known in the business of education. But it was not just his talents in theatre that brought us together. As a Cinematographer, he created a company called Cinesphere. Located in a 3,000 square foot warehouse just off campus, he created special effects for the Movie Meteor, the version with Sean Connery. The cover photo of me standing on a "fall away platform," designed for the shot of the meteor hurdling towards earth says it all. I think the appropriate caption is "What? And give up showbiz?" I have another newspaper clipping of Cinesphere shooting 35MM segments of "wire explosions" out in the San Fernando Valley. The "powder man," or officially, the pyro-effects person, was Cliff Wenger Sr. and his son Cliff Jr. They blew up the N.Y. Twin Towers models and "trash bags of black powder" hanging from a cable. Prophetic huh? I learned you do not approach the explosion scene until the "all clear" is given! I was attempting to retrieve a fish eye lens Byron rented from the bottom of the now destroyed towers! Byron and I remember another shot, where Byron got hit in the back and I got my eyebrows singed! At the various set ups for the movie, a "photo-sonics 35 MM High Speed Motion Picture Camera" was used for the avalanche effects. This is the same camera that was used for the famous "bullet through the padlock" TV commercial. Basically, the camera runs at speed, and captures so much information, that when it is slowed down to normal speed, it looks like it is in "slow motion!"

An independent contractor by name of Bruce Hill provided the equipment. His brother Phil was the operator. Cinesphere also produced a 20'0" diameter "world globe" for the Holiday inn chain International chiefs Event in Memphis, TN. This globe contained fiber optics illustrating all of the Holiday Inn International franchises. Plus, it rotated 360 degrees and had an outer "platform ring" for dancers! All of the "curved" pie slices for the globe were created using a "hot lamp" mold. We all took turns pushing that plastic into the form under a tent of aluminum foil to contain the heat! That's dedication! The event in Memphis was a black-tie affair, and all of us had to dress up to be there as the "running" crew! Cinesphere was also the production group that created the rock formations and "animated spaceship with sparkler" for the Universal Studios Tour "Flash Gordon" show. Byron is a dedicated professional and helped a number of us get into I.A.T.S. E., 33! Although we all worked many hours, between our Cal State responsibilities and Cinesphere, he always was a true gentleman, a good friend and he paid well too!

William Cruse. Byron worked under the direction of William Cruise for the movie – Meteor. I worked on one assignment with Bill at the old Howard Hughes Studios building for a movie called - Devil Dog, Hound of Hell! It was very interesting to watch the transformation of a beautiful German Shephard into a growling "Hound of Hell" on command! I acted as a grip, there was a "trainer," and a beautiful German Shephard who became the "Devil Dog!" It was Bill's group that assigned several effects shots to Cinesphere. They included the Tsunami, Avalanche and the Twin Towers demolition. Bill's film credits include Rush Hour 2, Rules of Engagement, Meteor, The Green Mile, Volcano, Executive Decision, Clear and Present Danger and The Hunt for Red October, among others. He has numerous credits for Art Direction, Visual Effects, Art Department and Production Designer.

Clokey Productions

Ruth Clokey. Producer for Davey and Goliath. A very quiet and strict Lutheran Lady who dressed impeccable always! Ruth continued the talents of Clokey Productions on the Davey and Goliath Series for the Lutheran Church. I'll share this really great story about Pete's Kienow's out take surprise for Ruth, at one of our mornings "dallies." (Dallies is a term for watching the previous days "canned" or rough film footage) Ruth wasn't known for her funny personality, so Pete decided to liven things up and add something special to his animation work from the day before. The scene is Davey, tied to a tree with a gag over his mouth. Davey is obviously in distress and Pete's animation emboldens the script in every way. Suddenly, there is a "swoosh", an object passes by Davey, very close to his head! Davey looks to camera left, where the shot cuts to an arrow just next to his head, still quivering from the impact. Davey does a double take; his eyes change to saucers and with a look of sheer terror, the shot ends! The room is deadly quiet. Finally, we can't help ourselves and everyone is on the floor laughing! I recall Ruth not being very pleased, but only Pete could get away with it! Just a note. A typical stop motion animator was expected to produce only 20 seconds of usable (canned) film per day. Sneaky Pete regularly provided twice that-with every frame a stop motion Gem!

Raymond Peck. Series Director for Davey and Goliath – Ray set the studio atmosphere of the animator's studio workspace! Set up with open workstations for each stop motion animator in the 6,000 SF warehouse building (a former plumber's shop) in Azusa, CA, Ray always had classical music playing in the background. Besides being a terrific film director, Ray was also a cinematographer, production manager and model maker for the Gumby series.

Pete Kleinow. Known as "Sneaky Pete", a Stop motion animator, steel guitar musician for "The Flying Burrito Brothers" Rock band, studio musician (Joan Baez, Jackson Browne, The Byrd's, Joe Cocker, Rita Coolidge, Eagles, The Everly Brothers, George Harrison, The Steve Miller Band, Joni Mitchell, The Rolling Stones, Ringo Starr, Stevie Wonder, Spencer Davis,

Linda Ronstadt and more) and special effects technician for major motion pictures! Pete used to practice his steel guitar at lunch at the studio. He also produced the most amazing Davey crowd scene for the special "School, who needs it? I witnessed his manipulation of over 30 puppets, each one moving (Pulling hair, spit balls, etc.) while Pete did a tracking shot (a camera move on a curved track with a slow wide to close up shot) of Davey and Goliath in the front of the classroom. One frame at a time! I was fortunate to be invited to Pete's wake in Joshua Tree, CA. There were only five of us Art Clokey, Creator of Gumby – first met outside my studio window when his yellow Porsche drove up onto the sidewalk in front of me and came into the art department. The last time in 2007 at his anniversary of Gumby gala in San Francisco. For some reason, although I didn't know him, when I went up to him to thank him for getting me into the biz, he held on to my wrist and wouldn't let go! He just wanted to talk! A Very special moment and memory!

Doug Beswick. Animator, model maker, machinist and special effects creator. Doug was my first and remains one of my best friends. Doug's assistance in the props I made and especially his guidance in mixing "skin" colors for the puppets was an important part of my growth as a model maker. Doug also partnered with me to produce an extraordinary model fire truck called "Snuffy" for Mark Wilson productions. I toured the United States with mark and Snuffy where he appeared on television shows such as Captain Kangaroo, Wonderama and Bozo, the Clown. That firetruck, a scale working model of a larger golf cart size prop that toured with us for fire week, had a hat that "tipped", moving lips on the radiator, headlights for eyes that turned left and right and drove both forward and backwards. All by remote control. That's a story in itself! Doug hired me as a "grip" (basically a do this-do that job) for an effect he was doing for the movie "Cremators". The movie plot had something to do with Indians being rolled over by a gigantic ball of flames! I was the "moving" man for the fire ball. My first "grip" position! Doug's small studio in Azusa was shared with Rick Baker. Together, they co-created the creature "Octa man" in 1969. Imagine, Ricks earliest make up effect and I didn't even know Rick at the time! It was years later, I met Rick at a Gumby Fest in Glendora, CA in 2014. The City celebrates Gumby and claims the Gumby studio as their own! A section in the Glendora library is devoted to Clokey Productions! Rick has come a very long way from Octa Man! To date, he has garnered seven Academy Awards for special effects and make up from the Academy!

Harry Walton. Another Clokey alumnus, Harry is a visual effects artist, cinemaphotographer, special effects stop motion animator, camera technician and model maker, among his other talents. His credits are impressive with over 85 film credits over his career in special effects. You might know him for his work on the Pillsbury Doughboy and the Ralston Purina Stagecoach commercials, Robocop, Innerspace, the Abyss and Howard the Duck among his many credits. Harry and his family lived in Novato, CA where we moved when I went to work for ILM in 1989. I just happened to look over the pool at my children's swimming meet, and saw Doug and Harry standing there watching the same meet! How's that for fate? Our kids were on the same team and we didn't even know it!

Terry Smith. A model maker, Terry was the son of Hal Smith, the voice of Davey and Elmer Fudd. His father was also an actor, with his role as the town drunk in the Andy Griffith series for television. Hal came to the shop just once at the Glendora Studio. The "voice overs for Davey were taped in Hollywood. Playing "film reel frisbee" was a highlight at the studio when "management" was away at the recording studio! We were such "devils!"

Tim Frawley. Tim was quite a character, no really, a character actor! As a model maker, Tim worked on the background scenery for Davey and Goliath. Tim was also a stuntman for television and movies and is credited with Gunsmoke, Bonanza, Wagon Train and the movie Play Misty for Me, Directed by Clint Eastwood.

Tim also "doubled" for one of the Cartwright boys" on Bonanza. His stories of practical jokes on the various sets were memorable and made our lunch time, very special!

Euro Disneyland

Yves Valante. I met Yves at the A.O.R Scenic Shop in Paris. He was working for the Lido show "Bravissimo" as a scenic designer. Yves started his career in 1980 as an assistant designer on the Lido show Cocorico." He went on to design his first show, Hot Shock in 1984 at the old Lido De Paris on the Champs Elysées. His work at EDL began in 1988 as a show estimator under LMB, transferring to EDLI as a show set designer for Frontierland with show producer Jeff Burke. In February of 1992 as EDLI opened on April 12th, he was hired by Lido to become the permanent designer and architect of the Lido De Paris on the Champs le Elysees where his work continues today. Yves is also a professional magician and performs at many functions throughout France. This included a special birthday gift to our daughter Andrea, with a personal performance at her 8th birthday celebration at our home in Lesigny! I want to thank Yves for everything he did for me and my family in Paris during our relocation! He is a true gentleman and a consummate professional! Merci Bon Amis!

Aaron Haas. What can you say about a young man that travels all the way to France after graduating from the University, knocks on the door of Le Pascal completely unannounced, and gets himself a job on the EDL project? Hoot spa comes to mind! Aaron not only did a terrific job assisting us in show and ride estimating in Paris but found time to keep us all informed with his weekly "newspaper" of "happenings at EDL!" a publication we all looked forward to reading.

Aaron has since kept moving forward through some very high-profile construction companies! Currently, Vice President of Design and Construction at The Howard Hughes Corporation since February 18, 2017. His previous work included positions at major corporations such as Walt Disney Imagineering and Caruso Affiliated. At Disney, Mr. Haas worked on various stages of large complex projects, including Eurodisneyland in Paris, France; Disney's California Adventure; Walt Disney World's Animal Kingdom and other attractions. At Caruso Affiliated, he worked on award-winning developments, including the Americana At Brand in Glendale, CA and 8500 Burton Way, Los Angeles, both mixed use luxury apartment and retail projects. Mr. Haas is a graduate of Arizona State University with a B.S. in Construction Engineering and minor in Real Estate Development. A great story and well deserved!

About the Author

Carl is a cost control specialist, developing project estimation and cost control functions for the theme park industry. His estimating/budgeting education and experience of over 40 years include these major entertainment companies; Walt Disney Imagineering, George Lucas's-LucasArts Attractions, the National Broadcasting Company (NBC Burbank, CA) Renaissance Entertainment Corporation and RIVA Entertainment, Bechtel Corporation and Scenery West. His volume of cost work exceeds $5 billion on prestigious entertainment projects including EPCOT, Walt Disney World, Disneyland, Tokyo, Disneyland, Disneyland, France, New World, Hawaii, Magic World, Dubai, Motiongate, Dubai, The Virginia Renaissance Faire, Fredericksburg, Disney Stores, Texas Wild, Dallas, among others.

Mr. Jablonski is also a miniature model maker and has created miniatures for both film, television and live theatricals.

Mr. Jablonski holds a master's degree in Scenic Design and Theatrical Lighting and a bachelor's degree in Technical Theatre. He is also a Certified Professional Estimator in show construction.

ABOUT THEME PARK PRESS

Theme Park Press publishes books primarily about the Disney company, its history, culture, films, animation, and theme parks, as well as theme parks in general.

Our authors include noted historians, animators, Imagineers, and experts in the theme park industry.

We also publish many books by first-time authors, with topics ranging from fiction to theme park guides.

And we're always looking for new talent. If you'd like to write for us, or if you're interested in the many other titles in our catalog, please visit:

www.ThemeParkPress.com

· ·

Theme Park Press Newsletter

Subscribe to our free email newsletter and enjoy:

- ◆ Free book downloads and giveaways
- ◆ Access to excerpts from our many books
- ◆ Announcements of forthcoming releases
- ◆ Exclusive additional content and chapters
- ◆ And more good stuff available nowhere else

To subscribe, visit www.ThemeParkPress.com, or send email to newsletter@themeparkpress.com.

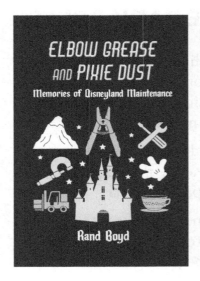

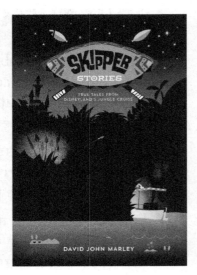

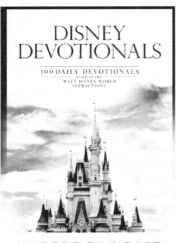

Read more about these books
and our many other titles at:

www.ThemeParkPress.com

Made in the USA
Las Vegas, NV
08 March 2021

19244424R00128